Compliance Management

Compliance Management

A How-to Guide for Executives, Lawyers, and Other Compliance Professionals

Nitish Singh, PhD, and Thomas J. Bussen

 PRAEGER

AN IMPRINT OF ABC-CLIO, LLC
Santa Barbara, California • Denver, Colorado • Oxford, England

Library of Congress Cataloging-in-Publication Data

Singh, Nitish, author.
  Compliance management : a how-to guide for executives, lawyers, and other compliance professionals / Nitish Singh, PhD, and Thomas J. Bussen.
      pages cm
  ISBN 978-1-4408-3311-3 (hardback) — ISBN 978-1-4408-3312-0 (ebook)
  1. Corporate governance–Law and legislation–United States.   2. Commercial law–United States.   3. Business ethics–United States.   I. Bussen, Thomas J.   II. Title.
  KF1422.S56   2015
  658.1'2–dc23   2014041800

ISBN: 978-1-4408-3311-3
EISBN: 978-1-4408-3312-0

19 18 17 16   3 4 5

This book is also available on the World Wide Web as an eBook.
Visit www.abc-clio.com for details.

Praeger
An Imprint of ABC-CLIO, LLC
ABC-CLIO, LLC

130 Cremona Drive, P.O. Box 1911
Santa Barbara, California 93116-1911

This book is printed on acid-free paper ♾

Manufactured in the United States of America

Contents

Preface

A business's reputation is significantly affected by the business environment: scandals, prosecutions, and investigations of any one company foster public skepticism of all business, raising the stakes for companies to have well-trained professionals and rich corporate cultures of "doing the right thing." Laws and regulations impacting businesses are extensive, and professionals must be familiar with a wide variety of subjects in order to spot issues and manage compliance risks effectively.

Research also increasingly supports the notion that more compliant and ethical businesses see increased productivity across a range of measurements. The purpose of this book is to provide corporate professionals, law students, and business students with a one-stop, hands-on guide to creating and managing an effective compliance program. The book specifically outlines practical tips and best practices in compliance management. In this book we have attempted to provide a simplified understanding of compliance with various laws related to international business compliance, wage and labor compliance, environmental compliance, antitrust issues, and other areas.

However, this book provides the authors' subjective evaluation of best practices for compliance. Numerous regulations are covered through the lens of compliance management. This is not meant to serve as a legal handbook, but rather as a compliance handbook. We attempt to combine our compliance expertise with expert opinions and best practices to provide practical guidance on compliance management. Thus, we sincerely hope that we provide the reader with a comprehensive understanding of various aspects of compliance management. The most important thing a reader can take away from this book is ethical knowledge and the conviction to "do the right thing." We hope to continue to share ethics and compliance insights via our blog www.ethicsresources.org. We also encourage our readers to contact us with their stories, best practices, and other compliance insights, so we can create a rich discussion around these issues via our blog and other formats.

This book is divided into three major sections, which take the reader through the foundations of compliance management, critical success factors for compliance management, and an overview to compliance with specific laws.

In Section I: Importance and Foundations of Compliance Management, readers will gain an understanding of the importance of investing in a compliance program and developing a culture of "doing the right thing." This section will also introduce readers to ethical foundations and ethical decision-making strategies. Finally, readers will be exposed to the role of corporate governance, corporate responsibility, and the importance of the Federal Sentencing Guidelines for Organizations (FSGO) in compliance management.

In Section II: Critical Success Factors for Compliance Management, readers will develop a better understanding of how to manage and implement an effective compliance program. Specific strategies for managing various facets of a compliance program will be outlined. We will also share examples and best practices with readers to better integrate theory and practice. More specifically, readers will learn about critical aspects of compliance management such as training and communication; preventing and investigating fraud; risk management, auditing, and control; and evaluating compliance program effectiveness.

In Section III: Mitigating Risk: A Brief on Compliance with Various Laws, readers will gain specific insights into compliance with various laws that govern different aspects of a business undertaking. This section will be useful for both a legal and nonlegal audience as it provides a simplified and brief overview of compliance with important laws applicable to a variety of organizations across industries. We will cover compliance with laws related to international business, money laundering, employment, the environment, and antitrust issues.

Finally, before we conclude we do want to acknowledge several people who helped us with research insights, cases, best practices, editorial services, and other inputs. Thank you especially to Aaron Appelbaum for providing us with constructive feedback and editorial guidance. We are also thankful to the following experts who provided us with rich insights and guidance: Kara Tan Bhala, Lyn Boxall, Steve Casazza, Ron Gieseke, Brendan Keating, Gary Levine, Michael Keating, Dr. Seung Kim, Aley Raza, Jeroen Tetteroo, and Mark Whitacre. Thank you all.

Section I: Importance and Foundations of Compliance Management

CHAPTER ONE

Why Doing the Right Thing Matters

Managing compliance is not just a functional necessity—it's a critical component needed to successfully navigate the turbulent global environment and deliver against the business strategy—especially in the wake of high profile cases and recent events around the world.

Bobby Kipp, partner, PwC[1]

It's Monday morning, and Paul is just sitting down at the kitchen table for a cup of coffee. He opens the *Wall Street Journal*—like he does almost every morning—and lets out a small gasp. His company is on the front page, its name in big bold letters, cited for alleged compliance failures and employee misconduct. Before he can digest the information, his phone rings; his caller ID shows that it's the CEO of the company. This is bad. "Paul," his boss begins, "have you seen the front page? You're the head of compliance. We have to show the market that we're making changes. You know how it is. You're gone." He hangs up.

And then Paul wakes up. It was all a dream—or rather, a nightmare—but Paul knows this could be reality one day. Paul's been putting off improvements to his company's compliance program, but today he resolves to begin making improvements.

Compliance professionals and executives are not as isolated from this nightmare scenario as they once were. Regulatory pressure for effective ethics and compliance programs (hereinafter "Program" is used to refer to an effective ethics and compliance program) has been increasing ever since the United States Sentencing Commission (USSC) passed the Federal Sentencing Guidelines for Organizations (FSGO) in 1991. However, recent scandals involving Enron, WorldCom, Tyco, Freddie Mac, AIG, Lehman Brothers, and others, have also had a significant impact on modern regulatory compliance. These glaring misjudgments and compliance failures resulted in criminal actions that led to record fines and increased regulatory scrutiny designed to prevent future criminal violations.

Thus, today more than ever, having a Program can directly impact a company's bottom line by minimizing the risk of fines, penalties, and employee wrongdoing, and by strengthening its corporate culture and reputation among its stakeholders. As businesses recognize the importance of the compliance function, the role of the compliance officer is also becoming more important, elaborate, and sought after. Unsurprisingly, the Bureau of Labor Statistics projects continued growth in the employment of compliance officers through 2022.[2]

I. Defining Compliance

Compliance means adherence to, or conformance with, rules, laws, standards, and policies. It also implies a sense of accountability and an obligation to uphold pertinent codes of conduct. From a more legalistic perspective, corporate compliance entails devising a formal internal system of policies, procedures, controls, and actions to detect and prevent violations of laws, regulations, rules, standards, and policies.

Ethics forms the foundation for a company's Program and the code of ethics/conduct (hereinafter "Code of Conduct"). While the Code of Conduct helps set the overall corporate tone toward compliance expectations, a company's Program should be a series of integrated mechanisms designed to address all aspects of compliance breaches. A company's Program can only emerge when basic operational components of a Program are in place. These key components of a Program include: top management commitment; compliance organization (structure, function, and assigned responsibilities); standards and procedures to detect and prevent fraud; and effective mechanisms for communication, training, auditing, control, evaluation, reporting, and corrective action.

II. The Importance of Compliance

The FSGO creates a consistent approach to deterring organizational wrongdoing by providing universally enforceable sentencing guidelines for similar crimes. The FSGO also sets forth mitigating conditions, including decreased fines and penalties for effective Programs. In fact, companies with effective Programs can see their fines reduced by up to 95 percent. Meanwhile, companies without effective Programs may see fines increased by up to 400 percent.[3] The 2004 amendments to the FSGO further highlight the need for organizations to have strong Programs. Specifically, these amendments strongly encourage companies to adopt a compliance-oriented culture by exercising due diligence to prevent and detect criminal conduct.[4]

The Sarbanes-Oxley Act of 2002 (SOX) requires public companies listed on a stock exchange to have a Program in place. Furthermore, Rule 206(4)-7 of the Securities and Exchange Commission's (SEC) Investment Advisers Act requires companies to appoint a chief compliance officer and implement a Program to prevent violations of federal securities laws.[5]

More recently, the Dodd-Frank Wall Street Reform and Consumer Protection Act of 2010 (Dodd-Frank), with new provisions for heightened whistle-blower awards, is further motivating organizations to practice self-regulation by developing formal channels for detecting and reporting violations. Under Dodd-Frank, eligible whistle-blowers are entitled to an award of between 10 percent and 30 percent of the monetary sanctions collected in actions brought by the SEC. From 2011 through 2013, the SEC received 6,573 whistle-blower tips and complaints. In 2013, whistle-blowers were awarded over $14.8 million.[6]

Numerous other laws mandate that companies have a Program with strong policies. Navigating the regulatory environment requires that companies develop an overall compliance management framework to handle the complicated assortment of laws and regulations. For example, certain provisions of the Federal Acquisition Regulations (FAR) require government contractors to implement internal controls, a Code of Conduct, and a fraud hotline to improve compliance management.[7] Since 1995, the top 100 cases alone against federal contractors resulted in more than $42 million in fines amid revelations of hundreds of instances of misconduct.[8]

The increased enforcement of the Foreign Corrupt Practices Act (FCPA) is leading to a rash of anticorruption Programs. In March 2014, the Department of Justice (DOJ) fined Marubeni Corporation $88 million for foreign bribery charges under the FCPA. In that case the DOJ cited the company's lack of an effective Program at the time of the offense and its failure to self-report the wrongdoing as key reasons for the large criminal fine.[9] Noncompliance can lead to enormous monetary losses and permanent reputational damage. To further illustrate the importance of an effective Program, the next section provides additional examples of violations and fines.

III.   The Cost of Noncompliance

The following are examples of compliance violations and fines:

- *Bribery/Corruption:* In 2008, Siemens AG paid U.S. authorities almost $800 million in penalties under the FCPA.[10] As of this writing, this is the largest penalty imposed under the FCPA.
- *Price-Fixing and Failure to Self-Report:* In 2011, Bridgestone was fined $28 million for price-fixing and FCPA violations in the marine hose industry, but it failed to disclose that it was also involved in price-fixing of automotive parts. In 2014, when Bridgestone finally pled guilty to automotive price-fixing, the DOJ took into account its past failure to fully disclose wrongdoing and fined the company $425 million.[11] This case serves as a reminder to self-report compliance breaches and fully cooperate with government authorities in all aspects of an investigation.
- *Fraud and Kickbacks:* In 2013, Johnson & Johnson made history for its part in one of the largest health care fraud settlements in U.S. history. It paid more than $2.2 billion for illegally marketing drugs to patients and paying kickbacks to pharmacists. This case highlights the severe damage that can result from gaps in a company's compliance management Program.[12]
- *Discriminatory Lending Practices:* In 2011, the DOJ agreed to a $335 million fair lending settlement—one of its largest—against Countrywide Financial Corporation for discriminatory mortgage lending practices against African American and Hispanic borrowers.[13]
- *Environmental Crimes:* In 2009, BP agreed to pay almost $180 million to settle Clean Air Act (CAA) violations. Pollution control violations alone amounted to $161 million of the settlement.[14]
- *Consumer Fraud:* In 2014, the DOJ imposed almost $1.2 billion in financial penalties on Toyota for issuing misleading statements to consumers about safety issues in Toyota and Lexus vehicles.[15]

IV.   Benefits of an Effective Ethics and Compliance Program

A DOJ attorney explained that when deciding whether to prosecute employees and companies, the key inquiry is whether the violation occurred *in spite of* the Program or *because of* a faulty or nonexistent Program. When management maintains an effective Program, the DOJ is far more likely to prosecute an individual employee rather than the entire company.[16]

A comparison of two well-known cases illustrates this point. Over a several-year period beginning in the mid-1990s, Siemens made over $1.3 billion in illegal payments to government officials.[17] The company's poorly managed Program greatly influenced the unprecedented $800 million in fines and penalties it received. In the mid-2000s, a Morgan Stanley top-level manager engaged in foreign corruption and personal enrichment.[18] Since a high-level manager had committed the violations, the bank was potentially exposed to severe fines and penalties under the FSGO. However, Morgan Stanley's effectively integrated Program led investigators to prosecute only the individual wrongdoer, saving the bank from significant fines and penalties.

Siemens's fraud involved more money than Morgan Stanley's violations. But, according to a DOJ attorney familiar with the cases, the relative strength of each company's Program ultimately dictated the extent to which each company was held accountable. Siemens, with 400,000 employees, employed only six compliance lawyers who presided over a "toxic" ethical culture.[19] Morgan Stanley, with 60,000 employees, boasted 500 compliance officers, and high-level compliance managers had a direct line to the board of directors.[20] Meanwhile, comprehensive training was instituted throughout Morgan Stanley and the Program was subjected to regular oversight and close scrutiny, including by third-party agents.[21] Finally, when Morgan Stanley discovered the violations, it hired an outside law firm to review documents and interview relevant parties.[22]

The lead DOJ attorney assigned to the Morgan Stanley case acknowledged that even an effectively managed Program will not prevent all violations. As the DOJ attorney said, the "compliance program did not work, [but] it does not always work."[23] The point is that (just as the FSGO requires) a good faith effort was made by Morgan Stanley in this case to prevent and then correct the breach, and to avoid recidivism. Though prosecutors are not bound by the FSGO, this case illustrates the important role an effective Program plays when prosecutors decide whether to prosecute organizations for compliance failures.

Even if a company is prosecuted, the FSGO promises the possibility of reduced penalties and fines for those organizations with effective Programs. Indeed, according to the FSGO, even "the failure to prevent or detect the instant offense does not necessarily mean that the program is not generally effective in preventing and detecting criminal conduct."[24] An otherwise liable company can therefore see its fines and punishments significantly mitigated, should it successfully proffer evidence of an effective Program. In some cases, fines may be reduced up to 95 percent.[25]

Complying with the FSGO standards for an effective Program helps companies reduce their exposure to liability under other federal regulations as well. For instance, the FSGO has inspired regulations under the SEC, the Environmental Protection Agency (EPA), the Department of Health and Human Services (HHS), the Department of Veterans Affairs (VA), and the DOJ's Antitrust Division.[26] Even the Internal Revenue Service (IRS) promotes voluntary compliance, offering amnesty for self-reporting a diverse array of violations.[27] Companies failing to institute an effective Program are often required to institute a well-conceived Program as part of a negotiated settlement with the DOJ.[28] Consequently, the FSGO permeates virtually every phase of compliance, from setting compliance standards to prosecution and sentencing. Those companies with an effective Program only stand to benefit.

A Program not only serves as a mitigating factor for punishments, but it also reduces the likelihood of violations occurring altogether. According to Patricia Harned, CEO of the Ethics Resource Center, employees of companies with Programs are 60 percent less likely than employees at companies with ineffective Programs to say they feel pressured to break the rules or disobey the law in order to do their jobs.[29] Similarly, observed misconduct, including illegal activities and corporate misconduct, drops 66 percent when companies implement and maintain a Program.[30]

For the reasons discussed above, expending resources to build a Program is a form of insurance against catastrophic legal liability and organizational decline. The issue isn't simply the fines and penalties of a government investigation and citation; the organization also risks increased regulatory scrutiny in all aspects of its operations, including loss of licenses, reputational harm, and difficulty attracting top talent.[31] But Programs are not all about avoidance. They are also integral to organizational proficiency.

Companies with effective Programs often see organizational improvements that ultimately lead to a healthier bottom line. With a Program in place, employee engagement reportedly increases by 44 percent.[32] Research shows a correlation between a strong Program and less disciplinary action and employee sick time taken, and a consequent decline in human resource costs.[33] Employees who believe their company acts ethically consistently work harder and longer.[34] Research into the inverse correlation between employee misconduct and effective Programs is in its early stages, as is research into the direct correlation between revenue and effective Programs. But the above statistics and other recent studies continue to support the view that there is both correlation and causation. In short, all things being equal, a company with a strong Program will generate more revenue and find itself exposed to less liability than its less-compliant peers.

V. The Evolution of Compliance Management in the United States

"Vicarious liability." It's a term that makes corporate general counsel squirm. It means that an organization (or any "principal") can be held liable for the acts of employees (or any "agent") acting wrongfully within the scope of their employment or in furtherance of organizational objectives. This legal concept results in organizational liability for a wide variety of improper actions on the part of employees and agents, including regulatory and ethical violations. Vicarious liability thus supports the trend of expanding compliance-oriented practices.

Early 20th Century: The history and growth of internal compliance Programs can be traced back to the founding of the Food and Drug Administration (FDA) in 1906.[35] Though the FDA was initially only responsible for public safety concerns, its founding began a trend in which corporations considered compliance as part of their operating environment. Modern regulatory compliance emerged more formally in the American corporate arena in the 1950s, when high-profile antitrust-related prosecutions impacted companies in the heavy electrical equipment industry.[36] Thereafter, companies began adopting what today are considered the rudimentary forms of antitrust compliance Programs. Comprehensive compliance Programs would later follow.

1970s: Further impetus for corporate self-regulation emerged in light of numerous financial scandals and the discovery of illegal campaign contributions during the Watergate scandal. In the 1970s, the SEC and IRS revealed rampant corruption in corporate America characterized by a culture of bribery and kickbacks.[37] As it became clear that multinationals based in the United States were also bribing foreign government officials to gain business advantages, the public recognized that self-regulation and informal compliance Programs were not enough to curb corporate misconduct. Consequently, lawmakers passed the FCPA in 1977 to restore public trust and deter misconduct. The FCPA pressured companies to adopt more formal compliance policies relating to bribes, kickbacks, accounting practices, and other business conduct.

1980s: The role of ethics and compliance officers emerged in response to scandals in the defense industry during the 1980s.[38] These industry-wide scandals brought defense contractors together to form the Defense Industry Initiative on Business Ethics and Conduct (DII). The DII prescribes ethical principles for business conduct, including promoting and enforcing written Codes of Conduct and reporting misconduct to appropriate government authorities.[39]

The 1980s were also plagued with scandals in the financial industry. Corporate misconduct in the savings and loans industry led to the collapse of major financial institutions. The Federal Deposit Insurance Corporation (FDIC), which insured the accounts housed at these failed financial institutions, was stretched to its limits.[40] This led to the passage of the Federal Deposit Insurance Corporation Act of 1991 (FDICIA), which resulted in increased oversight of insured entities.[41] Meanwhile, high-profile insider trading cases outraged the public and resulted in Congress passing the Insider Trading and Securities Fraud Enforcement Act of 1988. This law required financial institutions to establish Programs to prevent insider trading by personnel.[42] These laws, therefore, all required organizations to strengthen internal compliance Programs.

Finally, in 1984, Congress used its authority under the Sentencing Reform Act of 1984 to create the USSC. This powerful commission is responsible for articulating the sentencing guidelines of U.S. federal courts.

1990s: As an extension of the Sentencing Reform Act, the FSGO became effective on November 1, 1991. The FSGO applies to corporations, partnerships, labor unions, pension funds, trusts, nonprofit entities, and governmental units.[43] These guidelines were designed to further two key sentencing objectives: "just punishment" and "deterrence." "Just punishment" refers to the relationship between the sentence and the degree of blame attributable to the offender. "Deterrence" refers to incentives offered to organizations that effectively prevent and detect misconduct.[44] These guidelines thus incentivized self-regulation and were a decisive milestone in facilitating the development of modern Programs.

In 1999, the Holder memo further developed the sentencing guidelines by setting forth the "Principles of Federal Prosecution of Business Organizations." The principles provided standardized factors to be considered by federal prosecutors when deciding whether to charge corporations with wrongdoing.[45] In 2003, the Thompson memo revised the Holder memo to include mandatory guidelines for all prosecutors. The Thompson memo comprised the revised set of principles, including factors that federal prosecutors must consider in determining whether to charge a corporation. These factors include: (1) seriousness of the offense, (2) pervasiveness of wrongdoing, (3) past conduct, (4) timely disclosure, (5) willingness to cooperate, and (6) existence and effectiveness of the Program.[46] Whether a Program is effective is determined, in large part, by reference to the Seven Pillars of an effective compliance and ethics Program, as set forth in the FSGO.

Early 2000s: The 21st century began with some of corporate America's biggest financial scandals. The fraudulent financial and accounting practices exposed during the Enron and WorldCom scandals led to loss of investor confidence. The WorldCom scandal alone destroyed an estimated $175 billion of shareholder wealth. Additional accounting scandals involved companies such as Tyco, Halliburton, and Arthur Andersen.[47]

In response to these scandals, Congress passed the Sarbanes-Oxley Act (SOX), which was signed into by then-president Bush in 2002. "The Act mandated a number of reforms to enhance corporate responsibility, enhance financial disclosures, and combat corporate and accounting fraud, and created the Public Company Accounting Oversight Board, also known as the PCAOB, to oversee the activities of the auditing profession."[48] In fact, section 406 of SOX requires public companies to disclose whether senior financial officers have adopted a Code of Ethics. Under SOX, "Code of Ethics" means written standards that are reasonably designed to deter wrongdoing and promote honest ethical conduct; avoidance of conflicts of interest; compliance with applicable laws, rules, and regulations; full, fair, accurate, timely, and comprehensible disclosure to the SEC; prompt internal reporting of any violations of the Code; and accountability for adherence to the Code.[49] SOX has been instrumental in driving increased transparency and deterring fraud and misconduct.

Mid-2000s: In another milestone year for strengthening the modern compliance movement, the 2004 amendments to the FSGO required companies to promote an organizational culture that encourages ethical conduct and strengthens commitment to compliance with the law.[50] These revisions place more emphasis on high-level oversight of Programs, training and evaluating employees, internal and external risk assessment, and monitoring to enhance an organization's ethical culture.

Post–Great Recession Reforms: The Great Recession started in 2007 with the subprime mortgage crisis in the United States. This crisis culminated in 2008 with the bank failures of Bear Stearns and Lehman Brothers, followed by the most significant stock market decline since the Great Depression. This crisis caused 8.8 million people to lose their jobs while household wealth declined by a staggering $19.2 trillion.[51] The government bailed out Fannie Mae and Freddie Mac, the auto industry, and a large portion of the banking industry via the Emergency Economic Stabilization Act of 2008.[52]

It seemed that the earlier scandals involving Enron and WorldCom, and the regulatory initiatives thereafter, had barely made a dent in corporate America's appetite for risky business ventures and unscrupulous lending practices. The American public was outraged as $700 billion went toward bailing out the same institutions that had caused the public to lose trillions of dollars in wealth. To restore public confidence and prevent misconduct that could initiate another economic collapse, Congress passed the Dodd-Frank. Dodd-Frank is the most significant regulatory reform in decades and implicates nearly every aspect of the country's financial services industry.

The FSGO and SOX are two key pieces of guidance impacting current developments in corporate compliance. In addition, Dodd-Frank promotes transparency and accountability while its whistle-blower provisions are a further impetus for organizations to self-regulate. Accordingly, the following sections explore in more detail the key compliance implications of these legislative initiatives.

VI. The Federal Sentencing Guidelines for Organizations (FSGO)

The FSGO advises the courts on penalties for organizational legal violations and sets clear standards for organizations to develop Programs that detect and prevent criminal conduct. Prosecutors, though not bound by the FSGO, may also make prosecution decisions based on whether organizations meet the standards of an effective Program under the FSGO. The FSGO has thus forcefully shaped modern compliance and encouraged organizations to implement effective Programs.

The FSGO takes a carrot-and-stick approach: organizations with Programs that meet FSGO standards tend to get reduced penalties for wrongdoing, while organizations with subpar Programs receive tougher penalties. According to the FSGO, "such compliance and ethics program shall be reasonably designed, implemented, and enforced so that the program is generally effective in preventing and detecting criminal conduct."[53] As a result, many organizations now have Programs that are based on FSGO standards.

The Seven Pillars: Seven broad factors, widely known as the "Seven Pillars of an effective compliance and ethics Program," are identified by the FSGO and contribute to an effective Program:[54]

1. *Processes and Procedures*: Creating standards, processes, and procedures to prevent and detect criminal conduct.
2. *High-Level Oversight*: Providing oversight by high-level personnel for implementation of a Program. This pillar also provides guidance on appointing both high-level and operational personnel for effective implementation of the Program.
3. *Excluding Bad Actors*: Due diligence to prevent anyone who behaved illegally in the past from obtaining a position of substantial authority.
4. *Communications*: Effectively communicating Program policies and procedures throughout all levels of the workforce and to all other relevant agents.
5. *Ongoing Monitoring*: Taking reasonable steps to monitor, detect, and report criminal conduct, and to audit the Program. The Program should ensure mechanisms are available that enable retaliation-free, anonymous reporting of criminal conduct.
6. *Enforcement*: Enforcing the Program consistently, and adequately balancing incentives and disciplinary measures (the "carrot and stick"), to prevent and detect criminal conduct within a workforce.

7. *Self-Reporting:* Periodically assessing the risk of criminal conduct and, upon detection of any such misconduct, taking appropriate actions to prevent a recurrence.

The Culpability Score: After determining the offense and the base fine to be imposed on an organization for criminal conduct, the court then calculates the organization's culpability score. The culpability score takes into account the severity of the violations and any mitigating factors in order to either increase or decrease the severity of the punishment imposed on the organization. The ultimate culpability score is reached by adding or subtracting points as a result of aggravating and mitigating factors.[55] The score then correlates to a defined range of fines and/or jail time for the offense.

Aggravating Factors:[56]

- High-level personnel were involved in or tolerated criminal activity.
- Prior history of misconduct by the organization.
- Violation of a judicial order, injunction, or condition of probation.
- The organization's willful attempt to obstruct or impede justice at any point during the investigation, prosecution, or sentencing.

Mitigating Factors:[57]

- At the time of the offense, the organization had an effective Program as outlined by the FSGO.
- The organization self-reported the offense to appropriate government authorities, cooperated with the investigators, and accepted responsibility for its criminal actions.

VII.   The Sarbanes-Oxley Act of 2002 (SOX)

SOX consists of 11 titles and almost 70 subsections setting new or enhanced standards for U.S. public company boards, management, and public accounting firms. From a compliance perspective, the key sections include: 302, 401, 404, 409, 802, and 906.[58]

- Sections 302 and 404 outline the key role of a company's internal auditing and reporting functions. These sections outline responsibilities for adequate fraud risk assessment and ensure that internal controls are properly designed, implemented, and evaluated to prevent and detect fraud.[59]
- Section 401 is intended to prevent the fraudulent use of off-balance sheet items, as in the case of Enron. This section requires that published financial statements accurately represent information and include all material off-balance sheet liabilities, obligations, or transactions.[60]

- Section 409 requires companies to clearly report any material change in the financial or operating condition of the company.
- Section 802 "imposes penalties of fines and/or up to 20 years imprisonment for altering, destroying, mutilating, concealing, falsifying records, documents or tangible objects with the intent to obstruct, impede or influence a legal investigation."[61]
- Section 906 relates to sections 302 and 404, as it requires the CEO/CFO to ensure that all financial reporting is fair and compliant. This section also outlines criminal penalties in the form of fines and imprisonment.[62]

SOX also includes protection against whistle-blowers (Section 806) and criminal penalties for retaliation against whistle-blowers (Section 1107).[63]

VIII.   The Dodd-Frank Wall Street Reform and Consumer Protection Act of 2010 (Dodd-Frank)

Dodd-Frank was signed into law by President Obama in 2010, and it arguably represents the most important financial reform since those of the Great Depression. Dodd-Frank is infamous for its vast legislative scope and its thousands of pages of rules and guidelines. The multifaceted act implicates nearly the entire financial industry and economy, including commercial lending, consumer lending, derivatives, brokers-dealers, hedge funds, investment banking, community banking, whistle-blowers, investor advocacy, and more.[64]

Dodd-Frank's primary objective is to identify and prevent future interruptions and collapses of financial institutions. According to its authors, Dodd-Frank is designed "to promote the financial stability of the United States by improving accountability and transparency in the financial system, to end 'too big to fail,' to protect the American taxpayer by ending bailouts, to protect consumers from abusive financial services practices, and for other purposes."[65] Some salient features of Dodd-Frank include:

- Establishing the Consumer Financial Protection Bureau (CFPB) to protect consumers from predatory business practices. Its role extends to enforcing federal consumer protection laws, restricting deceptive/unfair practices, taking consumer complaints, promoting financial education, monitoring consumer risks, and preventing discrimination in consumer finance.[66]
- Avoiding institutions that are "too big to fail" by creating the Financial Stability Oversight Council (FSOC). Established under Dodd-Frank, "The Council is charged with identifying risks to the financial stability of the United States; promoting market discipline; and responding to emerging risks to the stability of the United States' financial system."[67]

- Establishing the Department of the Treasury's Federal Insurance Office (FIO) to monitor all aspects of the insurance sector, ensuring that underserved communities and consumers have access to affordable insurance products. FIO also advises the Treasury and other federal agencies on insurance matters.[68]
- Implementing section 619 of Dodd-Frank, known as the Volcker Rule, which "prohibits banks from engaging in short-term proprietary trading of certain securities, derivatives commodity futures, and options on these instruments for their own accounts."[69] It also requires banking institutions to implement an internal compliance Program to effectively comply with the provisions set forth in the Volcker Rule.
- Extending the authority of the Public Company Accounting Oversight Board (PCAOB) to oversee audit reports of brokers and dealers and to share information with foreign auditor oversight authorities.[70]
- Amending the Securities Exchange Act of 1934 to provide whistle-blower incentives and provisions. The SEC is authorized to pay awards (10–30 percent of collected money) to eligible whistle-blowers who provide high-quality and original information leading to enforcement actions that yield sanctions of over $1 million.[71]

This is only a brief overview of Dodd-Frank. As its voluminous nature suggests, its reach is extensive, and compliance is an intensive proposition.

Conclusion

The rush is on to create an effective Program—replete with Codes of Conduct, compliance officers, reporting hotlines, and training modules. Companies, like people, respond to incentives. And there is now both a carrot and a stick for effective and ineffective Programs, respectively. New regulations are coming online at a rapid pace, and organizations failing to stay vigilant while navigating this fluid regulatory framework face severe fines and penalties. Organizations with effective Programs can see their fines and penalties mitigated, and may avoid prosecution altogether.

CHAPTER TWO

Dealing with Ethical Challenges

I. Business Ethics: The Foundation for Compliance Programs

Business ethics deals with the ethical business standards, codes of good conduct, rules, rights, and morals that govern the interactions and relationships between an organization and its stakeholders, including society-at-large. Simply put, business ethics addresses the responsibilities or obligations that a company, as a steward, has toward all its organizational stakeholders. These stakeholders are not limited to the business's employees, but also include customers, suppliers, investors, government, society, the environment, and all other entities that impact, or are impacted by, the business.

What Are Ethics?

A Word from Kara Bhala, Seven Pillars Institute

"Ethics is a guide to human conduct using reason. An agent chooses the best morally right action in a situation based on reason, in light of the interest of each individual affected by the action. Ethics therefore, is the theoretical basis for compliance programs.

We need to know why an action is right or wrong. Ethics gives us the explanations based on a theoretical body of knowledge stretching back two thousand five hundred years, for the western moral tradition, and an even longer period of time for the eastern moral tradition."[1]

Some argue that, since the core motive behind a business is profit maximization, only profit-maximization activities should be undertaken.

Historically, the notion that businesses exist solely for obtaining maximum profit fed the public's cynicism toward businesspeople. In Japan and England, for example, nobility of past centuries tended to look down on merchants. In India, the business class is still today relegated to the second-lowest caste, just above the "untouchable" caste, in a four-tier caste system. The ancient Greek god of merchants, Hermes, was also the god of thieves,[2] and taught his lessons or morals through deception and trickery.

The perception that businesspeople are shrewd and untrustworthy contrasts with the view that businesspeople drive the technological advancements that benefit society—in areas including but not limited to medicine and health care, transportation, agriculture, manufacturing, and information technology. The reputation of business, particularly in the United States and much of the developed world, is a step above that of centuries past. But recurring business scandals (think Enron, WorldCom, and Arthur Andersen) mean that questions are never far off. Aggrieved consumers may boycott companies, scandalized populations pass restrictive laws against corporations, and, where the reputation of corporations is poor, young talent finds alternative careers to pursue.

Maintaining a positive perception requires not only that a business comply with the law, but also that its compliance efforts are derived from an ethical vision that is consistent with the public's notion of how a business should act. Exceeding ethical expectations rather than simply abiding by them requires that companies engage in proactive moral imagination. Moral imagination is "a form of reasoning that serves as an antidote to decision environments that normally lead to morally defective choices."[3] Moral imagination demands abandoning the blind pursuit of profits and embracing a wider appreciation of the impact that businesses have on stakeholders and society-at-large.[4] Moral imagination not only creates a business enterprise bolstered by pillars of integrity and moral certitude, but also can increase a company's long-term profitability.

Accordingly, identifying the underlying causes of misconduct is a prerequisite for complying with, and eventually exceeding, legal requirements. Misconduct and lapses in judgment generally occur when individuals lose their moral grounding, or when an organization's insufficient ethical foundations and moral imagination fail to instill the importance of "doing the right thing."

In light of fragile public opinion, and in an ocean of complicated regulations, the ethical foundation is an essential, but often neglected, aspect of compliance. When developing an ethical foundation, businesses have two choices for instilling a high ethical standard among employees: First, the business can attempt to outline and then teach thousands of complicated rules to its employees. Alternatively, the business can instruct employees on how to think ethically when making decisions. The latter approach is more effective (and more efficient) since it makes employees more likely to consistently comply with laws, even without necessarily understanding the full breadth of laws to which they are subject.

II. The Importance of Ethics Training and Education

Can organizations really teach employees to behave ethically? It's a mushy and spiritual goal, some might say. Besides, people are going to do what they're going to do. Businesspeople live in the realm of realities, finite numbers, and tangible products. But ethical training does work, and in measureable ways.

The idea that people are "going to do what they're going to do" regardless of training is based on the idea that ethics are innate. But this is an overstatement. Our upbringings, our communities, and our cultures are influential, even decisive, in shaping our ethical perspectives. This is why laws exist. This is why religions set forth rules ("Thou shall not kill," "Thou shall not steal," etc.). People have been teaching one another to act ethically since the rise of civilizations, and this should continue throughout individuals' personal and professional lives.

Further, in contrast to the view that ethics is too abstract to teach or measure—the "it's mushy" argument—the effectiveness of ethical training can indeed be quantified and measured. For instance, trainers using advanced psychometric testing can help organizations assess training effectiveness by measuring things like ethical awareness of an issue, ethical judgments that employees may make when confronted with a specific ethical dilemma, and more. This also means that we can measure whether employees believe top management acts ethically; whether managers engage in discriminatory hiring practices; or whether international workforces believe corruption, bribery, or conflicts of interest are appropriate in the workplace.

The data derived from these tests help organizations quantify the compliance risk associated with each employee, allowing companies to address gaps in ethics training and thereby reduce the potential for ethical violations within their organizations. This means training the workforce to recognize its own subconscious biases and beliefs; educating the workforce to uncover the fallacies inherent in so many biases; and implementing standards and procedures to encourage the type of behavior that is appropriate for the organization. This process isn't about telling people what is moral.

Morals are the beliefs of individuals. This is about shaping ethics. Ethics are broad, and each organization can and should have a set of ethics that individuals, even those with varying morals, can all follow.

Lastly, organizations cannot simply ignore ethics. Around the world, the trend toward ethical behavior is clear. Almost every country in the world now outlaws bribery. Even China, with its long history of bribery in the name of *guanxi*, or connections, is in the midst of an unprecedented crackdown on corrupt actors. And domestically and internationally, transparency is at an all-time high. The Information Age is fully upon us. More often, companies are being exposed for past wrongs for which they might not have been cited in the past. For instance, Apple faced an enormous public outcry after it was revealed that a third-party manufacturer for the company, Foxconn, was treating its employees inhumanely.[5] Those that refuse to see the writing on the wall may escape pressure in the immediate term—or they may not. But even if they do, the shadow of unethical behavior is long, and retribution is patient.

Consequently, ethics training and education is important for three main reasons: (1) an effective ethics Program greatly influences employees' behavior, (2) the effectiveness of ethics training is quantifiable, and (3) organizations around the world are increasingly being held to higher ethical standards. Accordingly, companies should perpetually focus on updating compliance-training programs and educating employees on ethical behavior.

III. Benefits of Ethics Training and Education

As the previous section demonstrates, ethics can be taught. In fact, ethics training and education is central to developing a culture of compliance since it provides employees with the knowledge needed to confront key ethical challenges and make decisions that comply with national laws and company values. This section discusses how ethics training and education is imperative to a company's long-term success.

1. Ethical business practices help cultivate a culture of trust, goodwill, integrity, and compliance. Where an ethical culture reigns supreme, organizations see fewer ethical violations, compliance breaches, and fines. An ethical orientation in an organization serves as a sort of insurance policy against fines and litigation costs, as well as unruly employee behavior and employee misconduct such as harassment, bullying, and discrimination. Perhaps most important, a strong ethical culture enhances employee morale, which positively impacts productivity and company performance.

2. An ethics training program is part of the foundation of a company's long-term competitive advantage. A strong ethics training program fosters a culture of respect, fairness, and prioritizing long-term relationships over short-term gains. Businesses that have solid relationships with suppliers, distributors, and employees are more insulated from external economic and reputational threats.

3. Research shows that goodwill and a favorable reputation have a positive impact on companies' bottom lines, since customers who perceive a company to be ethical often give that company the benefit of the doubt when the company is accused of a regulatory violation.[6]

4. Research has also shown that ethical and socially responsible companies tend to attract and more readily retain talent. Employees who are treated fairly have a sense of goodwill and organizational trust, which translates into a happier and more productive workforce.[7]

5. Shareholders and other external stakeholders also value companies with reputations for acting ethically. An ethical reputation signals to shareholders more transparency, less risk of wrongdoing, a better compliance culture, and, ultimately, future growth and success. In fact, some organizations, such as Ethisphere, have responded to customers' and investors' demands for ethical responsibility by publishing rankings of the most ethical companies. An entire emerging category of investors promotes socially responsible investing (SRI). SRI entails investing in well-managed and profitable companies that are also committed to upholding social, environmental, and governance standards that benefit society.[8]

6. Lastly, emphasizing business ethics is instrumental in ensuring that corporations act in the best interests of not only their shareholders but of society-at-large. When companies behave unethically, society pays the price in terms of corruption, product failures, worker rights abuses, profiteering, and social inequality, which cumulatively threaten the fabric of our social and economic system.

IV. Understanding Right and Wrong

So what is morally or ethically right or wrong? Answering this question requires exploring the process of ethical reasoning. Morals tend to be socially learned, largely unconscious precepts of personal behavior based on self-evident rules of what society deems appropriate conduct.[9] Ethics are generally accepted standards that provide guidelines for conduct in various situations and professions. Thus, unlike morals, which are more personal, ethics tend to be groups-based. Organizations and professional associations tend to institute these ethics in the form of Codes of Conduct.

However, research has shown cross-cultural differences in ethical beliefs, perceptions, attitudes, and behavior.[10] American managers, for example, view bribery and theft as an ethical issue whereas German and Austrian managers view bribery and theft as a moral issue.[11] Although eating beef is customary in many societies, hundreds of millions of Hindus in India consider it immoral due to religious reasons. And almost 160 million people in India are still treated as "untouchables," suffering under oftentimes inhuman conditions.

As the above examples show, the customs and practices of one culture may be seen as unethical in another culture. Multinationals and companies operating abroad must consider how this will affect behavior within their organizations, and when dealing with partners, clients, and competitors. Organizations must therefore consider, prior to engaging in organization-wide ethics training, the following:

- How do we come to an understanding of what is moral or ethical?
- Is our understanding of morals superior to others?
- Shall we impose our morals and ethics on other cultures?
- Is there a set of universal ethics?

Before elaborating on the process of ethical reasoning, it is helpful to understand what causes personal variation in moral judgments and behaviors. At an individual level, moral judgments are broadly guided by either an idealistic and relativistic orientation, or some combination of the two orientations. Idealistic and relativistic orientations then further guide the specific ethical reasoning approaches that people apply in their ethical-decision-making processes. The following paragraphs elaborate on the idealist and relativist points of view and delve into various ethical reasoning methods.

V.   Idealism

Idealism is the moral belief that ethics are universally applicable regardless of culture or conditions. In other words, idealists believe that certain conduct is always unethical or immoral regardless of where and why it occurs.

To help illustrate the concept of idealism, consider the United Nations' founding document, the Charter of the United Nations. This document sets forth principles, or moral and ethical boundaries, regarding interactions among different countries. For instance, Chapter I, Article 1 sets forth the following universal principles: (1) respecting "equal rights and self-determination of all peoples"; (2) "promoting and encouraging respect for human rights" without discrimination based on "race, sex, language, or religion"; and (3) prohibiting the "threat or use of force against the territorial integrity" of any country. The UN comprises more than 190 countries, which claim to uphold these universal principles.

Idealists would argue that these ethical boundaries be upheld in all situations, without exception. In other words, these principles are so superior that compliance with them should be imposed on all UN member states, and that any deviation from these principles constitutes a moral and ethical breach.

Idealism is an attractive philosophy because of its simple application. For the idealist, a particular behavior is either morally or ethically permissible, or it is not. Certain restrictions on women's rights in Saudi Arabia, for example, are immoral and unethical for the idealist who believes that discrimination based on gender is never permissible.

On the other hand, idealism is unattractive because of its rigidity. It may be, for example, that the majority of Saudi Arabia's population supports certain restrictions on women's rights in order to preserve the country's ancient religious traditions. However, for the idealist, cultural considerations or other extrinsic factors cannot justify a deviation from certain principles.

Moreover, what is ethical is a varying concept across time and culture. At one time, human slavery was considered a part of the social fabric of many countries and cultures. Today, slavery is not only illegal, but also widely acknowledged as immoral and inhumane. Similarly, several cultures and religions consider same-sex marriages or adoptions to be taboo and even unethical, while other cultures and nation states are more open to permitting same-sex couples the freedom to marry or adopt. In practice, then, the universal set of ethical principles that idealists espouse are open to interpretation, and can be interpreted differently in different cultures, during different time periods, and in different situations.[12] This undermines the claim of universality.

For idealists, the well-being of society is contingent on the application of a set of ethical values or principles, rules, and laws.[13] Cultural imperialism is one variant of idealism. Cultural imperialism implies that one's national and cultural Code of Conduct and moral principles are superior to all others. Nations throughout history—including the ancient Roman Empire and the British Empire—have practiced cultural imperialism. But, in fact, one culture's highest ethical principle may mean nothing to another culture, as the example of women in the Saudi society shows.

The purpose here is to not espouse one philosophy over another, but instead to reinforce the point that it is not easy to establish universally accepted rights and wrongs in life or in business. Organizations embarking on ethics training are advised to acknowledge and account for these variations in ethical perspectives and cultures. One may believe one's culture is superior to all others, but such a monopolistic viewpoint is unlikely to fall on receptive ears in the multinational, multicultural workplace.

VI. Relativism

"When in Rome, do as the Romans do."

Unlike idealists, relativists do not believe that morals and ethics are universally applicable. Instead, they believe morals and ethics vary between cultures. The relativistic point of view says there is no absolute right or wrong. Aligned with this view is the idea of cultural relativism, wherein morals and ethics are not universally determined but culturally determined. According to cultural relativism, no one culture's values or ethics are better than any other, and judgments pertaining to right and wrong or good and evil are products of the cultures and societies in which we live.

Consider again the universal principles set forth in the UN Charter, namely, the right to self-determination, the protection of human rights, and the prohibition of the use of force. Unlike idealists, who argue that deviating from these principles is never permissible, relativists would contend that exceptions may exist based on cultural or other extrinsic factors. For instance, compared to the idealist who believes that gender discrimination is never permissible, relativists may perceive Saudi Arabia's restrictions on women as a cultural norm. In other words, if the people in Saudi Arabia view certain restrictions on women's rights as necessary to comply with religious traditions, then no other country can assert that Saudi Arabia is acting unethically.

Relativism is an attractive philosophy because it is more flexible; it accounts for practical and cultural considerations when determining whether certain conduct is moral and ethical. For instance, relativists may argue that the United States should refrain from imposing a free-market economy on Cuba if Cuba's citizens prefer communism. Idealists, on the other hand, may argue that free-market economies are the most productive and should be imposed on all countries.

Taken to its logical extreme, however, relativism is untenable.[14] In Nazi Germany, for example, the persecution of Jewish civilians and others was permitted by parts of the population. But in Nazi Germany, as in South Africa under apartheid, universal principles prevail in denouncing such actions.

Consequently, a company must determine the type of conduct that it will not consider permissible. For example, companies generally have companywide zero-tolerance policies toward intentionally stealing from the company or sexually harassing a coworker. Such a prohibition is derived from idealism since the ban on these two types of conduct is universal throughout the company.

On the other hand, management's policy toward salespeople offering gifts to clients may vary based on geography. For instance, salespeople based in the United States may be prohibited from offering cash gifts to potential clients, since this could be construed as bribery. Meanwhile, the same company's sales team in parts of Asia may be permitted, based on appropriate guidelines and policies, to give small cash gifts when attending the weddings of customers or clients, because such cash gifts are an integral aspect of many Asian cultures. This variation in gift-giving policy is derived from relativism, since the policy is based on the ethical and moral principles of different cultures.

VII. Ethical Reasoning

The above section covered the underlying philosophies behind individual moral judgments. In this section, ethical reasoning methods are explored. The three broad categories of ethical reasoning are (1) teleological ethical systems/consequentialism, (2) deontological ethical systems, and (3) virtue ethics. While examining the ethical reasoning perspective, consider how an individual with a relativistic moral orientation and an individual with an idealistic moral orientation might differ in their analysis of an ethical situation.

Teleology/Consequentialism: Consequentialism holds that an act is judged as morally right or wrong based on the consequences of that act. (Remember that what is right or wrong will vary with the situation for a relativist, but will apply universally for an idealist.) Consequentialism further breaks down to include: utilitarianism, distributive justice, and ethical egoism.

Utilitarianism is the belief that if an act produces the maximum possible good or the greatest happiness, it is therefore a moral act.[15] Some criticisms of utilitarianism are that it fails to explain how to determine the greatest good, and that it remains, in essence, an "ends justify the means" principle.

Distributive justice is the consequentialist belief that a moral or ethical act is one that is "fair." Imagine you are about to enter an entirely alien world and, although there is inequity, you don't know whether you will be poor or wealthy, educated, healthy, influential, or powerful. What type of society would you create? How would you allocate resources? The just society is the society that we would all create if we had such a "veil of ignorance" about our ultimate role within that society.[16] From a societal perspective, distributive justice therefore pertains to the perceived fairness of how costs and benefits are distributed.

Virtue Ethics

A Word from Kara Bhala, Seven Pillars Institute

"Aristotle, the first person to systematize ethics as a discipline, had a practical way of viewing ethical conduct. The term for Aristotle's form of moral philosophy is 'virtue ethics.' A person is virtuous by possessing and practicing the virtues every day. To be virtuous is to do the right thing for the right reason, at the right time, in the right way.

While we have the capacity to act virtuously, the virtues are acquired through daily practice and doing. We become just by doing just actions and brave by doing brave actions. This idea of becoming ethical through practice and constant doing is inherent in compliance programs. We keep doing what is right as laid out in relevant rules and laws. Doing the right thing then becomes part of our nature."[17]

Ethical egoism is the consequentialist belief that an action is considered right or wrong based on the extent to which it helps enhance an individual's rational self-interest.[18] This theory is premised on the idea that a society thrives when each individual focuses on improving his or her own quality of life. Ethical egoism is often criticized as focusing too much on the individual while ignoring the welfare of society.

Deontology: According to the deontological category of ethical reasoning, a person's conduct should be guided by a set of universal laws that can be applied in every situation and every action.[19] Thus, it is based on the idealistic orientation of universally applicable guiding principles. A common criticism of deontology is its lack of moral or ethical flexibility.[20] For instance, a dogmatic deontologist who believes that killing is always wrong may then refuse to defend himself against a violent criminal for fear of inflicting death on the perpetrator.

Virtue Ethics: According to virtue ethics, a person's conduct should be guided by that individual's experiences and personal perception of what is moral or ethical in any given situation. Unlike consequentialist and deontological approaches, which focus on outcomes and universal principles, virtue ethics focuses on the character traits that dictate the process for how an individual makes moral and ethical decisions. Thus, virtue ethics focuses on describing and understanding the virtuous character traits that drive an individual's moral and ethical decisions.[21]

In summary, ethical reasoning comprises three broad categories, which include consequentialism, deontology, and virtue ethics. Consequentialism judges a person's conduct based on the impact it has on the individual and society. Deontology judges a person's conduct based on universally accepted principles of what constitutes ethical and moral behavior. Lastly, virtue ethics judges a person's conduct based on how that person learns from experiences to make the right decision in different situations.

Compliance departments should remember that the workforce will rely on these different ethical reasoning perspectives, each of which has its own limitations and strengths from a corporate compliance and ethics perspective. Moreover, analysis of a workforce's moral perspective—either idealistic or relativistic—may provide insight into the ways in which the workforce will respond to ethical challenges.

VIII.   Ethical Reasoning in the Workplace

Using this overview of moral philosophies and ethical reasoning perspectives, think about the moral and ethical perspectives to which you subscribe, and whether your coworkers, supervisors, or employees may subscribe to different perspectives. Below are some additional considerations for a fuller understanding of how people make moral and ethical decisions.

The Hybrid Approach: As the name suggests, this approach refers to the application of the three categories of ethical reasoning simultaneously. For instance, a company's management may subscribe to the belief that employees deserve a minimum of two months' notice before being laid off (deontology). However, due to a sudden economic collapse, management may be forced to immediately lay off 10 percent of the workforce in order to save the company. By preventing collapse, the company will save the other 90 percent of its workforce from unemployment (consequentialism). This example illustrates that following one belief under ethical reasoning is potentially impractical and even harmful, since many factors may influence whether a particular behavior is moral or ethical. Accordingly, all ethical decision-making styles have blind spots. The hybrid approach is attractive because it requires consciously considering and revealing ethical blind spots. This practice is developed by enhancing one's ethical awareness of issues and challenges that generally arise in society, as well as those that are specific to a given workplace or environment.

The Resolution of Factual Misunderstandings Approach: In an international context, ethical disagreements may not actually be based on moral precepts but, instead, on mutual misunderstandings and miscommunications.[22]

People everywhere tend to have some sense of right and wrong and adhere to certain values that they feel are universally applicable. According to former UN Secretary-General Kofi Annan, for instance, the values of peace, freedom, social progress, equal rights, and human dignity are universal values, and thus enshrined in the Charter of the United Nations.[23]

Thus, by consciously ensuring the facts are adequately understood by all parties, the prevalence of certain core human values means that agreements can be achieved in a transcultural context on a wide variety of matters.

For example, as noted earlier, bribery is considered unethical in many parts of the world; it is thought to undermine the fabric of society. In China, by contrast, prohibitions against bribery might actually be viewed as unethical. Where rule of law has historically wavered, relationships and trust have served as an integral substitute in China and other countries.[24] Consequently, the use of family networks and influence is more acceptable in collectivist cultures like China than what may be considered acceptable in Western, individualist cultures. But in China, this is not bribery; it is considered protecting one's relations and, ultimately, contributing to societal harmony.[25] When one considers China's long period of civil war in the 20th century (and throughout much of its history), this begins to make sense. Ultimately, the universal value of social progress is inherent in both cultures, but historically differing experiences have resulted in a divergence as to the means to that end.

The Code of Ethics and Core Values Approach: Companies today regularly provide their employees with an ethics-based Code of Conduct to use as a guide when faced with ethical dilemmas. Many companies also find it helpful to discuss ethical dilemmas and offer ethics-based training, using the company Code of Conduct as a framework, so employees can practice handling inevitable ethical conflicts. Finally, encouraging employees to submit ethics-related questions to various departments, including legal, compliance, and HR, may allow for a cross-functional analysis of a situation and a more informed response to the particular ethical question.

The Headline Test Approach: Individuals can determine whether an approach is permissible by asking themselves, "How would this look displayed on the front page of the newspaper?" In other words, if the individual would be embarrassed by such publicity, then the questionable conduct should probably be avoided.

The Golden Rule Approach: This approach refers to the ethics of reciprocity, which is based on reciprocal responsibilities to ensure justice for all, beyond just friends and family. The golden rule, which derives from most major religious teachings, essentially encourages individuals to treat others the way they would want to be treated.

By stressing some of the above approaches, organizations can help bridge the moral shortcomings of their employees.

IX.   Ethical Issues in Business

Various business disciplines have developed ethical principles and Codes of Ethics to guide professionals in ways most relevant for those in the profession. Although the core idea of ethics and ethical decision making is the same across job functions, each profession presents different and complicated ethical challenges. This section outlines some common ethical issues in the fields of accounting, finance, human resources, marketing, and international business.

Ethical Issues in Accounting and Finance: Ethical issues in accounting and finance often relate to transparency, conflicts of interest, fraud, disclosures, and reporting. Unfortunately, the public is not isolated from ethical violations that occur within these professions. For instance, financial- and accounting-related ethical issues were eventually revealed to have contributed to the 2008 Great Recession, which devastated the global economy. Some common ethical challenges in the finance and accounting professions emerge around the following issues:

- fair and accurate reporting of financial data and statements
- falsifying documents and creative accounting
- misappropriation of assets through embezzlement, deception, and false expense claims
- appropriately disclosing conflicts of interests
- insider trading
- money laundering
- fraud related to financial statements, taxes, insurance, securities, and mortgage

Ethical Issues in Human Resource Management: An organization's HR department deals with all personnel matters and is therefore confronted with many ethical challenges that arise with managing people, policies, and procedures. HR departments often face ethical challenges in the following areas:

- recruitment, mergers and acquisitions, and layoffs
- discrimination, harassment, and bullying

- workplace diversity management
- workplace safety and fair working conditions
- compensation and performance evaluations
- privacy, confidentiality, and security
- health care issues

Ethical Issues in Marketing: Marketing departments generally focus on product management, pricing, advertising and promotions, customer service, and distribution and logistics. The following are examples of ethical challenges that frequently arise in marketing departments:

- price discrimination, price-fixing, price skimming
- deceptive advertising, stereotyping, puffery, negative content, green washing
- customer privacy, data protection, confidentiality, spam
- product returns, warranties, guarantees, shipping
- product safety, fair trade, consumer welfare
- responsible managment of social media

International Business Ethics: As globalization advances, more companies are coming into contact with different cultures and legal systems. Unsurprisingly, ethical issues related to international business are increasingly prevalent. Businesses with an international component are often presented with ethical issues related to:

- cross-cultural communications
- bribery and corruption
- human rights
- climate change, pollution, and social responsibility
- employment practices pertaining to workplace safety and wages
- industrial espionage, intellectual property, and piracy

Conclusion

The notion that businesses should be focused solely on maximizing profits is coming to an end. Companies are realizing that they are not only accountable to their stockholders, but to a larger constituency, the stakeholders, whom they directly or indirectly impact. The stakeholder theory goes beyond the stockholder and emphasizes that businesses are also responsible to constituents, including employees, suppliers, customers, and society in general.[26]

Consequently, organizations must focus on encouraging an ethical workplace culture, and thereby earning the trust and respect of society and consumers. With diverging cultures, it is essential that organizations account for the varying ethical and moral perspectives set forth in this chapter. Additionally, organizations must strive to find the glue to bind together a cogent ethical culture through common understanding and the identification of universally held values.

CHAPTER THREE

Corporate Governance, Corporate Responsibility, and the Environment

Corporate governance is vital to the integrity and functioning of financial markets. It is intended to maximize corporate efficiency, enhance shareholder value, minimize risk, and work in the long-term interests of all stakeholders. Unlike corporate governance standards, which are dictated by laws and intended to protect shareholders, corporate responsibility goes beyond regulatory demands and also seeks to affirm companies' voluntary commitment to all their stakeholders. Corporate responsibility takes into account the broader role of society and the environment in shaping a company's long-term strategy. Corporate governance and corporate responsibility are essential to a corporation's sustainable competitive advantage. They also help mitigate regulatory risk and account for shareholder demands, thereby supporting long-term growth through investments in society and stakeholders.

This chapter considers issues related to corporate governance and explores the links between corporate responsibility, society, and the natural environment.

I. Why Corporate Governance?

It is essential to ensure that organizations abide by laws and are not guided by the interests of influential executives to the detriment of other stakeholders, including society-at-large. The 2008 financial crises and corporate scandals demonstrate how a lack of strong governance mechanisms enables powerful executives to profit at society's expense. Deficiencies in corporate governance thus manifest at a macroeconomic level in the form of unstable financial markets and the disruption of the entire economy.

The Asian financial crises of the late 1990s illustrate how economic disasters can occur when financial liberalization is not moderated by strong governance mechanisms. Some key governance failures that exacerbated the Asian financial crises include: cronyism, high debt ratios, lack of oversight by financial regulators, predatory lending, and majority-owned family businesses that enriched themselves at the expense of minority shareholders.

Similarly, in the early 2000s, scandals at Enron, WorldCom, and Tyco demonstrated how corporate governance shortcomings can bankrupt a company and its unsuspecting shareholders. These scandals led Congress to pass the SOX. SOX created new standards for corporate accountability and outlines specific penalties for corporate misconduct.[1] Intended to strengthen corporate governance mechanisms, SOX mandates that public companies establish various board committees to oversee risk management, executive compensation, accounting practices, and internal controls. Despite the new standards imposed by SOX, questionable corporate conduct led to the Great Recession less than 10 years after SOX was passed. The 2008 Great Recession consisted of large bank failures that highlighted widespread governance failures pertaining to risk management, including lack of board oversight and compensation structures. This led to more risky behavior to produce short-term profits.[2]

In response to these governance failures and other regulatory gaps, Congress passed the Dodd-Frank. Dodd-Frank is the most sweeping financial regulation reform since those of the Great Depression. Corporate governance provisions of Dodd-Frank include:

- shareholder approval of executive compensation and "golden parachutes," or severance packages
- executive compensation disclosures, such as pay-for-performance
- disclosure of potential conflicts of interest regarding how consultants are compensated
- compensation clawback policies, which allow a company to recover an executive's pay if financial statements are discovered to be noncompliant
- the disclosure of hedging policies[3]

Corporate governance is constantly evolving. National governments and international bodies are perpetually modifying the regulatory frameworks to increase corporate transparency and accountability.

II.   The Scope of Corporate Governance

Broadly, corporate governance is a system of checks and balances implemented to guide all corporate conduct and foster long-term growth. More specifically, corporate governance is defined as "[p]rocedures and processes according to which an organization is directed and controlled. The corporate governance structure specifies the distribution of rights and responsibilities among the different participants in the organization—such as the board, managers, shareholders and other stakeholders—and lays down the rules and procedures for decision-making."[4] Corporate governance mechanisms are intended to provide managerial oversight of risk-taking activities to help protect all of an organization's stakeholders.

Internal stakeholders generally include nonexecutive employees, management executives, and the board of directors. External stakeholders can include shareholders, creditors, suppliers, regulators, reporting organizations, society, and the environment.

Corporate governance provides companies with direction, leadership, and an ethical orientation so that the organization can better manage:

1. Accountability and transparency among stakeholders
2. Shareholder welfare and maximizing shareholder value
3. Risk management
4. Long-term strategic thinking and corporate performance
5. Compliance with laws and regulations
6. Financial reporting and fiscal planning
7. Mitigating conflicts of interest among stakeholders
8. Executive performance and compensation
9. Management development and succession planning
10. Corporate citizenship or responsibility toward society and the environment

III.   Principles of Corporate Governance

The key principles of modern corporate governance are guided primarily by domestic laws and international standards, including the Cadbury Report, the Organisation for Economic Co-Operation and Development (OECD), and SOX. These domestic laws and international standards are based broadly on notions of accountability, transparency, and fairness. Listed below are key principles that guide corporate governance.[5] Some of these principles are codified by law, particularly for public companies, but all help to identify best practices for both public and private companies.

1. Develop the corporate governance framework to promote transparency and foster consistency with the rule of law.[6]
2. Protect shareholder rights, ensure equitable treatment of all shareholders, and allow shareholders to exercise their rights by participating in general meetings.[7]
3. Recognize the rights of stakeholders as established by law or by mutual agreements. Stakeholders should be able to freely communicate to the board their concerns about illegal or unethical practices without their rights being compromised.[8] SOX, for example, offers significant protection for corporate whistle-blowers.[9]
4. Promote transparency, including the timely and accurate disclosure of financial reports and other material matters concerning corporate health. SOX, for example, requires that public companies routinely evaluate internal controls related to financial reporting in addition to mandating that the CEO and CFO certify financial reports.[10]
5. Maintain a board that provides leadership and checks and balances for proper governance. The board will assist management with understanding and prioritizing the company's strategic, operational, financial, and compliance risks. The board will be driven by the long-term interests of the shareholders and ensure adherence to the highest ethical standards and to corporate citizenship.[11]

- Board members have skills, experience, time, and resources to adequately exercise objective, independent judgment with regard to corporate affairs. The board maintains a strong independent streak by including nonexecutive directors.[12]
- The board establishes an independent audit committee for appointing, compensating, and overseeing the external auditor.[13]
- The board provides effective monitoring of management and is accountable to the company and the shareholders.[14]
- The board provides oversight of the compensation system by establishing a remuneration committee. This committee should ensure adequate disclosure of remuneration policies and its relation to company performance.[15]

6. To engender integrity and ethical leadership, companies have a Code of Conduct to guide directors and executives in their decision making.[16]

IV.   Corporate Governance Structure

Corporate governance mechanisms tend to differ across countries since these mechanisms are often related to country-specific factors such as financial markets and banking systems, corporate ownership structures, and legal systems. These cross-border differences in governance mechanisms also lead to divergent board structures. In the United States, for example, companies tend to follow a one-tier model in which both executive and monitoring functions are assigned to one board. On the other hand, in countries such as Germany, companies often adopt a two-tier model in which monitoring and executive functions are separated by supervisory and management boards, respectively.[17]

However, as global markets become increasingly integrated, corporate governance standards are becoming more harmonized throughout the international community. Ongoing globalization, the integration of markets, and the free flow of capital all strengthen the trend toward harmonizing corporate governance mechanisms around the world. Generally, three major actors exist in the corporate governance structure:

1. *Shareholders:* Shareholders invest in the company and thus exercise ownership rights either way.
2. *Board of Directors:* The board, generally of a public company, is elected by shareholders of a public company to oversee shareholders' interests and provide management oversight.
3. *Management:* Management consists of the corporate officers responsible for day-to-day operations.

In theory, these actors operate as a system of interdependent relationships striving to maximize corporate performance. The board and management are responsible for ensuring that the organization meets its commitments to all internal and external stakeholders, including investors and legal, societal, and environmental commitments.

A. Board of Directors

The board of directors constitutes the highest governing authority in a publicly traded company. Directors have a fiduciary duty to act in the best interests of the corporation and its shareholders. This, in turn, means protecting the property or assets of the company's stockholders. For example, financial advisors have an obligation to act in the best interests of their clients just as boards of directors have an obligation not to advance personal interests to the organization's detriment.[18] Directors' fiduciary duties fall into two main categories:[19]

1. *Duty of Loyalty:* Directors and officers must set aside their self-interest and act in the company's best interests. This requires that directors consciously identify and avoid conflicts of interest. Directors should handle any potential conflicts of interest with full transparency, honesty, and integrity.
2. *Duty of Care:* Directors and officers are legally required to exercise prudent and sound business judgment. In practice, directors and officers are not held accountable for bad business decisions so long as they have exercised due

diligence in making an informed decision. They may be held liable, however, where the business decision was improperly influenced by a conflict of interest or some other dereliction of duty.

Over the years, boards have grown larger. Ron Gieseke, assistant secretary at Fortune 500 utilities company Ameren Corporation, says that this is the result of boards placing more of an emphasis on the risks associated withh a company's business. As board members recognize the board's capacity to influence a company's success, the board is also more involved than ever in key corporate decisions.[20] Since many decisions require a broad range of knowledge, there is also an increasing emphasis on attracting board members with different backgrounds of experience and expertise. In this way, expertise, rather than patronage or connections, reigns supreme at Ameren and other top corporations.[21] The board, in overseeing corporate operations, has several key responsibilities:[22]

1. *CEO Selection:* The board is responsible for selecting the CEO and evaluating whether the CEO is suited to ethically and effectively lead the corporation.
2. *Management Development and Succession Planning:* The board mentors the CEO, reviews senior management's performance and compensation packages, and creates succession plans.
3. *Effective Corporate Planning:* The board oversees strategic planning to ensure the company's long-term growth by evaluating and benchmarking a company's strategy and performance.
4. *Risk Oversight:* The board is responsible for providing risk oversight pertaining to strategic, financial, and operational risk factors, among others.
5. *Compliance Oversight:* Gieseke says that boards are much more hands-on today than they were even 10 years ago, and "compliance is at the core of what they're looking at."[23] The board and upper management are responsible for setting the tone at the top by creating an ethical and compliant corporate culture where a company's policies, procedures, and practices comply with the law.
6. *Budgetary Oversight:* The board reviews and approves annual operating plans and budgets.
7. *Financial Reporting/Disclosure:* The board must thoroughly evaluate accounting and financial reporting systems and ensure that all financial disclosures are accurate, reliable, and complete, and that they adhere to relevant laws and standards.
8. *Monitoring Efficacy of Governance Practices:* The board must monitor and assess the effectiveness of its governance practices, committees, and processes.

In addition to these key responsibilities, boards also deal with other issues, including informal consultations with management, director nominations, conflicts of interest, and corporate citizenship. However, despite its seemingly vast responsibilities, the board is not intended to interfere in the company's day-to-day management. Nor is the board involved in organizational structure and personnel decisions, as these primarily fall under the purview of the CEO and other officials.

B. Board Structure and Committees

In addition to exercising sound and independent judgment, the board must also have sufficient expertise and knowledge to effectively oversee corporate risk management. A board of directors should consist of members with diverse industry expertise in areas such as financial management, risk management, corporate strategy, corporate citizenship, and compliance.

Boards of directors often create committees to improve the firm's organization and operation. These committees generally include the audit committee, compensation committee, and governance and nominating committees. However, the number and composition of committees varies by organization and can also include other committees, such as an executive committee, a risk-management committee, a leadership-development committee, a finance committee, and a sustainability committee.

1. Audit Committee: The audit committee primarily oversees a company's financial risks, financial reporting processes, and internal controls. Increasingly, audit committees are expanding to include the evaluation of all organizational risks. This may mean reviewing security issues, operational problems, data privacy concerns, and other issues.[24] At Ameren, for example, management from various departments in the organization creates "heat maps."[25] These maps show the severity of an issue, including whether the risk is being adequately handled.[26] Says Gieseke: "Mak[e] sure that you're always stepping back and asking what can go wrong, what are the risks out there."[27]

The audit committee should have a strong independent streak and should thus include nonexecutive directors.[28] SOX enhanced the role of the audit committee by requiring that a company's auditors report to the company's audit committee, and not simply to management. Audit committee members are responsible for assessing management's application of accounting principles and financial insights pertaining to financial reporting compliance and disclosure procedures. Consequently, committee members must understand accounting principles and financial reporting requirements.[29]

2. Compensation Committee: The compensation committee primarily assists with creating and implementing senior executives' compensation plans.[30] This committee also ensures that compensation policies reflect the core principle of pay-for-performance, or performance-based compensation systems, for senior management. Some of the other responsibilities include overseeing the management of pension funds, approving stock option awards, and recommending board compensation.[31] U.S. law requires that members of the compensation committee retain independence from management.

3. Corporate Governance and Nominating Committees: While the audit committee oversees compliance and other areas of the organization, the governance committee creates policies and procedures, many of which are ultimately relied upon by the audit committee.[32] This committee is primarily responsible for making recommendations to the board regarding the board's composition, size, term limits, nominating process, diversity, and compliance with the Code of Ethics and governance laws and regulations.[33]

Since the governance committee is responsible for setting compliance policies and procedures, committee members should bring a variety of skills so that each board member can expertly evaluate risks in certain areas.[34] The board of a large company like Ameren, for example, may include the CIO, the CFO, the corporate secretary, and the CEO or president of another company.[35]

Gieseke also recommends that the committee have at least one meeting a year to review pertinent policies and procedures.[36] At this meeting, the committee can raise questions and seek additional information from those within the organization who specialize in those topics.[37] Additionally, those experts may be asked to report on any pertinent updates or changes that the committee should consider.[38]

V. From "Comply or Explain" to "Comply or Else"

Adhering to voluntary codes for corporate governance is common practice in several European countries and is based on the concept of "comply or explain." The "comply or explain" governance approach was first promoted by the Cadbury Report of 1992 as part of corporate governance practices in the U.K.[39] The principle behind this approach is that each organization is different. Boards, therefore, require flexibility in determining an organization's corporate governance structure. In other words, it would be impractical to subject boards to one-size-fits-all regulations. Accordingly, companies could either voluntarily adopt regulator-endorsed governance standards or explain why they would rather use alternative means of achieving good governance.

However, after several high-profile corporate scandals throughout previous decades, many countries have adopted a "comply or else" approach. This approach entails promulgating corporate governance laws and mandating that organizations comply with such laws.[40] Under this approach, companies either comply with governance standards as provided by the law, or they face sanctions. SOX, for instance, mandates clear accountability by key corporate officials for the accuracy of financial disclosures, establishes standards for external auditor independence, and provides standards pertaining to conflicts of interest and good governance.

Stakeholder Management

A corporation's long-term success is dependent on effectively managing stakeholder expectations. Stakeholders have the power to impose direct or indirect sanctions or, alternatively, reward a company for its services and ethical conduct. Corporations that choose to neglect social and legal obligations could face productivity-sapping backlashes, including hefty fines.

VI. Corporate Responsibility

From a narrow perspective, corporate governance centers on maximizing shareholder value and protecting shareholder rights. However, shareholders are only one of the stakeholders on which an organization depends for its long-term survival. Stakeholders constitute any group that impacts, or is impacted by, an organization's activities. Stakeholders include employees, the board, suppliers, regulators, creditors, customers, society, and even the natural environment.

Consider, for example, the environment. The environment provides corporations with a number of ecosystem services such as raw materials, fuel, and fresh water. But it also includes those ecosystems that are lesser-known but nonetheless crucial to the survival of the industrial economy. These less-visible ecosystem services might include carbon capture to mitigate climate change; nutrient cycling to keep ecosystems healthy; or processes such as air purification, pollination, flood mitigation, waste decomposition, and others. The value of the world's ecosystem services are said to contribute around $33 trillion per year to the global economy.[41] This number rivals the combined gross domestic product (GDP) of the world's top economies. The traditional Stockholder Theory—in which an organization considers only its investors—places little emphasis on protecting the natural environment, to the eventual detriment of all.

Consequently, the model of a corporation only accountable to its shareholders is morphing to encompass corporate responsibility toward all stakeholders. This approach is demonstrated by the Stakeholder Theory, which states that investor-owned corporations should consider the interests of all their stakeholders when making business decisions.[42] Thus, under the Stakeholder Theory, managers should act as agents of all stakeholders by taking into account stakeholder needs and interests when making corporate decisions.[43] Accordingly, corporate responsibility is broadly defined as a corporation's continuing commitment to *all* stakeholders so as to produce a positive economic, societal, and environmental impact.

Principles of the Stakeholder Theory are increasingly incorporated into modern corporate practices as more corporations embrace the idea of stakeholder management. These principles are embodied in terms such as corporate social responsibility, corporate citizenship, corporate sustainability, and corporate responsibility.

Corporate Responsibility

Corporate responsibility can be broadly defined as a corporation's continuing commitment to all the stakeholders that it impacts and is impacted by, so as to produce a positive economic, societal, and environmental impact.

VII.   The Triple (or Quadruple) Bottom Line

This sense of corporate responsibility and the resulting corporate impact on economic, social, and environmental dimensions is captured by the idea of the Triple Bottom Line. The concept behind the Triple Bottom Line is that the corporation achieves profit maximization in an environmentally and socially responsible manner.[44] Companies increasingly report their corporate performance based on the Triple Bottom Line, and use mandatory and voluntary reporting standards to disclose economic, social, and environmental performance. The Triple Bottom Line approach is also commonly called TBL, 3BL, People-Planet-Profit, and the Three Pillars Approach.

However, the Triple Bottom Line faces criticism as disproportionately favoring humanity over planetary or environmental factors.[45] Two components of the Triple Bottom Line—economic and social dimensions—favor humanity, while only one component—the environment—favors the natural earth. Critics argue that this approach inadequately accounts for harm done to the planet and its ecosystems. By incorporating the planet as another dimension—to create a "Quadruple Bottom Line"—companies would not only consider their impact on the environment, but also on the nonliving elements of the biosphere, including nonrenewable resources like metals and oil. Thus, the Quadruple Bottom Line considers the planet and the environment as factors in addition to social and economic elements.

Fundamental to the Quadruple Bottom Line is the concept of sustainable development, which argues that economic growth is balanced against the limits of what the planet and the environment can support. This is important not just for the long-term survival of companies, but for civilization as well. Sustainable development has been defined as "development which meets the needs of current generations without compromising the ability of future generations to meet their own needs."

Four key strategies for sustainable development are:[46]

1. Managing the ecological impact of population growth and resource consumption
2. Enhancing global food security by promoting sustainable agricultural practices and remedying imbalances in food distribution
3. Managing, maintaining, and preserving the long-term viability of ecosystem resources
4. Achieving ecologically sensitive economic development

Companies increasingly acknowledge the uncertainties caused by climate change and pressures on ecosystems. These environmentally induced uncertainties are, in fact, different from uncertainties in the business environment because they are emergent in nature, and are based on a complicated and often unpredictable web of ecological interactions. The uncertainties induced by climate change may impact ecosystem services, regulations, policy, technology, market mechanisms, stakeholder opinions, and societal expectations.

VIII.   Climate-Induced Corporate Challenges

Prudent compliance professionals routinely consider risks and uncertainties brought about by climate change when strategizing long-term plans. Moreover, these professionals ensure that an awareness of climate change and environmental responsibility percolates throughout the organization. The vision and direction from the top is important to set the tone and direction for the company to effectively handle long-term uncertainties induced by climate change. Some long-term uncertainties related to climate change include:

- *Resource Uncertainty:* Traditionally, businesses have taken for granted the services provided by ecosystems. Despite technological advances, most of the world's products and services today are based on industrial-era technology, which relies on the abundance of ecosystem services. This industrial-era technology is often inefficient, generating tremendous waste and further polluting the earth. It is widely recognized that ecosystem degradation resulting from human causes (toxic waste generation, natural resource depletion, greenhouse gas emission) is causing scarcity. Consequently, companies may face uncertainty with regard to the availability of natural resources, such as oil, minerals, fiber, top soil, clean water, and others. While renewable resources can be replenished by proper planning and conservation efforts, nonrenewable resources (such as oil), once depleted, can be very difficult to replenish naturally.
- *Market Uncertainty:* Changes in the natural environment can have unpredictable effects on markets. For example, uncertainties may arise due to the evolving nature of markets for ecosystem services. Prices may fluctuate wildly, or resources may suddenly become unavailable, thereby making consistent and predictable production problematic.
- *Regulatory Uncertainty:* Companies cannot predict how the regulatory framework will reflect policymakers' efforts to confront climate change. Whether companies can expect a flood of new regulations will depend on the extent to which lawmakers' constituents demand policy changes. Whether constituents demand policy changes will likely depend on the extent to which climate change actually impacts people. With these factors in mind, compliance professionals can only make educated guesses as to what future regulations may require. Regulatory uncertainty can be classified into four categories:[47]

1. uncertainty associated with the direction of the regulation
2. uncertainty and difficulty responding to the regulatory requirements
3. uncertainty relating to implementation and reporting requirements
4. uncertainty arising due to the interdependence of environmental regulations and other regulations

   Regulatory uncertainty makes long-term corporate planning difficult, increases risks of noncompliance, dampens innovation, and causes the loss of productivity. Proactive companies and industry trade groups should thus work actively with policymakers to shape environmental regulation. Smaller companies with fewer resources should, at minimum, fully understand current regulations and stay apprised of regulatory developments in order to reduce risks associated with regulatory uncertainty.

- *Societal Uncertainty:* Managing stakeholder expectations is crucial to a company's success. Firms must continuously monitor the expectations of various stakeholders. Stakeholders may have different, or even opposing, expectations related to environmental sustainability. This variance breeds uncertainty and challenges. For example, Monsanto's foray into agricultural biotechnology has led to a passionate debate over the use of genetically modified organisms (GMOs). On one hand, Monsanto's GMO crops help farmers use land more efficiently and increase Monsanto's revenues and its overall diversification, thereby satisfying several stakeholders. On the other hand, governments, environmental groups, and other public interest groups argue that genetically modified crops are under-regulated and potentially harmful to the environment, thereby angering several stakeholders. Although satisfying all stakeholders is a constant challenge, corporations that consider all stakeholder expectations in their business strategy tend to show more positive relationships between environmental and financial performance.[48]

Effectively managing resource, market, and regulatory uncertainty requires companies to create and continuously modify long- and short-term plans that address imminent and potential future changes in these three areas.

Companies that take into account environmental sustainability and societal considerations tend to achieve better corporate performance.[49] Examples of better corporate performance include the following:[50]

- better management of stakeholder expectations, and thus better corporate branding
- better regulatory compliance and mitigating costs associated with noncompliance
- sustainability-based innovations and new business models to maximize market potential
- increased resource efficiency resulting in waste reduction and lower costs
- increased product differentiation
- better accounting of ecosystem services and internalization of ecosystem costs
- improved access to capital as more banks and institutions take into account corporate sustainability
- attracting, retaining, and motivating human capital

IX. Sustainability Reporting

Increasingly, corporations are disclosing and reporting nonfinancial measures of performance related to corporate responsibility. This trend toward sustainability reporting can be attributed to increasing awareness of corporate responsibility, stakeholder pressure, and climate change–induced pressures to sustainable growth. For instance, companies now issue reports to disclose their environmental, social, and governance (ESG) performance. Several voluntary reporting standards and guidance for ESG reporting exist, including:

- *The Global Reporting Initiative (GRI):* GRI is a voluntary reporting framework that allows companies to report on governance, environmental, human rights, labor practices, societal, product responsibility, and economic performance indicators.[51] The GRI's main advantage is that it allows the reporting organization to report only on information that is important to the organization or its stakeholders. Another advantage is that the GRI serves as a baseline for other reporting frameworks and indices. As a result of this overlap, an organization that performs a thorough GRI report may use this information to fulfill other reporting bodies' requirements.

- *International Organization for Standardization's (ISO) Guidance on Social Responsibility (ISO 26000):* ISO 26000 outlines principles of social responsibility with respect to governance, human rights, labor practices, environment, fair operating practices, consumer issues, and community involvement and development.[52] It provides a good guiding framework, but it is not a reporting organization.
- *Carbon Disclosure Project (CDP):* This reporting agency's framework relates primarily to environmental and supply-chain management rather than societal and governance-related reporting.[53] The CDP's online response form is particularly valuable because it ensures that the data reported from participating organizations is recorded in a consistent format, which allows for a comparative sustainability analysis. Like most of the other frameworks, the CDP allows for some variability among business sectors.
- *UN Global Compact (UNGC):* The UN Global Compact sets forth 10 universally accepted principles on which organizations report, and to which organizations should adhere. The principles include areas of human rights, labor, the environment, and anticorruption. Organizations have broad discretion in determining what, specifically, to report within the framework of each principle.[54]
- *Organisation for Economic Co-operation and Development (OECD) Guidelines for Multinational Enterprises:* These guidelines for multinationals address issues pertaining to human rights, employment and industrial relations, the environment, bribery solicitation and extortion, consumer interests, science and technology, competition, and taxation.[55] Instead of dozens of specific criteria to report, the OECD provides best practices of ethical prescriptions relating to an organization's Triple Bottom Line. Whenever specific disclosures are applicable—such as the reporting of greenhouse gas (GHG) emissions—the OECD looks to the GRI as the preferred reporting method.
- *Dow Jones Sustainability Indices (DJSI):* The DJSI is a family of indices that compile sustainability data on companies based on certain criteria. It serves as a benchmark for investors who value sustainability when making investment decisions.[56] The DJSI tracks a relatively comprehensive set of criteria that addresses most aspects of any of the covered frameworks, including the GRI, which is the most comprehensive framework. The DJSI also ranks participating organizations. These rankings incentivize organizations to invest in sustainability goals. The DJSI is not a reporting framework, but rather a global sustainability benchmark.

Sustainability reports should be balanced, reliable, transparent, exhaustive, and timely. Organizations must decide which reporting framework best meets its goals. Accordingly, organizations should do their own analysis of various sustainability reporting approaches to answer the following questions:

Which aspects of the approach are valuable to the organization?

Which aspects fall short in helping to assess the needs of the organization's stakeholders?

What are the limitations to each approach? For example, are any limited to a specific industry or region?

Which approaches are the most valuable? That is, which provide the most comprehensive and useable sustainability information for stakeholders?

Many organizations use several of these approaches to enhance their sustainability-reporting efforts to stakeholders. In addition to using these approaches, organizations may produce extensive sustainability reports that outline their performance on environmental, social, and governance-related factors. Companies also seek verification and affirmation of their sustainability efforts.[57] Such efforts are crucial to instill investor confidence and enhance transparency, reliability, and accountability of corporate responsibility–reporting efforts.

Conclusion

Corporate governance standards are continuously changing to reflect society's demand that an organization be accountable to all its stakeholders. Corporate scandals combined with financial crises are key drivers of this evolution. Additional research on the effects of climate change and the enhanced corporate performance of companies that take an inclusive stakeholder view is also perpetuating the importance of corporate responsibility to organizational success. But organizations can, by and large, embrace these changes, for corporate governance helps protect the long-term interests of the organization.

CHAPTER FOUR

Risk Assessment and Structuring the Program

The first step to creating and maintaining a compliance Program is to complete a risk assessment. Risk assessments require identifying the "universe of compliance risk[s] facing the organization."[1] This is stage one, and it is responsive to the FSGO requirement to "periodically assess the risk of criminal conduct."[2] After identifying risks, organizations must assess the likelihood and seriousness of violating laws or experiencing noncompliance in the areas identified. This allows organizations to design the Program to reflect the prioritization of risks.

Organizations must then develop standards and procedures to respond to those risks, as well as specific pressure points. The results of the risk assessment also indicate the type of training to provide, as well as the appropriate delegation of tasks among a workforce. Organizations should also work to foster a culture of compliance and ethics, which bears on overall risk levels.

After the Program has been in place for a period of time—perhaps a year—the risk assessment should be repeated to determine whether risks have changed. Remember, the FSGO requires "periodic" risk assessments. At this time, organizations should also evaluate the effectiveness of the Program itself. Organizations should determine whether those policies and procedures are effectively mitigating risks, whether training is effective at changing behavior or improving understanding, and whether a compliant and ethical culture prevails. The results of this analysis bear on the risks associated with each of the previously identified issues, and changes should be made to "modify" the Program, in the words of the FSGO, on the basis of this updated risk assessment.

This chapter begins with stage one, the risk assessment process. The process for completing this assessment is examined by looking at both internal and external factors. The next several chapters then examine each of the Seven Pillars needed to build a Program, which is, remember, built on the back of this risk assessment. After theoretically constructing a Program, chapter 10 examines the process for evaluating the effectiveness of the Program.

I. Analyzing Risk Factors

A. Identify Primary Risks

Prepare, Prepare, Prepare: The Department of Defense (DOD) has a plan for every contingency, including, it is said, an apocalyptic world in which zombies run rampant across America.[3] While that may be a step too far, the DOD is instructive in that its preparation proves advantageous when faced with inevitable crises. So, too, should organizations prepare for (realistic) threats. Understand not just what the risks are, but also how you will mitigate the risk, and how you will act if the violation does occur.

But remember that the risks facing the DOD are not the same as those of, for example, Switzerland's Federal Department of Defence, Civil Protection and Sport. Similarly, no two organizations' risks are quite the same. The FSGO says: "When evaluating the risk of criminal conduct occurring, the organization should consider the nature of the organization's business. For example, an organization that . . . employs sales personnel who have flexibility to set prices shall establish standards and procedures designed to prevent and detect price-fixing. An organization that . . . employs sales personnel who have flexibility to represent the material characteristics of a product shall establish standards and procedures designed to prevent and detect fraud."[4]

A risk assessment requires evaluating both internal and external risks. The assessment should focus on the entire organization, including all divisions, major accounts, and even the compliance department, as well as competitors, third parties, and state and national legislation. Benchmarks should be used in an effort to understand the likelihood of a violation, and the seriousness of that violation should it occur.

B. Internal Risks

Be familiar with your organizational history and current practices, your employee's history, and your organizational culture. Review relevant documents, coordinate assessments with stakeholders, and interview employees and other stakeholders. Additionally, benchmark by comparing where you as an organization were previously versus where you are now—for example, look at the number of violations, or number of reports of possible wrongdoing. Additionally, you can perform a gap analysis of your own operations. This allows you to identify the gap between where your operations are currently and where you would like them to be in the future. Lastly, take your internal analysis and benchmark those against similarly situated organizations.

Organizational History and Practices: The prior history of the organization and its employees may indicate types of risks that the organization must prevent and detect.[5] Determine whether your organization has faced criminal or civil culpability for past violations of regulations. Companies may consider expanding this analysis to consider the legal history of competitors. Additionally, companies may benchmark their operations against those of similarly situated companies to determine whether they are performing well from a regulatory perspective.[6] Do realize, however, that past organizational history is less predictive of future events if processes, products, or customers have recently changed significantly.

Compensatory incentives, policies, and practices may affect organizations' risk portfolios. For instance, public companies that reward short-term earnings may inadvertently motivate financial fraud through the manipulation of financial statements; managers that are disproportionately rewarded on the basis of sales figures may neglect to penalize overly aggressive salespersons; and failure to properly compensate employees for overtime may lead to employment law violations. Again, benchmarking against industry leaders will provide insight as to your own organization's relative performance.

Employee History: Your current employees also subject you to risk. Employees with substantial authority should be vetted for any disreputable history prior to hiring. This is especially important for members of your compliance department. It may be that an employee has a criminal record for accepting, soliciting, or giving bribes; for sexual harassment of a former coworker; or for fraud. It is not unheard of for individuals to steal from a current employer in order to pay restitution to a previously victimized employer, for example. It's worth discussing these past violations prior to bringing the individual onto the payroll.

Additionally, consider the relative experience of employees—are they new to the organization or industry, or are they seasoned in dealing with risks? Where new employees populate the organization, institutional knowledge of risks and responses may be lacking.

Culture and Ethics: Ethical risk assessments are one of the least-developed areas of risk management,[7] but this is not an area to be ignored. As previously noted, lapses in business ethics harm relationships and result in negative financial performance.[8] Conversely, acting ethically is crucial to meeting strategic and financial objectives.[9]

Therefore, take steps to analyze the ethical atmosphere, as well as the nature of ethical breaches. Use a survey, or look for unusually high levels of turnover, to identify whether employees are satisfied with their jobs. Identify whether people are excited about the Program you are building. And once the Program is built, audit some of these same areas to determine whether impressions toward the company and the Program have changed.

Some organizations also pay particular attention to ethical orientation of managers and their commitment to acting ethically by requiring high-level managers to take in-depth personality tests prior to taking on new roles.

Interviews: Along with good, old-fashioned research and document review, interviews and surveys are particularly effective ways to determine the likelihood and potential seriousness of violations. Many compliance managers interview across all sectors of the organization—including within the legal and regulatory department—to hone in on key risk areas.

Ask employees about their knowledge and perception of relevant risks, laws, and regulations; any knowledge of violations; and the actions taken, if any, to minimize risks.[10] Interviewers should also ascertain whether employees receive effective and regular compliance training and are familiar with any existing Code of Conduct or other policies.[11] If risks have already been identified, a high degree of ignorance or apathy toward those risks or about how to respond to those risks signifies increased risks.

Ask employees, "How could I cheat if I wanted to?" "Are there ever any temptations to cheat?" "Has anyone here falsified books and records?" "Are there any temptations to do that?" "If I wanted to do so, where would be the easiest place to cheat or to falsify records?" "Are there any mistakes you'd like to self-disclose?" "Are there any areas where you're unsure whether you might have violated a policy?" "What could you be doing better?" These open-ended questions help employees to communicate those areas where they feel some exposure.

If interviews lead to concerns of a violation, an investigation should be initiated. However, interviews are generally not the time to criticize employees or suggest solutions. The interview is not an interrogation. Interviews are instead an opportunity to ask relevant questions, obtain information, and establish a rapport in order to follow up with the interviewee.[12]

However, questions of this type do create apprehension. Therefore, interviews are best conducted by an HR or compliance department professional: individuals who knows how to gather information without causing the interviewee to clam up. Some companies hire consultants who are not only trained in the intricacies of compliance-based interviews, but also offer independence and more credibility when claiming confidentiality. Outsourcing may be particularly advisable for close-knit or small companies, where anonymity is difficult or impossible to guarantee, and thus retaliation a real fear. If interviewed employees fear exposure and retaliation for speaking up about risks or wrongdoing of others, they are likely to hold their tongues. Best practices for employee interviews are examined further in chapter 9.

C. External Risks

Industry and Peer Comparison: Each industry has its own unique collection of risks. To determine the industry-specific risks facing the organization, ask what types of wrongdoing have been in the news and where competitors are facing problems, and look at the fines and penalties levied on others in the industry. Additionally, organizations should identify the legislation that applies to their business, and determine whether any significant regulations are plaguing the industry. This may include reviewing competitors' Codes of Conduct for hints as to their own perceived risk areas, referring to industry codes, and speaking with officers of industry associations to identify best peer practices. Additionally, individuals and groups may use social media, particularly LinkedIn and other channels that connect industry members, to share best practices or warn against high-risk areas.

When looking at others in your industry, benchmarking is essential. Why? Because much is to be learned by looking at the steps already taken by others facing the same, or similar, risks. Isolate best industry practices, and identify gaps you may have, through peer comparison. Industry conferences may be an optimal time to discuss best practices and benchmark.

When choosing peer organizations for comparison, consider the industry, but consider also operational similarities. For example, companies operating abroad have a separate set of regulations to consider. In such a case, comparisons with domestic competitors may be insufficient. Instead, look for comparable organizations that operate in the same geographic regions, and within the same or a related industry.

Customers and Other Third Parties: The FDIC has noted that customer "complaints may be indicative of compliance weaknesses in a particular function or department."[13] Internal complaints may also be indicative of problems. Evaluators should ask whether reports originate from particular business units or regions, as this could suggest underlying concerns with that unit or area of practice.[14]

Moreover, look at any risks associated with customers and third parties. Just as with employees, identify any history of legal or compliance violations. Oftentimes, "[third parties] are an intricate part of organizational operations that represents as great a risk, if not a greater one, as the organization's own staff."[15]

D. Distinguish the Ephemeral Risks from the Time Bombs

Risk Schematic: You've identified your risks. Now, you must prioritize those risks, considering both repercussions of a possible violation and the likelihood of a violation.[16] This is a somewhat subjective process, but the results of your benchmarks, interviews, and other reviews should help to make this decision. When considering the seriousness of a possible violation, account for legal, financial, and reputational impacts to the organization.[17]

The seriousness and the likelihood of a violation should each be weighed, for example, on a 1–5 scale, thereby creating a compliance-based risk schematic. As an example, an occurrence that is moderately likely to occur but brings extremely serious repercussions might merit a 3 and a 5 score, respectively. Multiply these numbers to obtain your overall score for that particular risk—in this case, 15 points.

Analysts can compare and contrast these risk scores ad nauseam by categorizing regulatory risks. For example, create a table with all regulatory risks divided by division, by geography, or by product. In so doing, organizations might find that a particular office or product has a risk score significantly higher than any other, for example. This is informative when allocating resources to mitigate risks.

Action Plan: After coming up with an aggregate score, action plans to mitigate those risks on the basis of those scores must be developed. Compliance managers should meet at least annually with business unit leaders from across the organization. Discuss the risk assessment results, and devise an action plan in response to those risks. Additionally, ensure that adequate resources are available to fund the action plan.

The importance of implementing the action plan cannot be overstated. The action plan serves as a road map to would-be prosecutors, and thus organizations are probably better off not completing the risk assessment at all if they're not going to act on the results.

E.   You're Done. Now Repeat.

Annual Updates: A best practice is to complete this risk assessment not just when creating a Program, but on at least an annual basis. Some organizations complete the assessment more often—perhaps quarterly or even monthly. This may be necessary for highly complex industries, for businesses with a troublesome history, or where the industry is in a state of flux. Organizations should also be open to completing a new risk assessment on an "as needed" basis, such as "when marketing a new product, entering into a new business venture, or facing a regulatory development that might affect the organization."[18]

Organizations should focus especially on any changes in their external or internal environment from the previous year. This includes determining whether any laws were passed that affect the organization, and whether the industry or organization is experiencing any new issues that were not previously integrated into the risk assessment. Expand the analysis to include any risks arising from new product offerings or business lines, new customers, and any organizational reorganization or downsizing that may put pressure on the organization.

Additionally, review your Program's effectiveness, and look to see whether risk perceptions have in fact been mitigated since the introduction of the Program. By remeasuring risk perceptions after implementing the Program, the organization can in some measure quantify the effectiveness of those changes. For instance, are policies and procedures effective? If the answer is no, organizations must dig deeper and determine what isn't working. This compliance assessment process is discussed further in chapter 10.

F.   Nuts and Bolts of the Risk Assessment

Operational Understanding: To perform these analyses, those completing the risk assessment should have a clear understanding of how the organization functions, including what makes it unique. If assessing a manufacturing company, for example, know where the water goes after equipment has been cleaned, understand the types of disasters that could occur within your facility, and know how you would handle those problems. By understanding operational issues, you are better able to grasp the types of risks specific to your organization, as well as the seriousness of repercussions should a violation occur.

Using All Resources: Conversely, those completing the risk assessment must understand that they are unlikely to be an expert in every area, and therefore they must draw on the expertise of others. Consult key stakeholders at all stages of Program development and implementation. Key internal departments include HR, legal, security, finance, and accounting.[19] The business leaders of these departments have the best grasp of the risks facing their units. External stakeholders that may be consulted include industry groups, regulators, and customers.

Responsibilities for the risk assessment might also be delegated by compliance subject area. Rather than having one person or department responsible for the assessment process, for example, organizations may decentralize compliance responsibilities among business units. This may be advisable for large organizations, where complexity of risks requires specialization of knowledge. However, it is important to ultimately centralize these findings so that the seriousness of risks can be evaluated and limited resources can best be allocated.

After identifying risks, it is time to create a Program that is responsive to those risks. So first things first-how do you design the compliance department in a way that advances compliance and ethics?

III.   Responsibilities and Penalties for Top Management

The failure of high-level employees to lead can readily undermine a company's Program. With this in mind, the FSGO requires that: (1) the "governing authority" of the organization has knowledge about the content and operation of the Program, (2) a "high-level employee" has authority over the Program, and (3) a manager (the "day-to-day" controller) is appointed and given sufficient resources to carry out the Program.[20]

The Governing Authority: The governing authority is synonymous with the board of directors or, if there is no board, the highest authority within the organization.[21] Governing authorities must understand the content and application of the Program, and also oversee the Program. This supervisory requirement is not to be taken lightly. It was incorporated into the fiduciary duty doctrine in at least one landmark case, *In re Caremark International Inc. v. Derivative Litigation.*[22] *Caremark* held that directors must ensure the organization gathers and evaluates "timely, accurate information" to "reach informed judgments concerning the corporation's compliance with law and its business performance."[23] Under *Caremark*, neglectful directors place their organizations at risk, but also expose themselves to personal liability under this expansive view of fiduciary duties.[24]

The High-Level Employee: A high-level employee is defined as one with "substantial control over the organization or . . . a substantial role in the making of policy within the organization."[25] Depending on the structure of the organization, this high-level employee may be a director, an executive officer, a division head, or someone with a substantial ownership interest.[26]

This high-level employee need not necessarily coordinate the day-to-day activities of the Program, but must instead be knowledgeable about the content and operations of the Program as a whole. The board should appoint one of its own or a trusted delegate to oversee the Program. Oftentimes, this is the Chief Compliance Officer (CCO).

Additionally, the high-level employee "shall promote an organizational culture that encourages ethical conduct and a commitment to compliance with the law."[27] This high-level employee may also be given responsibility for overseeing employee training and Program evaluations, establishing compliance- and ethics-related rewards and disciplinary standards, establishing mechanisms for handling employee reports, investigating claims, and managing the process for self-reporting to relevant authorities.

The Day-to-Day Controller: The day-to-day controller (the compliance manager) is responsible for managing the compliance Program. Depending on the nature and size of the organization, the high-level employee and the manager may or may not be one and the same. The manager will report up the chain to a senior manager or another, higher-level official. However, consistent with the board's need to stay informed, the day-to-day controller of the Program should at least have periodic reporting requirements to the governing authority. The organization should allocate sufficient resources to the compliance manager to ensure that his or her responsibilities can be fully carried out.

The high-level employee tasked with oversight of the Program and the compliance manager should both have reputations beyond repute. These are the ethical role models for employees. Character shortcomings in these individuals could thus undermine the corporate culture and the Program itself.

Due Diligence of High-Level Employees and Managers: The FSGO states that the organization should take reasonable steps to ensure that high-level personnel and managers with "substantial authority" within the organization are not tainted by past illegal conduct or other actions that would be inconsistent with an effective Program.[28] Moreover, the organization is expected to hire and promote in a manner that fosters an ethical culture.[29] Promotions and pay raises may thus be tied to compliance benchmarks, for instance, rather than (or in addition to) company profits or stock price.

A bad actor in a high-level position is anathema to corporate culture and a nightmare for legal counsel. If wrongdoing occurs and a high-level employee is in any way culpable, the organizational defendant faces significantly increased fines and penalties. If a high-level employee (or, in a company with more than 200 employees, any employee with "substantial discretion") "participated in, condoned, or was willfully ignorant of the offense," there is a rebuttable presumption that the organization did not have an effective Program.[30] One is willfully ignorant if one unreasonably fails to investigate a possible criminal violation.[31] Consequently, mere inaction by a maverick high-level employee could subject an employer to liability.

Where a high-level employee is implicated, the threshold to overcome the presumption that the Program is ineffective is very high. The organization must show that: (1) the Program manager had direct reporting obligations to the governing authority of the organization, (2) the Program detected the offense before discovery outside the organization or before such discovery was reasonably likely, (3) the organization promptly reported the offense to the appropriate governmental authorities, and (4) no individual with operational responsibility[32] for the Program participated in, condoned, or was willfully ignorant of the offense.[33]

Clearly, meeting the requirements of each of these factors is no easy task. It is thus extraordinarily unlikely that an organization will receive credit for an effective Program in the event a high-level employee or, in a large company, one with significant discretion, is implicated. For this reason, it is essential that an organization vet new hires and establish effective controls to ensure that high-level employees are ethical and in compliance with the Program. A Program must be sufficiently egalitarian to scrutinize all employees (perhaps especially) those at the top.[34]

IV. Structuring Considerations

Organizations must decide on the decision-making structure of the compliance department(s), including whether it is centralized or decentralized. They have to identify whether operations are concentrated in one area or region, or dispersed among international offices.[35] The department may consist of full-time employees, part-time employees, or independent contractors, or have portions outsourced. Individuals will need to be made responsible for audit, legal, risk management, human resources, and internal control functions.[36]

Organizations should talk with their primary regulators and obtain their views and recommendations.[37] Some regulations or associations may actually detail best practices. For instance, both the New York Stock Exchange (NYSE) and the Financial Industry Regulatory Authority (FINRA) require their members to designate Chief Compliance Officers (CCO), while the CEO and CCO must certify that processes are in place to achieve compliance with all applicable rules and regulations.[38]

Structuring the Compliance Department: Because compliance breaches by high-level employees significantly increase likely fines and penalties, independence between the compliance department and top management is essential. Policies and procedures should guide interactions between compliance and higher-level management, and thereby provide the compliance department with the independence it needs to thrive. Consider, for example, requiring board approval before the head of compliance can be dismissed, demoted, or transferred.[39] Additionally, clearly specify the criteria for his or her dismissal. To protect against the risk that the compliance manager will avoid a diligent investigation out of a sense of self-preservation, guarantee the compliance manager access to a personal lawyer at the organization's expense, in the event he/she is made a skapegoat, and consider including the compliance manager under the company's directors and officers insurance coverage (D&O).[40]

The organizational structure at all levels provides insight into the workability of the Program. Everyone from the CEO to compliance to staff-level employees should have their responsibilities and roles within the regulatory structure clearly delineated. Failure to do so may breed a sense of diffusion of responsibility and thus apathy; clearly identifying roles, by contrast, promotes a sense of accountability.[41]

Regulators believe the most effective structure is one where the compliance department is an independent operating unit within the organization, reporting directly to the board.[42] This maximizes independence and helps ensure the board is aware of compliance-related risks.

An alternative structure is one where the Program is an appendage of another department—for instance, legal. In this structure, the head of compliance may report to the legal department, but the compliance manager should also provide periodic reports directly to the board to ensure continued independence.[43]

A decentralized, wheel-and-spoke structure is another option. This features a small corporate-level Program that coordinates the overall Program, with dispersed Programs throughout the organization's business units. This structure may be ideal for highly diversified organizations, or those that operate across different legal systems or otherwise have diverse risk factors between units. Again, the compliance manager should periodically report directly to the board "about the status of the compliance Program, the resources required to maintain its viability, and the organization's response to identified compliance deficiencies."[44]

Of course, independence cannot be imposed where the will of top management and the board is lacking. Where the board is composed of the same individuals as the executive team, or is otherwise beholden to top management, there is likely no one to hold top management accountable for breaches. For example, U.S. Magistrate Judge Erin Setser held that then–vice chairman of Wal-Mart Stores, Inc. and head of Walmart International Mike Duke had knowledge that the company's Mexico subsidiary had engaged in a pattern of corruption years before such corruption became publicly known.[45] Nonetheless, high-level authorities within Wal-Mart allegedly failed to properly investigate the matter, and even terminated an initial investigation that had shown serious irregularities.[46]

Such willful blindness subjected Wal-Mart to numerous regulatory investigations, lawsuits, and a congressional investigation.[47] When the *New York Times* first broke this story in 2012, the company lost $17 billion in stock value in three days.[48]

Would the results of Wal-Mart's internal investigation have been different had a "lowly" compliance manager elevated such concerns to the board? Not likely. Duke served as president of Wal-Mart from 2009–2014, and is still chairman of the board. Independence between the company's top officer and its board was nonexistent.

Regardless of whether the accusations are legitimate, the lesson is that sometimes compliance is helpless to effectuate change internally. If you are in compliance, or if you are considering a career in this field, you must prepare to face the reality that top management may not always support compliance, and that the compliance department may even be used as a screen for unlawful behavior.

The good news is that such attitudes are becoming increasingly rare, as executives and directors recognize the high costs of noncompliance.

Compensation: The compliance department should operate with an eye on the regulatory well-being of the company, and not on its profit. This is because, at times, profits may be earned at the expense of acting compliantly. Compensation for compliance staff, therefore, should not be tied to the financial performance of the organization.[49] Instead, tie compensation to the effectiveness of the Program. It is also best to have the highest authority in the organization set the compensation of the head of compliance to avoid the risk or appearance of coercion or undue influence.[50]

Conclusion

Covered thus far were the steps for completing a risk assessment, as well as considerations when structuring a compliance department. It's time to fill in the shell. This means building a compliance Program with seven supporting pillars: policies and procedures, employee training, open communication by organizational leaders about risks and expectations, a mechanism for employees to report concerns, enforcement where wrong-doing occurs, and acting to avoid such wrongdoing in the future. Lastly, after everything is in place, circle back, completing the risk assessment again and also assessing the effectiveness of the new compliance Program. Each of these will be discussed over the next several chapters.

CHAPTER FIVE

Elements of a Compliance Program

Before examining the best practices of a Program through the lens of each of the Seven Pillars, a few notes of general import. First, the best practices of companies and across industries differ. The FSGO commentary notes that the determination of what is necessary to satisfy each pillar is affected by factors including: (1) applicable industry practice or the standards called for by any applicable governmental regulation, (2) the size of the organization, and (3) similar misconduct.[1] Through this language, the FSGO provides guidance as to the parameters of the compliance Program, while still allowing organizations leeway to tailor Programs to their individualized needs.

I. The Importance of Industry Practices

Companies should review the Programs and published processes of their industry's leaders. Where possible, companies should model Programs on recognized ethics and compliance leaders. A company's failure to follow applicable industry practice makes it less likely that a Court will find that the organization had an effective Program.[2] Conversely, companies may show a best effort to comply with applicable laws by modeling a Program on industry leaders.

Additionally, there has been a marked increase in the use of industry-specific Codes. These Codes, published by industry associations, provide direct guidance to their members. Because these Codes are created with an eye on the specific practices and risks facing companies within the industry, they are a valuable resource when creating a Program or evaluating the effectiveness of an existing Program. Further, the failure to abide by such standards is likely to adversely affect an organization that is claiming its Program was effective.

II.   Size of the Organization

Size—revenue, number of employees, and overall resources—is a vital factor in determining the depth and breadth of a Program. The operations of a global behemoth are not the same as that of a five-person firm, and the FSGO acknowledges that smaller firms will take an abbreviated approach to compliance relative to larger brethren.[3] The FSGO states that large organizations shall devote greater resources and formality to their Programs.[4] Additionally, large organizations should encourage small organizations, especially those with whom the larger company has a business relationship, to implement their own Programs.[5] Small organizations, by contrast, may use less formality, may rely on existing resources, and may use simple systems.[6]

However, "small organizations shall demonstrate the same degree of commitment to ethical conduct and compliance with the law as large organizations."[7] Small businesses should not assume they are too small to get the attention of regulators: small firms account for *three-quarters* of organizations sentenced under the USSC.[8]

Fortunately for small businesses, the FSGO goes into significant detail as to the specifics of a small business Program. An organization's governing authority (e.g., the president, owner, or CEO) may have direct authority over the Program, rather than simply exercising oversight while delegating authority. Training may take place at informal staff meetings. Monitoring can be done during regular "walk arounds." Modeling the Program on existing, well-regarded Programs and the best practices of similarly situated organizations is both acceptable and advisable.[9]

Large firms have the luxury of resources. The Allstate Corporation, for example, has attorneys in every U.S. state monitoring local developments. This is unrealistic for small companies that may, for example, have one head of compliance with far-flung responsibilities. Gary Levine, senior attorney at Allstate, emphasizes the importance for small companies' compliance managers to have an in-depth understanding of the business. "I can see a new law, and say with 90 plus percent accuracy whether we're going to open a compliance project. But you have to know the law, know the business, know the compliance program, or you have to know how the business operates."[10]

III.   Company History

A company's history, including its history of compliance and ethical breaches, is indicative of the standards needed to ensure adequate ethics and compliance programming. In fact, directors may even be held *personally* liable for failing to institute a Program that addresses past violations.[11]

When designing, modifying, or evaluating a company's Program, the nature of the industry must be balanced against the size and history of the organization. It may be that a small business in a heavily regulated industry and with a history of compliance violations needs to assert greater compliance controls than does a large business in a relatively unregulated industry. The FSGO requires that each company tailor the Program to its own needs. There is no one-size-fits-all solution. There are general practices and procedures that companies can draw from when creating their own specialized Program. It may be the company's president leading companywide training sessions, or it may be highly paid external consultants; the training may take place over lunch, or during a corporate retreat in a posh hotel. The form is unimportant. The substance of the issue is that the resources devoted to compliance should roughly coincide with the resources of the organization, the industry in which it operates, and the company's history of compliance violations.

IV.   Standards and Procedures

The FSGO states that companies must communicate the standards and procedures by which employees must abide. This is premised, of course, on the assumption that organizations have standards and procedures that they can communicate; in practice, many organizations operate with such a degree of informality as to lack codified standards and procedures. This section discusses the Code of Conduct, which is the primary, though not only, source by which organizations can codify internal standards and procedures.

Tricks of a (Highly Regulated) Trade

A Word with Allstate Insurance Company's Gary Levine

Think your job's stressful? Try sitting in Gary Levine's shoes. Levine is Senior Attorney for Allstate Insurance Company, and the book's authors recently sat down with him to better understand how companies in highly regulated industries respond to the complex regulatory environment they face. It's a "herculean effort," Levine calmly explains. The insurance industry is one of the most highly regulated industries in America. Unlike many industries, state-specific laws dominate.

With operations in all 50 states, Allstate must manage the laws of each state while somehow managing to keep a profitable business operative.

It's clear from talking with Levine that at Allstate, processes pave the way for compliance. Though he acknowledges that sometimes its compliance managers are reactive—"compliance is not static at all," he says—the reality is that even when things go wrong, carefully prepared processes guide the way out of the darkness.

Says Levine, "It's about keeping up with all of the changes, and fixing anything that we find is broken." To keep up with changes, Allstate looks for anything that could affect the company. Sometimes this is a law that clearly pertains to insurance, but other times they are laws that require changes on the periphery of this complex, Fortune 100 company. Attorneys therefore monitor legislative activities in each state and at the national level. This means attending legislative sessions, reviewing trade publications, and talking with regulators.

The challenge, when a new law comes down, is deciding how to act. Is an overhaul of the process needed, or will a tweak suffice? Allstate's product systems are largely automated, so "when you fix one thing, it might break something over here. From a systems standpoint, everything gets more complicated." And so "every time you make a change it costs money."

When new laws are passed, the local attorney provides the product compliance department—using a central mailbox—with notice of the law. The attorney notes when the law will become effective, "which is pretty critical." "The legislatures can have a very quick effective date on a very complex matter," Levine explains. The attorney also gives a high-level opinion as to how the law may impact the company.

Each week the mailbox is emptied, and the "triage process," as Levine calls it, begins. "In a very busy week we have upward of 40 reports, but maybe 10 to 20 normally." Both the potential exposures, as well as the complexity of implementing changes, are discussed at a meeting in which all relevant internal stakeholders are present. Levine estimates that one-quarter of these laws end up being actionable. Business experts and attorneys are both present at the meeting, and ultimately they decide whether further action is necessary or whether the company is already in compliance with the new law.

If the law requires action, a project manager is assigned the case, and a project management form is created—"basically, they will write up 'this is what we need to do to close this project.'" This is sent to the attorney tied to that region, who reviews the project task and signs off.

All outstanding projects are tracked during monthly meetings to ensure that progress is being made in a time frame consistent with the date on which the law becomes operative. Projects are color coded based on the effective date, so that a "red" project, for instance, means the law is nearing its effective date. Again, the triage attorney and business compliance manager come together. If something looks wrong, they're asking questions.

"Our business compliance folks are really good at moving things along, and that is what you have to do. You can't let projects die on the line, or languish. That's why you have to have regular meetings. You have to have a spreadsheet with all the projects on there, and you have to have someone that is engaged, asking questions, and challenging. That's where you determine whether there's a roadblock."

Once processes are in place, the issue becomes correcting any malfunctions within its automated and interconnected systems. For this, Allstate uses a "noncompliance" mailbox, just as it has a "new law" mailbox. A similar process of investigation and analysis proceeds to address any possible chinks in the armor.

Allstate is, says Levine, "very proactive as far as trying to correct items. It's very difficult to correct everything. If an individual messed up, that's less of an issue. When a regulator finds something out of compliance, they send a list of questions. And really what it is always getting at is, is it a system failure or an individual failure."

Levine stresses to clients the importance of anticipating questions from regulators. Before deciding on a course of action, ask yourself, *How are we going to answer such questions?* "If we can't formulate an answer defending a particular course of action, then we're not doing it. If you feel comfortable about your answer on the front end, then you're in much better shape if questions do arise."

It's the responsibility of the organization to help the regulators distinguish between intransigence, and one-off human errors. "Earning trust with your regulators is invaluable; it's easy to lose that trust, and it's hard to earn it. If you're a regulated business, you should know them. They're not your friends, but I think if they understand you're trying to do the right thing, it goes a long way. Regulators are not forgiving if you're not doing anything. They can understand things break. But they can't understand not having a compliance process."

After enacting standards and procedures, those rules are communicated via training and employee education, a topic that is taken up in chapter 7. Additionally, such communications should come from, or at least be authorized and approved by, top management. Setting the appropriate tone from the top is explored in detail in chapter 6.

A. The Central Import of a Code of Conduct

A Code of Conduct is one of the most visible manifestations of a Program; in fact, it sets the tone for the Program itself. It may be used to identify how the organization complies with aspects of the Seven Pillars—such as training, monitoring, and discipline—and should also identify primary areas of regulatory concern for the organization. For example, the Code may state that employees are expected to be familiar with the content of the Code; it should set forth, in broad terms, the consequences for violations of the Code; and it may refer to ongoing obligations of authorized individuals for monitoring and auditing of high-risk compliance areas.

Coverage: Extreme care should be taken in writing the Code. Organizations should anticipate that both internal and external stakeholders, including courts, will hold organizations to their Codes.[12] The drafter of the Code should, as an introductory step, identify the target audience of the Code, be it all stakeholders, all employees, or specific departments and positions.[13] For example, Aley Raza, chief ethics and compliance officer at the Emirates National Oil Company, writes that his company's Code of Conduct references relevant corporate policies and procedures, and embraces six elements: (1) people, (2) integrity, (3) customers, (4) stakeholders, (5) confidential and proprietary information, and (6) trust and compliance.[14]

A Code may also cover corporate ethics, human rights, labor, appropriate workplace behavior, possible environmental concerns,[15] insider trading, conflicts of interest, government relations, and reporting mechanisms,[16] while the modern trend is to include provisions on political contributions, and data privacy and protection. The organization's most prominent regulatory risks should also be covered in the Code. Industry associations and governmental agencies oftentimes publish guidance on specific regulatory risks and sample or generic Codes of Conduct. Though these Codes should not be adopted verbatim, they can serve as a valuable foundation for a customized Code.

Policy Statement: The Codes of corporate compliance and ethics leaders, including Colgate-Palmolive,[17] CH2M HILL,[18] General Electric,[19] and others, all include a "policy statement." A policy statement is an introductory provision to the Code and is ideally written by the company's owner, president, or CEO. The statement should summarize the policy and set forth goals, objectives, and broad-based principles, such as a commitment to ethics and legal compliance.[20] Along with waxing philosophical, many Codes also discuss the pragmatic reasons for the Program, such as the importance of maintaining a good reputation or the belief that compliant and ethical behavior is good for business.[21]

Simplicity Is King: An effective Code is not meant to be a catchall. It is impossible to provide a how-to for every situation that every employee might conceivably face. The policy statement should note the limitations of the Code and provide the contact information of authorized individuals so employees can report concerns and seek guidance in times of uncertainty. These contact persons may be from the HR or legal departments, managers, or from a company's hotline reporting system. Many Codes prompt employees to reflect before acting, and to ask themselves, "Is it legal? Does it follow company policy? Would I want this published in the newspaper?"[22]

In recognition of the sheer abundance of rules and regulations, a Code should focus on ethics. Remember the old proverb: give someone a fish and you feed him for a day; teach that person to fish and you feed him for life. Similarly, it can be an exercise in futility for complex organizations to try to teach employees countless different rules. Instead, they can provide a solid ethical foundation to those employees, thereby giving them the tools to make good decisions in a variety of circumstances. Additional recommendations for an ethically oriented Code are taken up below in Part B of this section.

An overly comprehensive Code is likely to confuse or bore employees rather than educate them. Instead, the Code should have a broad focus on the areas that pose the greatest risk. Companies with a high level of risk may publish a Code with a general overview of risks, and then distribute supplemental publications to employees on an as-needed basis. CH2M HILL and Colgate-Palmolive both publish a variety of supplemental Codes, such as a supplement setting forth the complex provisions and standards of the FCPA.[23] Oftentimes, each department has its own set of policies that apply. Additional instruction may be needed beyond department-specific policies where a regulation may be vague or subject to multiple interpretations.

Organizations are advised to publish a glossary of important terms and laws, thereby making the Code more user-friendly and increasing the likelihood that employees will turn to the Code when faced with specific concerns. A good Code will also use hypothetical situations to illustrate company expectations with regard to both regulatory requirements and ethical standards. For instance: *Q: Sally is invited to a meeting with competitors in which she believes collusive pricing agreements will be made. Should she attend? A: No. Sally should decline the invitation and bring the meeting to the attention of legal counsel.*

By focusing on situations familiar to the workforce, these examples help retain employee focus given what may be onerous or (let's be honest) occasionally boring subjects. Employees may also find that hypothetical illustrations can increase understanding of complex scenarios.

A "Living" Document: The worst thing a Code can be is a "paper Code." It should not collect dust on the bookshelves of senior management. It should serve as an integral guide for the Program as a whole. The FSGO requires that the Program be publicized within the organization,[24] and the Code plays a central role in the effective promotion of the Program. Moreover, Codes should be published on the company's Web site and intranet so that the workforce can readily access the Code on a moment's notice. Additionally, both the Code and other relevant policies may be communicated via newsletters, Web conferences, and during training.[25]

Companies often publish their Codes in multiple languages. Jeroen Tetteroo, senior localization manager at Language Solutions Inc., says, "When it comes to making big decisions, no matter the English-language proficiency of the person, people will want to read it in their own language."[26] If a company doesn't operate abroad, but does have employees for whom English is not a first language, effective translation of its Code may increase comprehension. Colgate publishes its Code in approximately 80 languages. CH2M HILL publishes its Code in every language its employees speak. Tetteroo warns, however, that translation is not a one-time endeavor. Once a company opens communications in the native language of an employee, it has created the expectation of continued communications in that language. So translating a Code should be "consider[ed]. . . an investment and not a one-off," and companies should be wary of translating their Codes if they are unable to follow through with ongoing linguistic support for their employees.[27]

A related option is to include videos in the digitized version of the Code. Global companies, for instance, can feature employees from around the world to instill a sense of unity, and to show the universal application of the Code.

The Company must do more than just pay lip service to the Code. If the Code outlines a process for dealing with a particular situation, or if rewards or penalties are promised for various behaviors, those provisions must be upheld. Employees may be required to affirm their commitment to the Program,[28] and the Code, as well as the Program as a whole, must be implemented and adhered to. As a DOJ attorney said, most companies have strong Programs on paper; it is the lack of enforcement and implementation that can get them in trouble.[29] Consequently, and as is taken up in detail below, periodic refresher training on the Code is recommended. This should take place at least once a year, but can be done in conjunction with other training sessions.

Expanding Its Reach: The FSGO Commentary notes that large organizations should encourage smaller companies, particularly those with whom it does business, to adopt their own Programs.[30] Many companies have instituted a Code of Conduct specifically for suppliers, buyers, and other business partners. These companies may require a contractual commitment from such organizations to comply with their Codes.[31]

For those organizations with the bargaining power to impose such demands, this signals to stakeholders and regulators a commitment to an ethical and compliant culture. Such a step also minimizes the likelihood that a company's partners will engage in regulatory violations for which the company itself could be held vicariously liable. The key is for a company to balance its own strengths with the legal sophistication of its partners, clients, and customers, to determine the appropriate path.

B. Ethics

Compliance-based versus Values-based Programs: Many companies—probably most—have compliance-based Programs.[32] As the name suggests, these Programs focus on specific regulatory risks facing the organization. By contrast, values-based Programs emphasize acting ethically and are unsurprisingly deemed most effective at deterring unethical conduct.[33] The compliance-based Program thus meets the FSGO's requirement to identify serious potential regulatory issues but, as demonstrated below, that is not all that the FSGO requires.

While the earlier versions of the FSGO stressed the need for an "effective compliance program," the 2004 amendments call for an "effective compliance *and ethics* program."[34] Regulatory regimes consistently tout the necessity of an ethical orientation in a compliance Program. In a paper held by the USSC, author Dr. Stephen Cohen writes that ethics "is now clearly part of the brief of compliance departments."[35] Therefore, to follow both the spirit and the letter of the law, a Program should be a hybrid of the values-based approach and the compliance-based approach. The Code is the most prominent way in which companies communicate this intertwining commitment to both ethics and compliance.[36]

Why Ethics Should Not Be Ignored: It is a challenge to keep up with ever-changing federal and state laws and regulations. For smaller companies, or even highly regulated large companies, it may be impossible to continually monitor and adapt to such changes.[37] Because an ethical approach teaches employees how to deal with a given situation rather than simply to meet the legal requirements, an ethically oriented Program and Code may prove more resilient to regulatory changes. This is particularly important for smaller companies, which often lack the resources to regularly evaluate changes to the legal landscape. Additionally, employees acting ethically are far less likely to violate regulatory requirements than those trying to gain every possible legal advantage, and may do better than their compliance-trained counterparts when dealing with the inevitable gray areas of regulatory compliance.

Ethics and a Culture of Compliance: A 2009 study showed that those companies with the weakest ethical cultures were five times more likely to experience misconduct than those with strong ethical cultures.[38] Implementing and emphasizing ethical decision making reassures employees that the company is committed to making the right decision. Because a primary incentive for external whistle-blowing is an individual's desire to remedy a perceived wrong, an ethically oriented Program will increase employees' faith that internal reporting is an effective mechanism by which issues will be resolved. Indeed, an ethical culture may be the most important step a company can take to avoid *qui tam* whistle-blowing claims.[39] While managerial support ultimately establishes the tone and culture of an organization, it is the Code that is foundational to setting the managerial commitment to the organization's cultural values.

A compliance and values-based Program allows a company to both identify and alleviate its specific regulatory risks, while also providing its workforce with the autonomy and satisfaction to act appropriately in a diverse range of environments. The Code of Conduct is the most visible part of a company's Program, and it is the starting point for mapping out this vision of an interdependent compliance and values Program.

Steps for establishing a compliant and ethical culture are discussed in detail in chapter 6.

C. General Policies

The Code of Conduct is just the starting point, as more detailed policies and procedures will likely be disseminated on an as-needed basis throughout the organization. Many of these policies and procedures will be responsive to specific regulatory risks. Consequently, suggested policies and procedures are set forth further within the regulatory chapters of this Program. However, there are general best practices that merit attention here.

How Many Rules Are Enough? It is evident that there is a Goldilocks rule when it comes to the volume and nature of internal rules. Research supports the proposition that wrongdoing increases both in situations where there are too few rules, and where there are too many rules.[40] Remember, rules are beneficial in part because they add clarity.[41] But where there are too many rules, people become frozen by the fear that they might break a rule.[42] Moreover, unduly burdensome rules may actually *create* offenders. This is referred to as resistance theory, which says that people resent threats to their freedom and rebel in order to regain that freedom.[43] For example, "if people are not permitted to receive business gifts at work, then they have gifts delivered to them at home."[44] And once they've broken the rule, the leap from accepting a clearly outrageous gift, as opposed to, for example, a fountain pen, is a small leap indeed.[45]

Moreover, punishing rule breakers is essential to upholding the integrity of the Program as a whole. But the more rules are in place, the more costly and time consuming it becomes to monitor for wrongdoing, and the more likely attention will slip or the rules will not be thoroughly enforced.[46]

Set Goals: Rules should be clear and achievable. Consider a corporation that sets a goal of having zero environmental violations in a year. If the organization typically suffers from many complex violations, this goal is so unrealistic as to pervert the effort. "I can't achieve zero violations, so why try to make any improvement?" or so goes the sentiment. Where a goal is perceived as being very hard to achieve, "people feel less in control of the situation, are less certain and committed, and more readily devote their effort to other things, such as taking precautions in case the goals are not achieved, which again takes up time which cannot be put towards achieving the goal itself."[47]

Similarly, goals that are too easily obtainable work as an inefficient ceiling, where people are motivated initially to achieve the goal but lose motivation once the goal is achieved.[48] Imagine that an organization states that its goal is to increase employee attendance at voluntary training seminars by 5 percent from the previous year. Once this goal is hit, the drive to further improve declines if there is no subsequent benefit for reaching 10 percent or 15 percent improvements, for example.[49] In fact, sometimes such improvements are indirectly discouraged.[50] For instance, maybe this year's attendance will serve as the base upon which improvements are to be made next year. In such a case, it is to the benefit of those involved to improve by 5 percent and meet the goal, but not to improve further so as to ensure that the next year's goal remains obtainable. Instead, set low, easily obtainable goals but present those goals as a floor rather than a ceiling. Once the first goal is achieved, the goals should steadily progress such that there are incremental rewards, but ambitious goals.[51]

Delineate Responsibilities: Everyone from the CEO to compliance to staff-level employees should have responsibilities and roles within the regulatory structure clearly delineated. Each policy should identify the target audience, as well as responsibilities and individuals accountable for upholding, enforcing, or abiding by the policy.[52] Failure to clearly identify responsibilities risks breeding a sense of diffusion of responsibility, which leads to apathy. Clearly identifying roles, by contrast, promotes a sense of ownership.[53]

Retain Records: Additionally, each organization should have a record-retention policy. Many types of wrongdoing are not discovered until years after the fact. By that point, the original actors may have moved on or forgotten about the issue. Documentation may keep organizations out of trouble; it facilitates internal investigations, and it may show regulators a good faith effort to avoid trouble. None of this documentation does any good, of course, if it all gets periodically discarded.

First, take an inventory of all records within the organization. Then, categorize the documents by functional business classifications.[54] The goal is to ensure that documents are not inadvertently destroyed, and also to maintain easy accessibility. Work closely with the IT department to create systems that make this possible. Additionally, work with business leaders to ensure the policy is consistent with other organizational goals.[55]

Next, set forth clear policies for each category of document. Clarify whom is responsible and accountable for record retention—either by centralizing the responsibility or putting unit managers in charge of their own documentation. Clarify further the length of time each type of document must be retained.[56] Public companies have numerous time requirements imposed on them by legislation, and so, too, does the IRS require all companies to maintain certain records. Furthermore, subsequent chapters show that various regulatory regimes impose record keeping requirements, such as companies that do business with the U.S. government or obtain licenses to export goods. Consequently, record-keeping policies should be responsive to the industry, geographic region, and business.

However, retaining records consumes server and physical space, and is thus costly. Organizations must therefore strike a balance that avoids retaining unnecessary records. This is best accomplished by determining a record-retention period for each record category.[57] All such approval periods should be approved by legal counsel.

Manage Conflict: Members of compliance departments are often perceived as an invasive species; given the breadth of its responsibilities, compliance often necessarily finds itself shouldering in on the traditional domains of other departments. Additionally, drawing lines directly from the compliance department to the board means bypassing high-level management, and this may lead to resentment. The compliance department may work closely with IT, legal, finance, and HR in designing, implementing, and enforcing the compliance Program. Compliance may also, however, find itself enforcing the rules of the Program against some of those same members. Compliance activities and responsibilities thus have the potential for conflict. An organization should clearly establish the boundaries of the Program and the compliance department's authority relative to other departments. The organization should also have a clear plan to deal with departmental conflicts.

D. Auditing and Monitoring Procedures

Organizations should complete the full risk assessment periodically; annually seems to be a generally accepted rule of thumb, though some organizations complete the assessment more frequently. But regular auditing and monitoring are also indispensable to an effective compliance Program.[58]

The terms "monitoring" and "auditing" are related, but they are not identical terms. A simple example may help distinguish the two concepts. If an employee exceeds the corporate price limit for a meal, a notification is sent to the compliance or accounting department, which may then seek further information about why the meal limit was exceeded. This is monitoring. Auditing occurs after the fact. An auditor may look back on all meal expenditures over the past year to identify any abnormalities. Note that both auditing and monitoring activities may be carried out with the use of internal controls, though at times manual efforts will also be required. Let's look at these terms in a bit more detail.

Monitoring: Ongoing monitoring is integral to the "timely identification of the risk of fraud and misconduct; timely identification (and remediation) of internal control deficiencies; deterrence of corporate malfeasance; production of accurate data to help the organizational decision-making process; [and] preparation of accurate and timely financial statements and other corporate records."[59] Furthermore, amid increasing regulatory enforcement, regulators, prosecutors, and judges oftentimes look to auditing and monitoring as a sign of good faith compliance efforts.[60]

The regulatory environment is constantly evolving, and new laws are regularly implemented. When new positions are created or technologies implemented, the business environment and risks may also change. Organizations should therefore constantly monitor the regulatory environment to determine whether new policies are required. This is accomplished by looking to changes in the organization that bring new risks, by reviewing industry publications, attending trade association conferences, and even actively monitoring state or federal legislative activities.

Examples include: monitoring the activities of new employees that are working in high-risk areas; monitoring expense reports; monitoring legislative developments; monitoring the adequacy of record retention; and monitoring internal controls, as discussed in the previous section. The specific types of monitoring are dependent on the nature of the risks. Additional areas to monitor will be provided during the legal and regulatory sections of chapters 10 through 15.

Auditing: Auditing focuses on identifying—on a periodic rather than a continual basis—noncompliance and other risky behavior within an organization. For instance, compliance often requires that employees seek legal advice for certain pre-established events, such as meetings where competitors will be present. Audits may periodically ensure that employees are seeking advice in those circumstances. If they aren't following those internal directives, those issues may be reported to management.

Audits should also be responsive to the organization's unique ethics and compliance risks. Organizations concerned about fraud may periodically audit expense reports submitted by traveling employees, organizations that are subject to the FCPA may periodically audit third parties, financial institutions may audit customers for money laundering risks, those with hourly employees may audit overtime standards, and manufacturing facilities might audit to ensure ongoing compliance with certification standards. Additionally, compliance-focused interviews should take place periodically; an optimal opportunity to complete an audit pertaining to risks or to the Program occurs during exit interviews or through questionnaires with departing employees.[61]

Where auditing or monitoring uncovers a problem, organizations should implement an action plan to improve upon the issue. Just as with the risk assessment, auditing and monitoring activities provide a trail of crumbs to the cookie jar for regulators. Consequently, identification of problems without remediation is disastrous for organizations.

Section II: Critical Success Factors for Compliance Management

CHAPTER SIX

Oversight and a Culture of Compliance

I. Why Tone at the Top Matters

By requiring that high-level employees promote an ethical and compliant organizational culture, the FSGO creates an affirmative duty for organizations to establish an appropriate tone at the top.[1] Time and again, a wide array of compliance experts point to the tone at the top as one of the most important elements of an effective Program. A company may have a stellar Code of Conduct and an excellent training program, but this means little without leadership. It is the leadership team that ensures employees take the Code of Conduct and training seminars seriously. High-level managers, whether or not they are aware of their influence, strongly affect company culture.[2]

Boeing, a Cautionary Tale: Between 1998 and 2001, Boeing committed three separate legal and ethical infractions—despite boasting a Program "acclaimed as a model for Corporate America," complete with a worldwide hotline for the reporting of violations, extensive ethics training, and even the presence of ethical advisors in each division.[3] However, a lackluster effort from top management to support an appropriate company culture and to stress the importance of legal and ethical decision making marked the downfall of the company's Program and ushered in a period of significant reputational deficit.[4] When top management loses interest, compliance managers lose influence.

That tone at the top is important is virtually a truism. In this case, managers apparently contributed to the deterioration of an ethical and compliant culture. Whether the spirit is for good or ill, management's attitude and expectations filter through the organization.

But, unsurprisingly, where top management supports the Program and its compliance managers, the likelihood of misconduct declines.[5] Employees who know they face punishment for poor conduct and rewards for good decisions are more likely to choose the latter. And when there is misconduct, there is an increased likelihood that employees will report it, thereby allowing the company to respond timely and appropriately.[6] This is not just good for avoiding liability, it is also smart business.

Tone at the Top and Whistle-Blowing: Oftentimes, whistle-blowers have reported to regulators, the media, or other external parties only after judging that nothing would be, or could be, done internally. Internal reporting structures alone, such as a hotline system for reporting violations, are thus insufficient. Management must also show a meaningful commitment to the Program in order to signal to employees that complaints will be dealt with in a good faith effort to remedy the wrong. This is how employers foster the all-important ethical culture and show employees that they need not fear retaliation, regardless of the nature of the misconduct alleged or the individuals implicated. We live in an age where whistle-blowing provisions of SOX, the False Claims Act, and other laws provide whistle-blowers with substantial payouts. Even if you have internal reporting mechanisms, most laws still allow whistle-blowers to bypass those mechanisms and remain eligible for payouts. Consequently, top management support is necessary to redirect reports to those internal mechanisms.

II.   How Managers Set the Tone

It is human nature for most people to follow their leaders, often without question. For this reason, whether the culture is toxic, ambivalent, or productive, employees are likely to line up behind management. Consider this experiment conducted by Stanley Milgram at Yale University:

The researcher three people, a researcher and two volunteers, were to take part in a memory research study.[7] But one of the volunteers was an actor, while the other volunteer was in fact the subject of the study. The subject was asked to be the "teacher," while the actor was chosen as the "student." The researcher, dressed in a white lab coat, then tied the student/actor to an "electric chair" and fastened an electrode to his wrist. A paste was applied, the teacher/subject was told, "to avoid blisters and burns."[8]

The researcher and teacher/subject then went into another room. The teacher/subject was to ask the student/actor questions, and for every wrong answer the teacher/subject was to apply a shock, at an increasingly high level, to the student/actor, using a machine in the room.[9] The switches were labeled, ranging from "slight shock" to "danger: severe shock."[10] The voltages ranged from 15 volts to 450 volts.[11] The highest two levels were simply labeled "XXX."[12] The teacher/subject was given a 45-volt shock by the researcher to prove the machine worked.[13]

The purpose of the study was to see how high of a shock the teacher/subject would administer, though in reality, no shocks were administered to the student/actor. Initially, the teacher/subject heard nothing from the student/actor in response to shocks administered. However, once the 300-volt shock was administered, a pounding was heard from the other room, and again at 315 volts. Then, silence. The student/subject was told that silence was to be taken as a wrong answer, and the next shock level should be administered.[14]

If at any time the student/subject hesitated, the researcher would state: "Please go on." After each additional hesitation, the researcher would state, first, "the experiment requires that you continue," then "it is absolutely necessary that you continue," and, finally, "you have no other choice, you *must* go on."[15] The research ended only after the student/subject had resolutely declined to administer the shock, or after the highest level of shock was administered.[16]

Almost two-thirds of the subjects administered the highest shock, 450 volts, and no student/subject ceased before reaching the 300-volt shock. This study has been repeated by other researchers, with similar results.[17]

Clearly, the teacher/subjects did not want to administer the shock. Most exhibited unusual symptoms, including sweating, trembling, stuttering, digging their fingers into their skin, and nervous laughter.[18] But still they continued following the direction of the researcher. The application of this experiment to business is clear. One-third of American professionals have been asked to do something unethical or illegal.[19] The results of this experiment beg the question, how many say yes when that request comes from a business leader?[20]

According to the researcher, Milgram, obedience is a "deeply ingrained behavior tendency . . . overriding training in ethics, sympathy, and moral conduct." But "obedience serves numerous productive functions. Obedience may be ennobling and educative and refer to acts of charity and kindness, as well as destruction."[21] Consequently, managers deeply affect the moral direction of the organization. Managers should be cognizant that tone is set virtually every minute of every day—from how the manager talks and acts to the consideration given to ethics and legality in light of daily decisions and strategy.

Ethical Culture: Imagine you have just taken the reins of a company following a public scandal, and your first goal is to establish an ethical and compliant culture. What do you do? As is so often the answer: it depends. Not all cultures are ethical, and not all ethical cultures are ethical for the same reason. Similarly, you may have a weak but very ethical culture, or a strong but very unethical culture. Compare the culture of an organization borne from an idealistic desire to "save the world," versus one started to "get rich fast." Think more broadly, and consider the ethics of a remote Andean tribe versus the occupants of a cosmopolitan city. Multinational companies may have many different cultures permeating their worldwide operations.

Consequently, when managers or compliance managers consider the factors of a compliant and ethical culture, they must be sensitive to the reality that cultural differences are abundant. If there is already a strong culture, they must determine whether that culture is ethical and consistent with an effective and efficient Program. Where the culture is strong but imperfect, they should strive to redirect the culture, rather than seeking to reverse course by fostering an entirely new cultural perspective.

By contrast, some companies have weak cultures. For instance, a company arising from the merger of formerly disparate company cultures may lack a sense of identity, as may a company that experienced a dramatic turnover among upper management. Companies with weak or nascent cultures present compliance challenges; they may require more resources and employee training than environments where the culture is well-established. But organizations with weaker cultures also present an opportunity, as committed managers can work with the compliance and legal departments to build a culture consistent with their own vision. This culture, regardless of its exact manifestation, should incentivize ethics and compliance while furthering the business interests of the organization.

Seven Factors: Once you've identified the starting point of the organizational culture, there are several steps to take to build, maintain, or strengthen an ethical and compliant culture. Muel Kaptein, in "Why Good People Sometimes do Bad Things," writes of seven essential factors.

1. Clarity of expectations
2. Strong role models among business leaders
3. Achievability of goals, tasks, and responsibilities
4. Commitment on the part of directors, managers, and employees in the organization
5. Transparency of behavior
6. Openness to alternative viewpoints and to discussing dilemmas and problems
7. Enforcement of sanctions for wrongdoing and rewarding good behavior[22]

Walk the Walk: As discussed elsewhere, where managers set a good example, misconduct declines. Alternatively, where managers don't follow the rules, the perception spreads that those rules are not really important. Consequently, there is a need for ethical leadership.[23]

An ethical leader has the courage to stand for what is right, even if what is right is not what others are doing. Says Kaptein: "Where others are silent, [leaders] speak. They demand responsibility."[24]

Don't Just Walk the Walk; Talk the Talk: It's the job of managers to keep employees focused on the task at hand while acting ethically and legally. Employees are more likely to behave more honestly and responsibly if the manager expresses his or her vision loudly and consistently.[25] For example, William George, the former chief executive of Fortune 500 company Medtronic, frequently spoke at employee gatherings about terminating a top sales employee for violating company ethical standards.[26] This indicated in no uncertain terms that the company was functionally devoted to doing the right thing, and that those acting otherwise were expendable. This message reinforces that employees should not be blinded by profit or personal objectives to the exclusion of acting legally and ethically.

Similarly, upon taking control of Salomon Brothers, Warren Buffett famously stated: "If you lose money for the firm by bad decisions, I will be very understanding. If you lose reputation for the firm, I will be ruthless."[27] It's a clear sign of a bad corporate culture when employees are afraid to raise bad news with managers.[28] Buffett was telling his employees that bad news is okay—in fact, it's part of the business—but if bad news is concealed, it has the potential to morph into something worse. That is where compliance breaches and negative PR flourish, and that is where Buffett is rightfully ruthless.

Use employee evaluations to gauge employees' commitment to compliance and support of an ethical workplace,[29] and to show in concrete terms that compliance must be considered along with other organizational objectives. This will reinforce that ethics is not just a buzzword to learn and quickly forget, but is a primary means by which a workforce will be judged, disciplined, and even dismissed or promoted.

Managers also implicitly send the right message by enforcing the provisions of the Code, fairly but consistently. The words of George and Buffett would have little effect if employees watched as unethical actors received promotions and bonuses. Consistent enforcement illustrates that a Program is prioritized over individual personalities and short-term gain.

Employers can also signal their commitment by stressing the importance of ethical and compliant behavior during the hiring process.[30] New employees should receive the Code of Conduct and a tutorial about the Program, and a "clear message that reporting concerns is encouraged, supported and valued."[31] At CH2M HILL, all new employees are required to affirm their commitment to the organization's Program as a condition of employment. These actions put new employees on notice that ethical and compliant behavior is part of the job description, and also reassure existing employees that a commitment to ethics and compliance is part of the vetting process for all new hires.

Training, taken up further in chapter 7, is also a way to demonstrate that a key ingredient of the organizational culture is ethics and compliance. Regular training, mandatory attendance, and even periodic assessments put employees on notice that they are expected to be familiar with the issues covered. Managers are encouraged to make appearances at training sessions, either to personally lead training seminars or to express support for the topics covered.

The Pygmalion Effect: Researchers Robert Rosenthal and Lenore Jacobson conducted an experiment in an American elementary school. Students took an IQ test at the beginning of the year. Teachers were then provided with a list of students who were likely to make an intellectual leap throughout the year. In reality, the students were randomly chosen without regard to actual IQ. At the end of the year, another IQ test was performed.[32]

The IQs of the students labeled "promising" increased by at least 12 percent more than those of the other students.[33] As the researchers explained, "when teachers expected that certain children would show greater intellectual development, those children did show greater intellectual development."[34] The teachers had not spent more time with these children. But they did establish a warmer relationship with them, providing more learning materials, providing more opportunities to respond to problems, and by providing higher-quality feedback on their work.[35]

The moral of the story is to treat your employees well and to show faith in them as people. If you expect your employees to act honestly, they're more likely to. Because of your trust you'll give off subtle cues to confirm that trust, and your workforce will seek to conform to your expectations.

Learn to Read Your Employees: Research shows that tiredness leads to mental, and ultimately moral, fatigue.[36] Research also shows that being under time pressure results in a similar phenomenon. This pressure, to meet a deadline or an abundance of tasks, causes us to shut down our moral radar in order to maintain focus on a limited area. Ultimately, time pressure causes moral blindness.[37]

Managers should therefore set reasonable expectations for the workforce, while keeping both pressure and working hours manageable. Not everyone handles stressful conditions equally, and therefore managers should look for warning signs of mental exhaustion.

Tone at the Middle: Research shows that people are more attuned to those with whom they can identify, while one's sense of responsibility declines as relationships become more distant.[38] For example, per capita street crime is far lower in rural areas than in urban areas, in part because more folks know one another in small towns.[39] The same is true in organizations. In larger organizations, employees are most often influenced by direct supervisors, rather than high-level managers who only make periodic appearances. Mid management support of the Program is therefore essential. And the compliance department as a whole should be visible. Send these workers out into the organization, have them introduce themselves, and explain the goals of the department.

High-Level Visibility: This research, indicating that familiarity breeds responsibility, also shows why it is so important for high-level managers to be visible supporters of the Program. Training may be an optimal time for managers to make such appearances. Additionally, the Code is a straightforward instrument by which management can demonstrate its commitment to compliance and ethics. CEOs often write the Code's introductory policy statement, and can also spearhead the distribution and publication of the Code.

A relatively recent development is the creation of the ethics officer. Management sends the undeniable message that ethics is prioritized by putting an ethics manager in the C-suite. These officers are often tasked with training employees in ethics, upholding and strengthening the ethical culture, and integrating the Program's ethical orientation with the compliance-based portion. In a nod to the multinational character of the organization, CH2M HILL employs "ethics ambassadors." Generally senior leaders geographically dispersed around the world, these individuals provide insight as to how to behave ethically within the many different cultures in which CH2M HILL does business. Employees should feel comfortable bringing ethical concerns to a company's ethics officers. Consequently, such officers should be perceived as trustworthy, competent, and independent. Even if an organization lacks the resources to appoint a full-time ethics officer, it should consider appointing "ethics champions" to serve similar roles, albeit more limited ones, in conjunction with their other responsibilities. These individuals can also be tasked with many of the above recommendations for fostering an ethical culture.

Conclusion

Employee culture is a top-down enterprise. Employees look to their supervisors for behavioral guidance. Because virtually all organizations rely on their employees to self-police and advise top management of ethical or regulatory concerns, setting the appropriate culture is a key step in ensuring the effectiveness of a Program.

CHAPTER SEVEN

Education and Training

This book covers numerous topics that may require training. For instance, an organization may train on types of ethical decision making, on utilizing whistle-blower hotlines, or on legislation such as the FCPA. To avoid redundancy, this chapter focuses on the procedural aspects of training, such as how to be a better trainer and the types of options available for training sessions.

I. Increase Understanding of the Problem, Then Teach the Rules

There are several steps to increase employees' absorption of educational materials. This includes post-training assessments, real world scenarios, and, maybe most important, earning the credibility of the workforce before the training seminar ever begins. As any compliance manager knows, the compliance department is infamous for its reputation for saying no. Compliance is seen as the group of people who doesn't know how to have fun. They inundate business with needless rules; they handcuff salespeople. They hurt the business, or at least that's the perception. Part of the problem is that, if it may be said, there may be some truth to this.

Why *You* (or Your Training Subjects) Shouldn't Engage in Fraud

A Word from Lyn Boxall, Fmr. General Counsel, Visa, Asia Pacific Region

"The point isn't that Siemens had $800 million in fines. That's actually too big of a number to mean anything to your people. The point is that you, and I'm talking to you the individual, you start getting investigated for months and months and months, and the only thing on your mind—when you're at work, when you're at home, over dinner, with your family—is am I going to get charged? What is going to happen? Then, the question, do I get a lawyer, do I sell the house? Because don't think the company is going to pay for your defense. You're going to have this cloud hanging over your head. And you have to ask, is it worth it?"

It's an incredible balancing act to manage diverse regulatory concerns while still maintaining a focus on the companies' core competencies. Some compliance workers are better at this balance than others. Compliance workers are trained to protect the company, but their jobs are part and parcel of the company: without a profit, there's no company to regulate.

That's one side of the story. The other side is that there are real risks that need to be managed, and oftentimes the regular workforce is skeptical. Compliance knows saying no to everything is counterproductive, but communicating this willingness to find creative, proactive solutions is essential. Imagine an employee calls and proposes new sales tactics for a slumping product. And the first time it's explained, it sounds like it won't be legal. But a good compliance manager tries to work with him or her, to develop a relationship and find solutions so they're seen as not just the enforcer, but also as a resource.

There are several ways you, as a compliance worker, can develop that relationship. Before you ever enter the classroom or a formal training session, work with your employees to help them understand your role. Give them the respect of educating, rather than mandating. And when training does begin, emphasize the importance of compliance and ethics to the success of the organization. Stress the consequences to the company—and, ultimately, to its employees—for violations of the law. Outline rewards for compliance and punishment for violations. And don't sell yourself short. Says Allstate's Levine, "When the legislature writes those laws, a lot of time they have no idea what your business is, they just write a law. And you have to take that law and put it on your process. You have to take that law and make it work as smooth as possible. That's adding value. Knowing the business and making the law work with your business."[1]

When employees understand what you're doing and why you're doing it, you have an audience that is more willing to listen as you explain its obligations under specific laws and regulations. According to the OECD, the failure to understand the laws themselves is a "deeply underestimated source of non-compliance."[2]

Customization: Given the enormous variety of regulations to which organizations may be subject, compliance education may require more than one-size-fits-all training. Instead, each division or office may need a tailored approach to training. CH2M HILL, for example, created its own in-house training video to ensure that employees learn policies, rules, and regulations that directly apply to them. Where new laws and regulations affect the role of employees, those employees should be trained to understand the change, and the implications of the change, for the organization and the individual's job function.[3]

Additionally, organizations may relate examples of noncompliance within the organization during training sessions. Organizations should also use visuals where possible to *show* the wrongdoing—for example, to show an accounting entry that was made to cover a hidden bribe—so that employees can recognize the subtle nature of the fraud. Real-world scenarios are a much more effective source of training materials than pure simulations.

Training Managers: Supervisors should receive training on employment and labor matters, ethics, and any other regulatory matters that affect their job functions.[4] Managers should be trained to spot risks and compliance issues and to know where to report such problems.[5] This complements ongoing monitoring and auditing efforts. Moreover, managers should be trained to properly discipline employees, including knowing what documentation to keep and when to involve HR.[6] Compliance managers should also undergo periodic training on new laws and regulations, trends, and best practices.[7]

Reaching All Employees: Training should include all employees who may be subject to regulations or who could expose the company to regulatory liability. The FSGO requires that managers, directors, employees, and agents receive "effective" training appropriate to their positions and responsibilities.[8] Consequently, training will differ for different categories of workers.

For example, there may be training that all non-U.S. employees must receive, training specific to lawyers or managers, or training for those in finance or accounting. Additionally, all new employees should go through a minimum level of training, such as an overview of the Code of Conduct, and how to internally report problems or wrongdoing.

For large organizations, keeping track of the training obligations of each category of worker is a challenge. Work with IT to automate these requirements into a system such as SAP, so that it is easy to look back at the end of each recording period to ensure that each employee has received his or her required training. This is also helpful when employees change roles, as the required new or supplemental training is easily identifiable. Moreover, the system may also be set to provide notifications in the event training isn't completed within a period of time. For instance, it is advisable to set a time limit by which new employee orientation must be completed (e.g., no later than 30 or 60 days from the date of the person's entering the organization).[9]

Companies should consider declaring training mandatory, especially where the likelihood or the severity of violations is high. Particularly susceptible organizations may even institute a zero-tolerance policy for absences from training, with delineated consequences for unexcused absences. At CH2M HILL, for example, both new and seasoned employees are required to review the company's principles annually, complete a training course, and pass a quiz on its key components. At minimum, e-mail and verbal reminders should be given regarding the date, time, and location of approaching training sessions.[10]

Ethical Training: Trainers should emphasize, as should the Code of Conduct, that the Program is not meant to cover every possible regulatory or ethical dilemma. As previously mentioned, the breadth of regulatory risk only serves to increase the importance of an ethical orientation, by which employees are prepared to take the initiative under uncertain conditions. Important ethical issues include handling conflicts of interest, gift giving, bribery, and financial integrity.[11]

Affective Priming: Research shows that self-image determines individuals' behavior. For instance, people who think of themselves as honest are less likely to steal from their company in order to avoid contradicting their self-image. But, perhaps surprisingly, self-image can be affected by activating particular images in the mind of the listener. If people are primed to think of a library, for instance, they're likely to talk more quietly; raise an image of old age, and they're liable to walk more slowly.[12] This is what is known as affective priming.[13]

Affective priming can also be used to positively affect levels of honesty. One study showed that levels of honesty increased when people were asked to write down the Ten Commandments.[14] This was the case whether or not the participants were Christian, or even religious. This exercise may not be appropriate for all organizations, but just thinking about being honest in the moment of temptation affects levels of honesty by activating the self-image of honesty.[15] Training sessions serve as an opportunity to provide this nudge.

Proactive Training: Use training as an opportunity to set goals. People are more likely to comply with rules when they have a sense of commitment to the plan and can visualize their own success in meeting that goal. Consider the following:

Employees at a company were asked to recycle more. A recycling bin was placed within a short walk of each desk. The employees were clearly instructed that the purpose was to increase levels of recycling, while the importance of recycling was stressed. However, levels of recycling did not increase.[16]

The company then changed its approach. Employees were asked to draft plans as to when, where, and how they would recycle. Within a week, the number of recyclable materials that were thrown in the waste-basket had decreased to one-eighth of the previous figure. A week later, the number of cups in the trash can had increased to one-quarter of the initial figure, but this average remained constant thereafter.[17]

The results of this case show that organizations should encourage employees to draft resolutions to improve upon their skills, to be more compliant, or more ethical. Moreover, if employees draft these resolutions as a group, the chances of success increase even more because individuals do not want to let the group down.[18]

Keep It Simple: Just as straightforward language is suggested for the Code of Conduct, it is similarly advisable to avoid legalese during training. Training should focus on real-world situations, case studies, or hypothetical situations that employees may face.[19]

Moreover, the trend is toward ever shorter training sessions, but with increasing frequency. This makes the information more digestible, reduces the time in which employees will lose focus, and thus increases the likelihood of retention. Increasing the frequency has the added benefit of ensuring the constant reminder (or "affective priming") of the information at issue.

Advertise Your Systems: Proper training reduces employee misconduct. Importantly, however, it can also increase the internal reporting of violations, while at the same time reducing the likelihood of employees incorrectly reporting violations (either internally or externally).[20] Thus, training may save companies from the time and expense of investigating and defending actions that well-meaning employees mistakenly believed were violations of some law, regulation, or policy.

Training should therefore emphasize the internal mechanisms by which employees may report violations, and identify situations in which reporting is appropriate. Training should also discuss how employees can safely report issues where senior management is, or may be, part of the problem.[21] Lastly, trainers should emphasize the antiretaliation provisions of the organization.

Training Options: Companies have several options when choosing the training format. The traditional, and still very popular, approach is classroom-style training.[22] This can be done one-on-one for new employees or in larger groups for regular training sessions. However, this is relatively costly, and may not always be a realistic option.

Another option is the fast-growing e-learning, or online training, platform. This method eases scheduling issues by allowing employees to access the course at their convenience and from virtually anywhere in the world. Online access to training materials allows employees to access the course repeatedly, thus refreshing their knowledge or helping to deal with specific concerns as they arise. E-learning may also feature interactive quizzes and tools for monitoring progress, thereby allowing organizations to better assess employee knowledge.[23] Some systems now measure the skill and knowledge levels achieved by individual employees.[24] Moreover, e-training facilitates record retention because it is easy to track the time and frequency of employee training.[25]

E-learning is most common in large organizations, where it is not feasible to gather tens of thousands of employees for one training session. Large companies generally provide computer-based training, and use in-person training as a supplement. In-person or classroom-style training is generally the most effective means of education and is reserved for high-risk areas at many companies. In-person training provides the opportunity for feedback and for employees to raise questions. Additionally, employees are likely to remain more engaged during in-person training than when following a session from their desks.

Because funds are limited, organizations should consider creative, alternative options as well.[26] For example, organizations may combine training sessions to achieve economies of scale.[27] Voluntary, continuing-education training, such as lunch-n-learns, may also prove valuable. Workshops improve communication and foster interactions. Compliance managers or business unit leaders might also rotate articles on the company's intranet to reach employees in a more informal manner.

Conclusion

Training is foundational to an effective Program. Just as the Program must be regularly evaluated to incorporate ever-changing regulations and business practices, so too should training take place at regular intervals. Without effective training, the Code of Conduct is likely to be misunderstood or underappreciated; the reporting hotline underutilized, ignored, or misused. Company culture is likely to suffer and, ultimately, the key asset of a company, its *employees*, will fail to further—and may outright hinder—the purposes of the ethics and compliance Program.

CHAPTER EIGHT

Understanding Fraud and Other Wrongdoing

There's a reason Mark Whitacre has been the subject of two books, a documentary, and a Hollywood film starring Matt Damon. His story of corruption, bravery, double dealing, and triple dealing, is unlike any story before or since. It is, as they say, a story that not even Hollywood could have dreamt up.

Mark Whitacre is the man that turned on his employer, Archer Daniels Midland Company (ADM), revealing what would become the biggest price-fixing case in American history. Every day for three years, Whitacre wore a wire for the FBI. He did this while perpetrating his own fraud, stealing $9 million right under the watchful eyes of the FBI. When confronted, Whitacre denied wrongdoing. He lost his immunity from prosecution, he lost his claim as an American hero, and he served nearly nine years in a federal penitentiary.

By all appearances, Whitacre is no longer the man he was 25 years ago, working for ADM. He tours the country, giving nearly 100 speeches a year to universities, corporations, and church groups. Today he's back in the C-suite, serving as COO at a biotech company dedicated to cancer clinical trials. But as Whitacre said, this is not the story of redemption or of a hero. This is the story of what not to do.

In 1989, at the age of 32, Whitacre became the fourth-highest-ranking executive at ADM. At the time, ADM was the fifty-sixth-largest company in the world, with over 30,000 employees. For the seven years Whitacre worked with ADM he averaged $3 million in annual compensation. There was talk of him becoming the next company president. "People would drive by our home and say, 'Mark Whitacre has it all,'" Whitacre recalls. Explaining why he risked so much, Whitacre speaks of a feeling of invincibility. "I felt like a rock star. I'd never failed," Whitacre said. "It was all successes."[1] And so Whitacre thought he was too smart, too good, to be caught.

In retrospect, Whitacre says, his career advanced too quickly. He'd spent eight years in school looking toward the future, but by this point his life had become focused on the 90-day increments in which earnings reports were released. Whitacre tells young people to always stay focused on the long term. "The long-term consequence is not worth the short-term gain. They may get a promotion or feel like they have X amount of money they wouldn't have had, but the long-term consequence [of ethical misbehavior] is not worth that."[2]

Ten Things Mark Whitacre Would Have Done Differently

1. Have a life-work balance.
2. Know your value system.
3. Adhere to the compliance program.
4. Have an organizational purpose, rather than just pursuing shareholder value.
5. Pursue ethical fitness: this means regular training to know how to act ethically.
6. ALWAYS do the RIGHT THING! No exceptions!
7. Be accountable for yourself and others.
8. Isolation is dangerous; surround yourself with trusted advisers.
9. ALWAYS think LONG TERM!
10. Live your life assuming everything you say or do could one day be in the newspapers (because for Mark, it was).

Whitacre has learned a lot of lessons. That will happen after nearly a decade in prison to reflect. But in the end his lessons are familiar ones. It can be seen with politicians, with athletes, and movie stars: an aura of invincibility. And it will be seen again, bigger and worse than the last time, according to Whitacre: "Fifty years from now the scandals are still going to happen. The key is to not be one of them."[3]

I.   The Anatomy of Fraud

In 2008, KPMG sponsored a survey of over 200 executives from across industry and government. The report found that nearly two-thirds of respondents felt that fraud and misconduct posed a significant risk in their industries, with 71 percent stating that fraud would result in a loss of public trust in their company. This section first analyzes why fraud occurs, then identifies types of fraud, as well as processes for uncovering and investigating wrongdoing. Understanding why fraud occurs is not merely academic. By recognizing root source causes, organizations can take steps to foresee and bypass fraudulent conduct before it ever occurs.

A. The Story of the Bagel

Let's start with a story about a man named Paul Feldman, as reported by Steven D. Levitt and Stephen J. Dubner in the popular book, *Freakonomics*. In 1984, Feldman, an economist, decided to quit his job and earn a living selling bagels.[4] Every morning he would deliver bagels to offices, along with a wooden box with a slot for consumers to pay for the bagels.[5] Within a few years Feldman was delivering thousands of bagels to 140 companies.[6]

What makes this case interesting is that Feldman was rarely present to collect payment; he would leave the bagels and move on, and so stealing would have been easy. The result? Most people paid for their bagels. Over the several-decade period that Feldman delivered bagels, 87 to 91 percent of people paid.[7] On average, only one money box was stolen per year.[8]

In this case, the stakes were low and thus the percentage of honest actors may be misleading. But still, this reveals three groups of people: those who paid fully, those who didn't pay, and those who actually stole the entire box of money. This accords with the truism that there are basically three types of people in the world: (1) those who will never steal, (2) those who cannot resist the urge to steal, and (3) those opportunists who will steal if they believe the circumstances are right.[9] Most people fall into the third category, and for this group of people internal controls and oversight are particularly effective because opportunists consider the likelihood of success.[10]

Whereas the always-honest and the always-dishonest are, for better or worse, mostly independent, opportunists are heavily influenced by what others around them are doing. Consequently, the opportunists of an organization, likely the majority of employees, are less likely to engage in wrongdoing when those around them are similarly honest, and more likely to engage in wrongdoing when others are breaking the rules.[11] Those people who will never steal are more likely to serve as allies of the organization and ethical stewards for those opportunists if they believe management is committed to doing the right thing.

B. The Fraud Triangle

The "fraud triangle" is commonly used to represent the conditions that drive fraud. Those conditions are: opportunity, pressure/incentive, and rationalization. By understanding these conditions, organizations can better control the actions of opportunists, and better uncover those who cannot resist the urge to steal.

Opportunity: The opportunity component of the triangle generally pertains to internal opportunities. Oftentimes, organizational controls and oversight are insufficient, and fraud is readily committed. For instance, internal opportunities arise where managers show distaste for ensuring oversight of employees, and where employees in high-risk areas are given free rein. But whatever the reason for the opportunity, employees are unlikely to actively seek out areas to perpetrate fraud. Rather, the opportunity presents itself as a temptation. It's sort of like putting a bowl of cookies in front of a child before dinner—though little Freddie may be able to resist, it's a lot safer to lock the cookies in the cabinet. An effective compliance and ethics Program goes far in locking away those cookies.

Pressure/Incentive: Where there is opportunity to commit a fraud, it is often paired with financial or other pressures. An alternative but related idea is that the incentives, the benefits of stealing, are simply irresistible. Maybe little Freddie missed lunch and can hear his stomach growling. He thus feels pressured to satisfy those hunger pangs, along with the incentive of enjoying a tasty cookie. Anecdotally, financial pressure and debts are cited as the most common drivers of fraud by fraud investigators. Employees may have gambling problems or they may be deep in debt and on the verge of losing a home. They may be unable to offer financial help to children starting college or facing a divorce that is dissolving hard-earned financial stability. These often-unexpected contingencies create pressures and increase the likelihood of wrongdoing.

Along with personal pressures, organizational and external pressures may also foster the temptation for wrongdoing. Think of your most demanding boss, or the horror stories relayed by friends and family about their bosses. Maybe the boss set unrealistic budget expectations. Maybe the boss acted in fits of rage, with underperforming employees fired, thrown away, and forgotten about. The risk of losing one's position or not obtaining a promotion brings financial pressure, reputational pressure, and ego effacement. Pressures also come from third parties, such as pressures to meet debt repayment obligations, to maintain public listing requirements, or to maintain market position in the face of an aggressive competitor.[12]

The amount of benefit to be gained also affects the likelihood of wrongdoing. Think back to the bagel experiment. In that case, the pressure and the incentive to steal was minimal because of the low cost of a bagel. But if, instead of bagels, Feldman was selling computers using the honor system, would the number of cheaters stay the same?

Rationalization: People often rationalize bad actions. They find a justification, an explanation that warrants an exception. Fraudsters may not be any different, just better at finding excuses. Often, fraudsters rationalize that they will pay back any money stolen, for instance. Employees who face layoffs or downsizing may believe they deserve a golden parachute. Mark Whitacre states that the impetus for his theft was the knowledge that he would soon be out of a job. He rationalized that he made $3 million per year and deserved a three-year severance package, so he would (and did) steal $9 million.

Employees may also take ethical cover in the belief that they have been wronged. Lost out on a promotion, or a raise? Go ahead and steal a little money; you probably deserved it. These fraudsters tell themselves that they work hard, and that they're only stealing what they're worth to the company; they tell themselves that everybody is doing it, and that nobody will be harmed by it. They tell themselves whatever they have to, so long as their pockets are filled.

Let's examine how each aspect of the fraud triangle comes together in a real-world case. In the early 2000s a secretary to Goldman Sachs executives stole about $7.4 million by withdrawing money directly from her bosses' personal bank accounts.[13] Her bosses were so rich, as it happened, that it took them years to notice the deficiencies. Asked why she stole the money, she responded: "Because it was easy" (opportunity).[14] For her illegal conduct, this modestly paid secretary obtained millions of dollars and purchased big toys that others might only dream of (pressure/incentive).[15] And the fraudster seemed to imply that her bosses' had all the money they needed, and that her role was analogous to that of a Robin Hood figure (rationalization).[16]

REASONS FRAUD CONTINUES

1. Belief employees are too honest
2. Belief it won't happen
3. Belief it will be caught if it does happen

REASONS FRAUD IS CAUGHT

1. 42.2% from tips
2. 16% management reviews
3. 14.1% internal audit
4. 6.8% on accident
5. 21% other

Source: http://www.acfe.com/rttn-detection.aspx

A Slippery Slope: Another destructive element of human nature is what will be referred to as moral slippage. Take the Goldman Sachs secretary: what ended up as a $7.4 million fraud started out as a relatively small $6,500 check forgery.[17] Research shows that every time one crosses a moral threshold, it becomes easier to cross the next one.[18] So, what often starts as small frauds—just enough to pay the bills or make up for the loss of a promotion—soon takes on a life of its own. Steve Casazza, former vice president of Nestlé Market Audit North America, relates the story of an employee falsely claiming expenses on a company credit card over a four-year period. The employee claimed and was paid just over $15,000 his first year, which roughly aligned with those of his peers. More confident by year two, he claimed $40,000, then $80,000 in year three, and over $120,000 by year four. At that point, the fraud had grown so large that it became virtually impossible to hide. Catching fraud is oftentimes not the issue; it's catching it before its inevitable growth.[19]

Gotta Love the Fraudsters: Casazza's story illustrates another unfortunate fact: fraudsters are often the last people one would expect to engage in wrongdoing. A fraudster is often a senior manager in his 50s that is well-liked, has been with the company for a long time, and has lots of responsibilities. Remember, fraudsters need the opportunity to commit the wrong, and this often presents itself to highly trusted individuals in high-level positions. In Casazza's story, the fraudster was highly respected internally and was identified as a possible successor to the department head. He was also active in local government and held an elected position outside of the company. The point is not to distrust everyone, or to lose faith in the good of people. The point is, however, that with clear-eyed focus, compliance managers should ensure that no employees are above the rules.

C. Types of Fraud

1. Asset Misappropriation: It is estimated that organizations lose 7 percent of annual revenue to fraud every year.[20] Asset misappropriation constitutes 90 percent of all frauds.[21] Asset misappropriation flourishes in cash-intensive businesses. The following are types of asset misappropriation:

a. *Skimming*: Diverting cash from the organization prior to its being recorded in the company's financial system. For example, a bartender may pocket a bill for a drink and never record the sale of that drink.

b. *Larceny:* Larceny involves diverting cash after it is recorded by the organization. This is a more complex type of fraud and is often perpetuated by misallocating cash to a different account, such as a personal account, and creating false entries to cover up for the missing cash. Organizations can reduce the risk of this fraud by segregating duties so that multiple individuals are responsible for the different stages of receiving and recording cash.[22]

c. *Fraudulent cash disbursements*: This is the misallocation of company funds. Some employees are quite ambitious in fraudulent disbursement schemes. In one case, a fraudster working for a public school district created a shell company, then billed the school for over $500,000 of repairs that either were not performed or were performed by school employees under the fraudster's supervision.[23] Due diligence on the "company" performing these repairs would have revealed the nature of this fraudster's actions.

d. *Payroll*: Fraudsters may overstate payroll by crediting additional hours worked or dishonestly paying for overtime. They may create compensation schemes—such as easily met bonus provisions—that give the cloak of legitimacy to cash disbursements. They may also put ghost employees into the system in order to collect their payments. Companies should periodically audit overtime to ensure that the work is consistent with the demands of the business. Additionally, hours worked beyond a threshold—for example, more than 80 hours in a week or 15 hours in a day—may warrant further investigation. Further, if multiple employees are using the same social security number or bank account number, it may signal the use of a ghost employee.[24]

e. *Expense reimbursement*: An employee may fraudulently overbill the company for an expense incurred, or may entirely fabricate an expense by creating false receipts. This could be as simple as overbilling for a meal while on business travel. Scrutinizing employee expenses, and making it known that such scrutiny occurs, minimizes the likelihood of fraudulent reports.[25] Additionally, internal controls should recognize unusual deviations.[26] Peer-to-peer comparisons can be informative: if the average employee spent $50 while in Bangkok for a night, why did Sally spend $250? Other red flags might include expenditures on nonwork days or holidays (including commercial holidays like Black Friday), purchases of gift cards, and expenditures for tuition.

f. *Inventory theft*: Unlike the previous types of fraud, inventory theft is a noncash fraud. For example, an employee of a clothing store may wear a pair of jeans and a T-shirt out of the store without paying. Maybe the fraudster wears the clothes out on a date or sells them online to convert the inventory to cash. Inventory fraud may also occur at the time the items are received, during which time the employee can simply "forget" to record an item on the company's records. Employees may also overorder materials—for example, by ordering more toner than the company needs, more liquor than a bar requires, or more materials than a construction site will use. The fraudster can adequately complete the job, since there's no shortage, and is free to sell the surplus through back channels.

Companies should clearly document the arrival of all new items. Duties should be segregated, so that the same employee does not order goods, record the receipt of goods, and disburse the goods throughout the company. Auditors should also ensure that costs of materials align with organizational requirements.[27]

For each of these frauds, an accompanying change in lifestyle may be observed. Let's return to the case of the Goldman Sachs secretary. The secretary had purchased an Aston Martin and a $900,000 yacht, and had taken to vacationing at her Cyprus beach home.[28] Consistent with her modern-day-Robin-Hood persona, she was extremely generous with friends and coworkers.[29] Clearly this was not the lifestyle of a modestly paid secretary, and if red flags had been raised, this fraud could have been uncovered millions of stolen dollars earlier.

Additionally, many of the more complex types of fraud require continuous legwork on the part of the fraudster. Consider the following situation: While out on maternity leave, a fraudster sneaks into the office every night after everyone leaves in order to balance accounts that, if left alone, would reveal her fraudulent activities. Fraudsters are often thought of as some of the company's hardest workers, but are in fact simply afraid to leave their computers. They know, as did the woman on maternity leave, that if someone else sees their records, the wheels will fly off. This is why so many employers require that employees use their vacation days and build in a segregation of duties.

2. Fraudulent Financial Reporting: As noted earlier, the sources of pressure to engage in fraud can be personal or external. Where the sources are external—such as the need to meet investor demands or managerial expectations—employees may feel pressure to fraudulently report on a company's or a division's performance. Personal pressures—such as the need to pay a bill—may also result in fraudulent reporting where bonuses, for instance, are tied to those metrics. The following are types of financial-reporting fraud:

Earnings management: Fraudulent earnings management is the "intentional, material misrepresentation of bottom-line results."[30] This may be done to improve year-end earnings, to smooth reported earnings, or to meet management expectations.[31]

Revenue manipulations: Types of revenue manipulations include:

- *Fictitious sales*: The recording of nonexistent transactions in order to inflate revenue. This typically involves phony customers or legitimate customers with exaggerated or phony invoices.
- *Channel stuffing*: This typically involves pushing unordered or unneeded products to clients. Again, this inflates revenue for the organization in the short-term by "booking" the sale. Unlike simply recording fictitious sales, this has the

added benefit for fraudsters that the inventory is in fact nowhere to be found when the outside auditor stops by.

- *Bill-and-hold transactions*: Companies cannot recognize revenue until the risk of ownership is transferred to the buyer.[32] Organizations improperly recognize revenue if the revenue is recorded prior to delivering goods (or legal ownership) to a buyer.
- *Round-tripping*: This fraud occurs when a company sells goods to another company (perhaps even a shell company or an insider-controlled company) with the understanding that the goods will later be repurchased.[33] No economic activity occurs, but, again in the short term, there is the appearance of a sale and business activity. Red flags signifying round-tripping activities include unusual side deals, significant sales to unknown or new companies, and a high number of products returned after the end of a reporting period.[34]
- *Delayed revenue recognition*: Whereas the schemes noted earlier aim to accelerate or fabricate revenue, in this scenario managers may delay recognizing, or booking, revenue where expectations for the quarter or year have already been met, or where subsequent periods are likely to fall short of expectations.[35] This is a form of income smoothing and is illegal.

Investors pay a premium for stability. Income smoothing, where companies either fabricate revenues or report legitimate revenues on a selective schedule, is done to "provide the illusion of consistent, positive, revenue streams."[36] Income smoothing is recognized by, among other things, unusually consistent revenue reporting. This is particularly true where the industry as a whole sees inconsistent revenues.[37]

3. Expense Manipulation: The previous financial frauds dealt with manipulating revenues. But remember the old adage: a dollar saved is a dollar made. Manipulating expenses may mean, among other things, failing to recognize expenses entirely, improperly capitalizing expenses, and improper depreciation and amortization schedules of assets.

4. Balance Sheet Manipulation: The most common type of asset manipulation is the overstatement of inventory, which in turn inflates assets.[38] To evade external auditors who would reconcile claimed inventory with actual inventory on hand, these fraudsters may report the "inventory" as in-transit so as to justify its absence, or they may simply have empty boxes and pallets that are claimed as inventory.

Additionally, companies must periodically write off goods, either because the product has expired, the technology is antiquated, or the product otherwise has declined in value. One form of fraud is to fail to write off products when the loss becomes known.[39] Fraudsters may also inflate accounts receivables to give the impression that the company is owed more than it really is or, where delinquents fail to pay their bills, the company may state that those accounts receivable have actually been paid by fraudulently inflating the cash receipts account.[40]

5. Improper Disclosures: Publicly traded organizations have an obligation to publicly disclose significant fraud by top managers, officers, or others in positions of trust. In the Walmart matter, for example, Wal-Mart Stores, Inc. is facing a suit from shareholders who allege the company improperly failed to disclose in its 2011 quarterly report the full extent of ongoing liabilities and risks arising from the allegedly corrupt actions of its Mexican subsidiary.[41]

It has been noted frequently in the previous chapters that high-level management should not be immune to internal rules, and that compliance managers need independence from high-level employees and should ideally report directly to the Board. If you weren't already convinced of the legitimacy of this structure, here's another reason: around *90 percent* of financial reporting fraud involves a high-level officer.[42] Remember, trust but validate, and validate with neither discrimination nor exception.

Chapter 9 presents tools to increase internal reports of wrongdoing and to investigate reports. While employees may be most likely to report wrongdoing that involves fraud or theft, the system as a whole is integral to revealing wrongdoing inclusive of both regulatory and ethical violations.

Identification, Investigation, and Enforcement

I. Whistle-Blower Programs

Benefits of Internal Reporting: Whistle-blowing is the act of disclosing what one believes to be wrongful or illegal behavior to a higher-level manager or to the public.[1] Laws increasingly provide monetary awards to whistle-blowers—report a violation of the law to regulators, and the whistle-blower receives a percentage of any eventual recovery in what is known as a *qui tam* lawsuit. The success of these laws is uncontroverted, and is written into the False Claims Act, numerous environmental laws,[2] military laws, and various state laws. Perhaps most prominent, Dodd-Frank includes a whistle-blower bounty in which reporters receive 10–30 percent of recoveries over $1 million.[3]

Therefore, an essential component of a Program is a process by which to report internal concerns of wrongdoing to the appropriate person in the organizational chain. For most Programs this includes (though it is not limited to) a hotline. A hotline allows employees to report misconduct, follow up on the status of investigations, and learn what, if any, actions were taken to remedy or avoid harm.[4] Reporting may allow the company to identify problems before too much damage is done. As previously noted, the most common way by which organizations and regulators uncover wrongdoing is through tips, and most legitimate tips come from employees. Companies that have hotline programs in turn receive 34 percent more legitimate tips than companies without hotlines.[5]

Effective reporting systems reduce external whistle-blowing complaints. A *qui tam* litigator noted that many employees report not to obtain possible cash payouts but to redress a personal wrong, to "do the right thing," or because the company failed to act.[6] Because money is not the primary instigator for most whistle-blowers,[7] an employee may just as readily report internally as externally when an effective internal reporting system is made available.

Uses of the System: Employees at all levels, in all divisions, and across all geographic sectors should be encouraged to freely report perceived or potential violations. Though not all concerns are validated, it is better to disregard an erroneous report than to be unaware of a legitimate violation. Companies may find it prudent to require that employees internally report known violations. This may be advisable policy in light of the myriad regulations that affirmatively require individuals to report known violations to the relevant regulatory agency. Consequently, individuals failing to so report may unwittingly subject themselves and, by extension, the company, to legal liability.

Additionally, employees should be encouraged to seek guidance when facing ethical or legal dilemmas. Unsure if the payment your manager wants you to make to a foreign official is a bribe? Don't guess, seek guidance. Stress to employees that compliance is important. It's not something to take chances with. And it's better safe than sorry to ask on something.

Structuring the System: Companies have several options when structuring their reporting systems. Some organizations choose to filter reports and complaints through the legal department. This may allow the organization to claim attorney-client privilege, and it is also a means by which organizations can effectively evaluate the possible legal ramifications of issues before deciding whether to report up the organizational chain to higher-level managers.

Alternatively, and for smaller organizations in particular, reports can go straight to the CEO or the board. Regulators consider this the most effective reporting method, though admittedly it may be unrealistic for large or highly diversified organizations.[8] An advantage of this structure is the implicit guarantee to employees that their concerns will not be lost in the bureaucratic shuffle. Additionally, by giving the compliance department direct access to the highest levels of the organization, it is rendered independent from those departments which may be subject to investigations or which may otherwise hamper due diligence efforts.

Lastly, outsourcing the reporting system to vendors is common practice. Outsourcing gives organizations access to experience and knowledge that they may lack internally. In essence, it cedes responsibilities to those third parties whose specialty is knowledge of the FSGO and, more generally, ethics and compliance reporting systems. This may also be a less-expensive option for organizations than retaining full-time, internal staff to handle sporadic reports. Moreover, independence of the hotline operator is self-evident when internal organizations are bypassed. Organizations choosing this option are advised to remember, however, that oversight is essential—simply outsourcing the process does not externalize responsibility.[9] To paraphrase Harry Truman, the buck stops with the organization.

A hotline is necessary, but not sufficient. Ultimately, hotlines are passive tools by which employees can raise concerns. But the job of the compliance department is also to proactively root out wrongdoing. Audit and evaluation procedures may reveal past or ongoing instances of wrongdoing, along with the systemic or underlying risks. As touched on earlier, exit interviews are also a valued, proactive method for identifying potential compliance breaches. Departing employees may have a particular incentive to bring a whistle-blower claim against the company. An exit interview, followed by the evaluation and follow-up procedures outlined below, may assuage that individual's concerns and thereby divert a whistle-blower action.

And don't forget to *ask* your employees. Many organizations require employees to certify that they will, prospectively, abide by the terms of the Program. But don't forget to ask for retrospective validations. Ask your employees to certify that they did not participate in or experience any compliance violations. These certification forms are provided to Ameren employees on an annual basis.[10] The certification includes an exception block, says Ron Gieseke, where they can say "I think I'm okay, except what about this circumstance?"[11] This exception block allows employees to raise concerns, even if uncertain whether an actual violation occurred. Gieseke says that teams then review the certifications, investigating on an as-needed basis.[12] As many as 5 to 10 percent of Ameren certifications lead to further investigation.[13] Moreover, "there's commonality of concerns," wherein employees consistently misunderstand some policy or regulation and, says Gieseke, "that sometimes will lead to changes in the policy."[14] Consequently, these post hoc certification forms are beneficial not only for rooting out wrongdoing, but also for analyzing the weak links in policies and procedures.

II.   Optimize the Reporting System to Increase Internal Reporting

Anonymity and Confidentiality: The FSGO specifies that mechanisms for reporting "may include" allowances for anonymity or confidentiality so that employees can report without fear of retaliation.[15] This anonymity or confidentiality is crucial, particularly where one employee is revealing the wrongdoing of another employee or concerns about a department's activities. One study found that 39 percent of employees didn't report misconduct because they feared their identities would not be kept anonymous.[16] However, employees should understand the limitations of confidentiality. If an employee reports a violation that is ultimately investigated by a regulatory agency, investigative powers may allow the regulatory agency to bypass assurances of confidentiality.

Anonymity is a challenge for smaller companies; this increases the import of clearly defined and enforced antiretaliation provisions. The myriad third-party vendors that operate corporate hotlines allow companies of all sizes to better protect anonymity and confidentiality.

Maintaining the Integrity of the System: There is no doubt that employees may abuse the reporting system. An employee could attempt to discredit a fellow employee when both are up for a promotion, or as payback for a perceived wrong, or even to divert resources while perpetrating his or her own fraud. Minimize this risk by communicating with employees. The Code of Conduct or employee handbook should explicitly state that employees using the hotline in bad faith, be it maliciously, recklessly, or by falsely reporting, will face disciplinary action up to and including dismissal and a civil lawsuit.[17] "Good faith" should be defined and antiretaliation provisions set forth in the company's Code of Conduct and during training sessions. "Good faith" generally indicates that while the employee does not have to be right about accusations leveled, he or she does have to believe that the information provided is true.[18]

Prior to launching a full-scale investigation, the investigator should consider whether the reporting employee could have a motive to fabricate. If no red flags arise and the investigation proceeds, the organization will have a strong foundation from which to separate legitimate, even if ultimately erroneous, reports from those that are entirely fabricated. However, under no circumstances should an organization retaliate against an employee reporting in good faith.[19]

Retaliation: A fear of retaliation is one of the top reasons that employees will not raise concerns or report misconduct.[20] Nonretaliation means ensuring not only that employees are free from the fear of punishment, but also that the company takes measures to ensure that reporting employees are not shunned or ostracized by colleagues. Beware of both direct and indirect retaliation. Direct retaliation is most easily identifiable, as this includes firing, demotion, reassignment, or poor performance reviews. For instance, an employee with consistently high performance marks who suddenly receives a poor review after reporting is a signal of direct retaliation. Such sudden changes in the status of the reporting employee should be investigated.

Indirect retaliation includes harassment, ostracism, and poor work assignments.[21] Identifying indirect retaliation or low-level forms of retaliation is a difficult endeavor. The company should consider actively monitoring the status of reporting employees. This includes retaining an open channel of communication with the individual[22] and setting internal controls to alert management to changes in salary, position, or employment status. Any concerns brought forth by the reporting employee should be well documented, investigated, and remediated.

Even actions that could be *perceived* as retaliatory pose a risk to the organization. Given its significant chilling effect on employees' willingness to report, real or perceived retaliation weakens, if not destroys, the efficacy of the entire Program. Additionally, perceived retaliation may well lead to wrongful termination lawsuits, along with bad public relations and diminished employee morale. This all speaks to the need for hypervigilance and dogged documentation.

The best way to protect against actual or perceived retaliation is to separate functions so that any employment decision—termination, demotion, change of position, and the like—is made by someone without knowledge that a complaint was made. This is part of why anonymity is so vital. Moreover, document problems with employees early and often to show a clear history of past issues. Sometimes companies are overly generous with evaluations. But when employees get fired for something that may have been happening over an extended period, but for which there is no supporting evidence, organizations are left with a weak defense. Be honest during evaluations, and maintain records showing past nondiscrimination of whistle-blowers.

Lastly, guaranteeing nonretaliation goes beyond formal mechanisms. An ethical culture is essential to encouraging employees to utilize a whistle-blower hotline.[23] Where that culture is lacking, trust, too, is lacking,[24] and so assurances of confidentiality, anonymity, and nonretaliation are less credible.

Incentives for Reporting: As discussed previously, people are hesitant to go against what is perceived as the group norm. Moreover, people are hesitant to question managers and supervisors. Therefore, encourage your employees to trust their instincts, and make it clear that no harm will come from reporting a suspicion or concern. Paired with a strong nonretaliatory commitment, providing rewards may increase the volume of internal reports.

There may be cases where monetary rewards are merited, such as where a significant fraud is uncovered, or in situations where reporting to governmental regulators would have led to a monetary recovery for that whistle-blower. In this case, the organization rewards the whistle-blower for reporting internally rather than externally, while (it is hoped) taking such steps as are necessary to remedy and self-report the wrongdoing.

But providing actual monetary rewards for reporting could backfire, leading to more frivolous reports. Companies should also consider demonstrating appreciation by rewarding ethical behavior on employee evaluations. Research suggests that, in some cases, rewards as simple as a verbal or written note of appreciation from a manager or department head may be effective.[25]

Availability of the System: Companies should also consider giving employees multiple mechanisms to report. Don't stop with a telephone number; provide an e-mail address and a mailing address, too. Some employees, wishing to remain confidential and fearful of leaving a digital footprint, may only trust postal mail when reporting violations.

Don't skimp on the details of your reporting system. Keep the hotline open 24 hours a day, seven days a week. Employees can call while the details and sense of injustice are fresh, from the perceived safety of home, or during an inspired burst of courage.

The hotline should also provide options for multilingual reporting. Most employees will wish to report directly to a supervisor or manager, rather than through a hotline. But where communication is problematic, this multilingual reporting option ensures that all employees feel comfortable expressing what may be complex, serious concerns.

The organization should transparently publicize its policy for handling reports. This will reduce ambiguity and thereby increase faith that the processes will protect the reporting employee and remediate the wrong. General Electric, for example, indicates in its Code of Conduct that it will assign an investigation team that brings expertise and objectivity; this team will determine the facts through interviews and/or documents, recommend corrective actions to appropriate management, and provide feedback to the individual raising the concern.[26] This language serves to reassure employees that the company is familiar with handling reports, is competent in doing so, and is diligent in seeing investigations through to their logical conclusion.

Promote the Program: The hotline's existence should be regularly publicized through all available channels. The organization should publicize the reporting program in the Code of Conduct, during training sessions, in companywide communications from senior management, on posters placed throughout the office, and on the company's intranet and Web site. CH2M HILL lists the phone number and e-mail address for its reporting hotline at the bottom of each and every page of its Code of Conduct, which leaves no question of its import and ready availability. Such communications should stress not only the means of reporting, but also that such reporting is easy and anonymous.[27] The commitment to publicizing a reporting system also goes a long way toward that ever-present goal of showing top-level buy-in of the Program.

Moreover, clarify the uses of the system. Let employees know whether they can call, not just to make reports, but also to seek advice or guidance. Ideally, employees will be free to report any variety of ethical concern or wrongdoing. But some organizations, due to resource limitations, for instance, may limit the hotline to a specific purpose. For instance, the hotline may be operated by a specialist in one area of law, such as the FCPA.

Lastly, organizations must remain sensitive to the personal difficulties that whistle-blowers face. In many ways, this is the ultimate no-win situation. Whistle-blowers risk being labeled "tattletales," but failing to act may lead to culpability or make them scapegoats if the misconduct is later discovered.[28] Never forget that many careers have been wrecked by good faith reporting, *and* by failing to report, and that makes whistle-blowing a profoundly frightening position to be in.

III. Investigating Reports

This section examines the investigation process from the initial stage, where organizations must make plans and choose investigators; to the investigatory stage; and to the final stage, in which findings are made and actions taken.

A. Early Stages

The Investigator: Investigators should freely exercise autonomy. For those companies choosing to use an ombudsman or other internal investigator, it becomes especially important to give that individual total independence from all but the highest echelons of the organization. Such independence should be stressed in the Code of Conduct and when publicizing the reporting mechanism. Additionally, the best investigators bring a reputation for integrity, either through prior work with the organization or through unique past experiences. Many investigators are retired judges, military officers, or FBI agents, or come from other positions of high repute.

Resources: Organizations must not handcuff their investigators. Their jobs are hard enough already. Provide investigators the resources and authority to live up to their titles and effectively *investigate*. This may include the resources to hire experts to assist in the investigation, the assured cooperation of all individuals within the organization, and access to relevant records.[29]

To Outsource or Insource? Just as organizations have the option of outsourcing hotlines, they must weigh the following pros and cons of internal versus external investigators:

1. *Cost*: Internal investigators may keep costs down for those companies large enough to retain full-time investigators. Outsiders are likely more cost effective for smaller or less regulated companies that may only rarely execute full investigations.
2. *Expertise*: Outside investigators bring specialization in investigating the areas of concern. Many vendors are former prosecutors and regulators, for example. Internal investigators, by contrast, may possess superior knowledge of organizational operating systems.
3. *Confidentiality*: External investigators give the appearance (which is often a reality) of increased independence over internal investigators.[30] This in and of itself may increase reports. While larger companies may adequately uphold independence, particularly through the use of ombudsmen or others that report directly to the board, the appearance of conflict may still be difficult to overcome.

Organizations may also consider appointing in-house or retained attorneys to investigate. If incriminating evidence is brought to light and the organization fails to self-report for any reason, this may allow the organization to invoke the attorney-client and work-product privileges with regard to investigatory findings.[31] Attorneys also bring particularized knowledge when the issue is one of regulatory or legal violations.

Sources of Information: Organizations should be receptive not only to hotline reports, but also to reports from law enforcement agencies, suppliers, or customers, and via employee surveys or interviews. The individual receiving a complaint should fully document the allegations.[32] If the complaint is received via the hotline service, the reporting employee should be thanked for making the report, and assured that confidentiality will be respected and that he or she need not fear retaliation.[33] Though employees should be given the option of anonymity when reporting, the investigator may need to contact the reporting employee for additional information, or to verify details. To expedite follow-up, determine whether the employee is amenable to disclosing his or her name or contact information to the investigator. Employees are more likely to waive anonymity where the office or organization manning the hotline is perceived as independent from the alleged wrongdoer. Additionally, encourage the reporting employee to follow up with any additional information.[34]

Groundwork before the Investigation: For any complaints bearing the imprimatur of legitimacy, immediately open an investigation with the goal of gathering all pertinent information.[35] Balance this, however, against the reality that not all reports are legitimate. Consider the potential consequences to the company and the accused if allegations are false, and mitigate those consequences to the extent possible.

Large organizations may have investigators dispersed by departmental expertise, while others may operate with one, centralized investigatory department. Depending on the investigator's level of specialization, it may be necessary to bring in professionals experienced in the area of alleged wrongdoing. This is particularly true where the allegation involves the violation of a complex law or complex organizational operations. Consider involving compliance, legal, or another such department that may play a role in investigating the action[36] and identify contact persons therein. The individual or team conducting the investigation must, however, be fully independent of the subjects of the investigation. Care should therefore be taken before bringing the issue to the attention of other, possibly conflicted, parties.

The Checklist: At the earliest possible stage, investigators should identify the steps that will be taken along the way in order to complete the investigation. Steve Casazza, former vice president of Nestle Market Audit North America, suggests answering the following questions prior to initiating the investigation:

- Who else may be involved in the wrongdoing?
- What is the objective of the investigation?
- Who needs to be made aware of the investigation?
- Who should be involved?
- What disciplinary actions might be appropriate if the reports are verified?
- Would the company support prosecution?
- What documentation needs to be gathered?[37]

The investigation itself will vary depending on the nature of the compliance issue. The investigation may require auditing billing practices; interviewing employees or other involved parties; reviewing contracts, laws, or company policies; or evaluating other business practices.[38] Carefully document all actions taken and all evidence discovered. This provides the resources to verify the accuracy and reliability of a finding, in order to defend any claims of wrongdoing, prosecute a civil claim against the accused, or support a criminal prosecution.

B.   The Investigation

A "Stealth Mode" Investigation: Some tips for investigators: Learn as much as possible and work to avoid enlightening the accused. Learn all you can by doing your research prior to initiating employee interviews. When interviews do begin, interview all potential witnesses before interviewing the accused. Keep the accused in the dark by executing the investigation in a prompt manner. Minimize time between interviews, advise all interviewed witnesses as to the importance of confidentiality, and if rumors of the investigation spread, consider accelerating the timetable for the interview with the accused. By catching the accused off guard, you have a significant first-mover advantage. The accused will not have time to prepare a defense, and any assertions may be readily fact-checked. Additionally, the accused's reaction to the shock of an investigation may prove informative.

The Importance of Surprise in an Investigation

A Word from Nestlé's Steve Casazza

"The most skilled investigators are able to execute their analysis in 'stealth mode,' accessing and analyzing data without leaving behind any evidence that could potentially alert a suspect that they are under the microscope. This can be particularly challenging when the investigator is forced to rely on the assistance of others to obtain physical or logical access to system records or transaction details. It is therefore essential that fraud investigators have unfettered access to the organization's records. Investigators also need to be highly skilled in data analysis and have the ability to maintain their investigation files on secure workstations and network drives in order to maintain the confidentiality of the data and the identity of those employees considered suspects."[39]

Interviews: During investigations, focus on identifying the conditions perpetuating fraud by looking for opportunities, pressures, and any rationalizations that might have led to wrongdoing. If, for instance, the individual is accused of misappropriating large amounts of money, the investigator may ask whether colleagues or friends have seen a change in the spending habits of the accused ("Did she buy an Aston Martin?" for example.) Consider also whether the accused faces pressures to commit a misappropriation, such as outstanding debts, or losing out on a promotion.

Prepare thoroughly for the interview. Set out questions in a way that makes sense or, at least, given that the interviewer may not want to guide the interviewee too closely, in a way that does not confuse the witness. It may be advisable to strategically ask the same question in a couple of ways to ensure you're getting the same answer, but interviewers should not actively create confusion.

Additionally, ask the accused to provide evidence to substantiate claims of innocence. If employees are accused of misappropriating funds, seek bank records from the accused; if an individual claims to have been at dinner with friends during an alleged collusive meeting with competitors, ask for a restaurant receipt.

All investigatory interviews should take place with at least three people present; along with the investigator and the interviewee, include a third party to observe conduct, serve as a witness if necessary, and possibly maintain security as well. Choose a neutral position for the interview. The investigator's office may intimidate the interviewee, while the interviewee's office may give the interviewee a psychological advantage. Meeting rooms are generally better than offices; something with a table, rather than a desk, may signal a commitment to solving a problem and working together. Use a private location—as opposed, for example, to a glassed-in conference room—where others in the office are not necessarily aware that an investigation is occurring.

The accused may feel desperate, and desperate people are prone to desperate acts. It is not unheard of for employees to allege that they were coerced or threatened during investigations, or subjected to false imprisonment. Casazza suggests that the accused always sit with an unobstructed path to the door so as to counteract any claims of false imprisonment or threats to physical safety. Nor should physical safety of the investigator be neglected in high-pressure investigations.

Additionally, pay attention to local privacy laws of foreign countries. In some countries, there may be restrictions on the type of investigatory interviews that are permissible. Talk with local counsel before conducting the interview to determine whether there are any laws that require attention.

C. Concluding the Investigation

Reporting Investigatory Results: At the conclusion of the investigation, the investigator will likely report to higher management. For investigators, this is the time to shine. It is a stressful, exciting time. Steve Casazza offers this advice to investigators about to file reports:

> Even the most highly skilled and experienced investigators can succumb to pressures during a high profile investigation. Sifting through reams of transactional history and piecing together a suspect's motives, opportunities, and rationalization requires the investigator to become personally invested in each case. When the evidence starts to come together, the investigator may

interpret data in a way that makes his/her hypothesis of what has happened start to look like the only possible reality. Excitement and pressure start to build, and can be further compounded when the investigator feels the need to update senior management on the progress of the investigation, or to finally get face-to-face with a suspected fraudster. It is at these times when effective investigators force themselves to pause long enough to take one final objective review of the facts. Taking just a few short moments to review the case from a "big picture" perspective can make the difference between solving the fraud case, or accusing an innocent employee of committing fraud.[40]

Additionally, the report should include all relevant factual details, including who was involved and what happened. Reports should indicate the seriousness of findings and investigators should consider providing a suggestion for avoiding the issue in the future. Most important, reports must be precise and objective. This is no place to protect friends. Your credibility as an investigator is on the line.

Follow-Up with the Reporting Employee: As noted earlier, General Electric's Code of Conduct states that employees will be apprised of developments throughout the investigation. This follow-up with the reporting employee is a low-resource, high-impact proposition. As noted above, most whistle-blowing occurs because employees feel wronged, either by the company itself or by an individual thereof.

The purpose of reporting systems is to encourage ambivalent employees to report and to divert aggrieved employees to internal mechanisms. But the job is not completed upon receipt of a report. Employees need to know their reports are taken seriously and acted upon. The follow-up should keep the employee informed about the status of investigation. Failure to follow up could reinvigorate an employee's pessimism about the company's culture. A common reason employees fail to report is a belief that nothing will be done.[41] If the report isn't made, perhaps the employee simply sits on his or her hands. Or, instead, the employee may take his or her complaint straight to a government investigator.[42] By contrast, an effective investigation is likely to dampen the reporting employee's zeal for bringing a whistle-blower suit against the organization.[43] Companies should thus strive to minimize response time and reduce the risk that an employee mistakenly believes his or her complaint has been ignored during the interim investigation period.

As discussed, accountability and enforcement are instrumental to maintaining an effective Program,[44] but these actions mean little without communicating managerial commitment to those policies. Therefore, let the employee know whether the investigation bears fruit, and what, if any, disciplinary actions or policy changes are taken to remedy any wrongs committed. If the employee insists on anonymity, provide that employee with a fictitious name or a number for purposes of identification and ask the employee to call back at a specified date and time for an update.[45]

D.   Enforcement and Discipline

Despite all of your best efforts, something goes wrong. A law or a rule is broken. Unfortunately, there is no panacea for assessing penalties under what are inevitably disparate circumstances.[46] Sally steals a million dollars; Mikey sends a rude e-mail; Ashley inadvertently but negligently breaches an important regulation; Bobby violates a company rule for the first time after 20 exemplary years with the company; Andy receives his sixth violation in six months.

Enforcement Means . . . Enforcing the Rules: Remember our discussion of opportunists in chapter 8. These are people that are heavily affected by their environment and by what those around them are doing. Where policies are not enforced, opportunists get the message that they, too, can engage in wrongdoing without consequence. Chapter 8 also talked about the slippery slope, in which wrongdoing tends to accelerate. Similarly, where enforcement is not equal to the wrongdoing, the behavior may not only continue, it may accelerate in severity.

It may be tempting to ignore small acts of wrongdoing. But the slippery slope effect means that wrongdoing of all types should not be ignored lest the small-time thief become a big-time criminal. Of course, small acts of wrongdoing should be treated differently than significant violations.

The Goldilocks Punishment: The Goldilocks rule, as seen in chapter 5, says that both too many and too few rules have a negative effect. It is probably no surprise that there's a similar rule where the penalties for wrongdoers are overly severe or too moderate.

On the one hand, punishments should not be too light, lest they fail to carry a deterrent effect. Additionally, wrongdoers may view light punishments as a quid pro quo—if they're willing to accept the punishment, they feel sanctioned to commit the wrong.[47]

On the other hand, the punishment for wrongdoing also shouldn't be overly severe in relation to the wrong. Because the consequences are more severe, and because opposition by the wrongdoer is more likely, enforcers look for clearer proof of wrongdoing before acting. This leads to a situation where enforcers are less likely to confront offenders when punishments are particularly severe.[48]

Consistent, Not Identical: While the exact parameters of the punishments cannot be delineated for each action, enforcement should be appropriate to the nature of the wrong. Most important, enforcement and discipline should be consistent and applied in a manner that is blind to internal politics or an individual's contributions in other areas. So the consequences should be the same whether it's Ashley who is out of compliance or your best friend Tommy perpetuates the wrong.

This consistent approach shows the appropriate tone at the top and can help establish the appropriate company culture. It ensures employees feel a sense of perceived fairness, as arbitrary decision making is removed from the equation. It also encourages internal reporting. Employees are not likely to report a violation if they think nothing will be done because the wrongdoer is a "rainmaker" bringing in big bucks, or a cousin of the boss, for example. Employees are your biggest asset in uncovering violations; don't provide them with a valid excuse to stay quiet.

Even after discovering that an employee has engaged in wrongdoing, subsequent investigations may be necessary to determine the extent of culpability. For instance, an employee that was trained on a topic may merit greater punishment than one to whom training was not offered. Or maybe training was offered, but upon inspection it is learned that the standards set forth were unclear. These and other issues are variables that should be considered.

It is difficult to come up with hard-and-fast rules for enforcement actions. Within organizations, managers may have different approaches to penalization. Therefore, it is important to clarify who has final authority for decisions and who merely makes recommendations. This responsibility, along with enforcement generally, should be constructed in conjunction with employment counsel and HR, as they will be implementing and possibly defending these actions.

Publicize Your Processes: To consistently enforce and discipline, companies must make efforts to preemptively outline the discipline meted out for various violations. This can be done in the Code of Conduct and should be emphasized in training materials. SAP's 2006 Code noted that "violations of the Code have serious consequences for employment" and that "any contravention of this Code will be internally investigated." The Code goes on to warn employees that violations could result in termination of employment and even actions in civil or criminal courts.[49] While the Code is rarely the appropriate place to state in detail the consequences for the vast array of possible violations, HR and management should have a clear plan for how varying levels of misconduct are to be handled.

Document Your Decisions: Document the date and time of any misconduct, and briefly describe the misconduct and disciplinary actions taken. This documentation serves as a precedential resource when determining the appropriate actions to take against wrongdoers. Documentation also, importantly, allows companies to head off allegations of wrongful termination or retaliation—such as for age discrimination or disability provisions—because companies can clearly point to a pattern of consistent and therefore nondiscriminatory application of company policies. As in many areas of compliance, enforcement issues may not arise until years down the line. In some cases this is how long it takes for a problem to manifest, while slow legal systems also mean delays are common. Documentation is thus about ensuring that where the human mind forgets, written documents recall.

The Big Picture: If the investigation suggests a wider issue rather than an isolated incident, the company should consider stepped-up training on the issue by updating its Code and otherwise evaluating the methods by which to mitigate the newfound risk. If the investigation arouses suspicions but fails to uncover the possible wrongdoer or to otherwise conclusively resolve the issue, training and other broad brush approaches may be the company's *only* path to rectify wrongdoing. At minimum, such training puts wrongdoers on notice that their behavior has aroused suspicions, and that they are unlikely to escape notice in the event of a recurrent breach.

Rewards: Enforcement is not all about punishment. Just as rewards may be appropriate for whistle-blowing, so, too, should systems recognize employees that consistently do the right thing, serve as leaders, or otherwise exceed expectations.

E.   Response and Prevention

The organization should take reasonable steps, as warranted under the circumstances, to remedy the harm resulting from a regulatory breach. These steps may include, where appropriate, providing restitution to identifiable victims, as well as other forms of remediation. "Other reasonable steps . . . may include self-reporting and cooperating with authorities."[50]

Self-Reporting: Companies are not given immunity from civil or criminal liability for self-disclosure of legal violations. They may, however, reduce their culpability score, which in turn minimizes fines and punishments. To receive credit for self-reporting, the company must act appropriately with regard to timing and the means of reporting.

There is no single threshold beyond which organizations should report. Instead, it's a facts and circumstances test. There are a lot of examples in which self-reporting was absolutely the right thing to do. But it's hard to say it's always the right thing to do. Organizations should do good, old-fashioned legal research and find out whether this is something that happened to someone else, and what the results were. Even with a pretty robust compliance Program, complete with subject-matter experts, there are times when getting an outside opinion may be the best option.

If the organization unreasonably delays reporting an offense to appropriate governmental authorities after becoming aware of it, then the company may not receive credit for having an effective Program in place.[51] However, companies are given time to conduct an investigation; indeed, they are affirmatively expected to investigate internally before reporting.[52] Accordingly, if after proper investigation and verification the company becomes aware of a violation, the company must report such violation to obtain credit for an effective Program.

Depending on the law or regulation at issue, the particular method by which the company must self-report may vary. For instance, the Office of Inspector General, the EPA, and other agencies clearly delineate the steps that an organization is to take when self-reporting to its particular agency. The FSGO requires that organizations report to the appropriate governmental authorities. If self-reporting is ineffective in the eyes of regulators, either because the incorrect agency was notified or the reporting procedures were not followed, it is likely ineffective for the purposes of the FSGO. Failure to follow such procedures may nullify any credit otherwise given under the FSGO for self-reporting a violation. Consequently, the individual authorized to report on behalf of the company should be familiar with the reporting requirements of relevant regulatory agencies.

Cooperate with Authorities: Additionally, even if the organization failed to discover a violation in its own right, the organization can mitigate its penalty by cooperating with authorities investigating claims of noncompliance. To obtain credit for cooperating with authorities, such "cooperation must be both timely and thorough."[53] Timeliness means cooperation begins contemporaneously to the organization's notification of an active investigation, and thoroughness means disclosing all pertinent information to those investigators.[54] To increase the likelihood of timely cooperation, the organization should take care to ensure that its compliance manager retains an open line of communication with regulators.[55] Such cooperation also serves to increase the likelihood that regulators will "play nice" with the organization, such as by warning the compliance manager about new laws and regulations or suggesting best practices.

When dealing with regulations, the law is often unsettled. Organizations, by necessity or happenstance, often operate in the gray. Surprisingly, regulators can be a resource. Organizations oftentimes call a regulator and say, *Hey, this is what we're thinking about doing. We think it's legal but we want to make sure you agree and approve.* Frequently, the regulator will work with the company, particularly where there's a pre-established relationship and a history of best efforts at compliance. Organizations should do what they can to operate in the clear—and the following chapters give advice on just that—but remember that regulators just may be another arrow in the quiver.

Acknowledge Mistakes: Lastly, the organization can reduce its culpability by clearly demonstrating "recognition and affirmative acceptance of responsibility for its criminal conduct."[56] The company can initially show such recognition and acceptance of responsibility where the organization's CEO or highest-ranking employee appears at judicial sentencing.[57] The organization should also act appropriately to prevent further similar criminal conduct, including assessing the Program and making modifications necessary to ensure the Program is effective."[58] This may, the FSGO states, include "the use of an outside professional advisor to ensure adequate assessment and implementation of any modifications."[59]

Conclusion

At this point in the book, each step of building, implementing, and enforcing a compliance Program has been covered. In the next chapter, the process for evaluating and ultimately improving upon the Program is covered.

CHAPTER TEN

Compliance Program Evaluation

I. Evaluating the Program

Compliance and ethics Programs are meant to evolve and grow; a one-year-old Program, for example, is not as mature as a seven-year-old Program. An out-of-date Program does little good in preventing or revealing violations, and an antiquated system is also unlikely to gain a court's approval as an effective Program.

In order to create the Program, organizations have ideally completed an initial risk assessment in which likelihood and seriousness of a violation were aggregated to quantify the overall level of risk. The risk assessment set forth in chapter 4 should be repeated on an annual or semi-annual basis. However, once the Program is in place, organizations should add a layer to risk assessment and evaluate how their compliance Programs are affecting risks. The Program risk assessment follows the same principles as the more general risk assessment. Organizations should use this information to identify risks that continue to fester, as well as areas of improvement for the Program.

In the creation of a Program, timelines should specify the regularity of evaluations, the individual or employee who will conduct the evaluation, and the process for improving upon deficient aspects of the Program.[1] While organizations should regularly evaluate regulatory and internal changes, it is suggested that organizations engage in an extensive evaluation of the Program's effectiveness at least every two years.[2] Compliance departments may partner with the audit committee to perform the following evaluations, which require both knowledge of compliance best practices and audit procedures.

The results of evaluations should be clearly documented. Such documentation is not only a requirement of a Program under the FSGO, but will also allow subsequent evaluators to analyze the changes from one period to the next. Documentation is also valuable evidence to courts and prosecutors of a goodwill effort to prevent breaches.

A.   Hotline Evaluation

Organizations should consider whether the hotline, or internal reporting system, operates as advertised. Benchmarks can be used to determine whether the hotline operates as well as it should and as well as or better than it has performed historically. Evaluators may identify whether:

- Reports to hotlines are anonymous
  - Evaluators should ensure the workforce actually knows about the hotline and that anonymity is an option, for instance, and determine whether individuals are willing to make reports when they suspect wrongdoing.
  - If there's a gap in knowledge, training may be in order. If there are leaks in which anonymity is not being upheld, the organization should consider initiating an investigation.
- The number of reports is increasing in quality and quantity
- The ratio of frivolous to bona fide reports is improving
- Patterns suggest an increase in reports out of certain offices, geographic regions, or industries, as this may signal a systemic issue
- Hotline staff are asking all relevant information during calls, asking about and explaining conditions of confidentiality and anonymity, and passing relevant leads onto the appropriate parties.

B.   Policies and Procedures

Evaluators should consider whether each policy or procedure effectively mitigates the risk at issue. They should also ensure that all policies and procedures are clear to understand. Evaluators may:

- Ask employees whether they can describe their responsibilities under a policy
- Determine if the roles and responsibilities of those delegated the task of implementing and enforcing the Program are clearly established
- Determine whether the policies and procedures are internalized—if compliance stopped asking, would the leadership still communicate the importance of the rules?
- Ensure polices are also up to date and reflect any organizational, industrywide, or regulatory changes.

C. Training

Evaluators should periodically look back to ensure that training is effective. Techniques to complete this assessment include:

- Providing post-training surveys to identify what information is or is not being internalized
- Identifying whether employees understand the training materials, and whether the materials are relevant to their work and a good use of their time
- Determining whether instances of wrongdoing decline after training takes place
- Measuring attendance, participation, and employee attitudes toward training sessions

D. Tone at the Top

Given top management's importance to an effective Program, evaluators should measure the tone set by top management. Evaluators can:

- Survey employees' feelings about management's commitment to the Program. Where employees perceive management as disinterested in the Program, or worse, as contradicting its precepts, illegitimate or immoral, managers should be put on notice that their behavior risks bringing harm to the organization.
- Review existing written policies, procedures, memoranda, and directives issued by management to analyze the regularity and content of such communications.
- Review manager's history of rewarding ethical or compliant behavior and punishing compliance wrongdoers,[3] as this may help identify whether management takes its compliance responsibilities seriously.
- Analyze how effectively managers integrate the Program with the goals of the company, as well as with day-to-day practices.[4]
- Identify whether management can identify the organization's core values and how the organization seeks to live up to such values.
- Verify that managers follow the rules. If there's a policy that prohibits dating within the organization, for example, then a CCO that is dating a colleague sends a message that the organization isn't really serious about the policy.

E. Organizational Structure

Procedures to evaluate the effectiveness of the compliance department's structure include determining:

- The degree of independence between the board and top management.
- Whether the compliance department is free of coercion from top management such that the department is assured a retaliation-free working environment.

- Whether the board takes steps to receive all relevant information from management and that the board understands compliance risks facing the company.[5] This information can be obtained with interviews, surveys, or discussions with board members; a review of policies and procedures; and an analysis as to whether those policies and procedures are followed.

F. Internal Controls

Evaluators should ask whether:

- Monitoring systems are sufficient and use up-to-date automated systems
- Internal reporting mechanisms are designed to encourage internal reporting
- Investigatory processes see reports of violations through to their logical conclusions

G. Resources and Compensation

Evaluators should determine whether:

- Sufficient resources are devoted to the compliance department. Insufficient resources not only weaken the department, but may also signal a lack of high-level commitment to the Program.
- Compensatory incentives for the compliance department employees are aligned with their responsibilities to mitigate ethical and legal risks. As previously discussed, compensation of compliance officials should be based on improvement to the organization's compliance and ethics performance.

II. Choosing the Evaluator

Corporate Knowledge: For anyone authorized to act upon an organization's Program, operating knowledge is essential. This individual should have knowledge about the policies, procedures, Code of Conduct, training procedures, and communication methods of the Program; the underlying business operations on which controls are placed; and the laws and regulations most applicable to the company.[6] Many organizations will want an evaluator who is familiar with common fraud schemes and specific techniques used to commit the fraud or misconduct to which the company is most susceptible.[7]

Character Traits: Professional skepticism is a prerequisite for an effective evaluation. The evaluator need not be cynical or suspicious of employees or organizational standards, but should employ a questioning approach and critically assess findings.[8] During employee interviews it is important not to blindly accept all statements as true. Instead, an evaluator should trust but tactfully validate. It may be unavoidable, but offending or frightening the interviewee will likely stop the flow of communication.

Furthermore, evaluators must be objective and free of conflicts of interest.[9] One area of potential conflict is where the evaluator and Program creator are the same person or otherwise lack independence from one another. Ideally this should be avoided, though small companies may have some flexibility in the eyes of the FSGO. If this arrangement is present, the company must determine whether there is a risk that the evaluator may hesitate to reveal information that would demonstrate deficiencies in the Program he or she created. At minimum, where the evaluator did create the Program, incentives to fabricate should be nullified: the individual should neither be rewarded for finding an effective Program nor disciplined for revealing deficiencies. If the individual that created the Program also has day-to-day control over the Program or any internal control systems thereof, the company should make every attempt to ensure a third-party-led investigation.[10]

Personal integrity may be the most important characteristic of an effective evaluator (and, incidentally, of an effective compliance manager). Evaluators and compliance managers both may face significant pressures in performing their duties. They may be seen as threats to some employees, including high-level managers. They also may be the subject of attempts at coercion, including bribes and direct or indirect retaliation. Accordingly, companies should take care to utilize evaluators who demonstrate the utmost professionalism and personal integrity,[11] not to mention a certain mental fortitude. If management is truly committed to compliance and ethics, the ideal evaluator and compliance manager is one who is committed to the law and the Program above all else. Ask yourself whether your compliance manager or evaluator would report *you* for failing to act in the face of a significant violation. If the answer is yes, you may have found the perfect person.

Internal versus External Compliance: Companies with sufficient resources may employ a competent and objective internal team of compliance professionals. However, outside consultants provide a ready mechanism for ensuring objectivity and freedom from coercion. In a possible nod to this reality, the FSGO specifies that steps to rectify criminal conduct may include the use of outside consultants to assess and implement modifications.[12] Additionally, because outside consultants need not be retained on a full-time basis, outsourcing the project to external professional experts may save money in the long term. This is particularly true of smaller organizations, where the need for full-time regulatory officers or teams is likely less pressing than at large companies. Whether internal or external, ensure the evaluator receives sufficient resources to carry out his or her duties.

III.   Improving the Program

The ultimate goal of an evaluation is to identify whether the company meets the FSGO's requirements for an effective Program, and whether from a subjective perspective those internal controls are likely to reduce risks. After interviewing employees, reviewing pertinent internal controls and regulations, and thereby evaluating the company's risks, the evaluator should implement appropriate changes. This may mean identifying areas to tinker with to improve efficiency, or it could require reconstructing entire portions of the Program. Based on the results, the evaluator may focus on shortening the response time to a hotline or improving confidentiality,[13] or rendering training more effective, the Code more intelligible, or a company culture better integrated. If evaluations or ongoing monitoring and auditing systems reveal specific instances or concerns of misconduct, the organization should initiate an investigation as detailed in chapter 9.

Conclusion

The best practices of this and previous chapters are necessarily generalized. Such is the diversity of organizations and industries that no detailed set of practices has emerged or is likely to emerge. Rather, organizations should evaluate the above factors and tailor a Program that is appropriate to their needs. Such needs vary with the size and resources of the organization and the severity of risks based on operational practice and its history of violations. The depth to which compliance and ethics practices should be integrated into the company is therefore at issue. Thanks to the Seven Pillars of the FSGO, however, the breadth is not at issue—*all* organizations are expected to touch on the same elements in composing an effective Program.

Nor are organizations' required commitments to their Programs in question. Regardless of the resources devoted to the Program, organizations small and large and across vast industries do well to remember that the FSGO expects from all the same degree of commitment to ethical conduct and compliance with the law.[14] That language, along with evidence that regulatory agencies do pursue a wide variety of organizations, is likely the primary reason behind the spur in Programs across the country during the last decade. For that reason, companies failing to abide by the FSGO provisions risk exposing themselves to legal fines and penalties along with an assortment of other nefarious repercussions.

The best way to encourage compliance, however, is to highlight the growing list of benefits flowing to organizations that have effective Programs. The positive effect on employee morale and retention, performance and attendance, and, ultimately, on revenue, are all reasons that companies should not view compliance as a necessary evil, but instead as an opportunity for improvement. Consequently, though the above best practices are necessary for full conformance with legal requirements, they are also essential to organizational efficiency and productivity.

A company's Program must be responsive to the specific regulatory risks it faces. Consequently, the following chapters of this book explore prominent regulatory regimes in detail, with the expectation that the best practices for conformance to each regulation will contribute to a more comprehensive and effective Program.

Section III: Mitigating Risk: A Brief on Compliance with Various Laws

CHAPTER ELEVEN

International Compliance

The Foreign Corrupt Practices Act (FCPA) is best known for regulating foreign bribery of government officials, but it also oversees accounting and internal control requirements for publicly traded corporations. Attempts to cover up bribery of foreign officials may result in improper accounting reports, leading some public companies to face charges under both sections of the FCPA. Both provisions of the FCPA are covered in this chapter, with an emphasis on bribery.

Top Ten FCPA Payouts of All Time

1. **Siemens** (Germany): $800 million in 2008
2. **Alstom** (France): $772 million in 2014.
3. **KBR / Halliburton** (USA): $579 million in 2009
4. **BAE** (UK): $400 million in 2010
5. **Total S.A.** (France) $398 million in 2013
6. **Alcoa** (U.S.) $384 million in 2014
7. **Snamprogetti Netherlands B.V. / ENI S.p.A** (Holland/Italy): $365 million in 2010.
8. **Technip S.A.** (France): $338 million in 2010
9. **JGC Corporation** (Japan) $218.8 million in 2011
10. **Daimler AG** (Germany): $185 million in 2010

—Provided by FCPA Blog (www.fcpablog.com)

It is difficult to overstate the importance of understanding and complying with the FCPA. For U.S. organizations operating abroad, this may very well be the most important regulation with which to comply, and it is here to stay. "It's an unstoppable train," says compliance specialist and former general counsel of Visa, Lyn Boxall.[1]

The FCPA has become the centerpiece of the DOJ's strategy for policing multinational corporations, whether headquartered in the United States or elsewhere. Prosecutions are up, way up. The top ten settlements in overseas bribery cases have all come since 2008.[2] Lanny Breuer, former assistant attorney general for the Criminal Division at the DOJ, said, "We are in a new era of FCPA enforcement; and we are here to stay."[3] Further, the DOJ is just half of the equation; the SEC has concurrent criminal and civil jurisdiction over the FCPA.[4]

Unlike some regulations under which enforcement tends to focus on the company rather than the individuals, under the FCPA individual employees are going to jail for violations. Along with monstrous fines that may be imposed on both the corporation and on individual wrongdoers, individuals face up to five years in prison for violations of the corruption provisions and 20 years for violations of the accounting provisions.[5] In recent years, numerous executives have been sentenced to multiyear prison terms for FCPA violations.[6]

It would be a mistake to believe that any organization is below the radar of the DOJ or SEC. But those inclined to take false comfort should know that actions arising from foreign bribery may lead to civil claims under federal securities laws, the Racketeer Influenced and Corrupt Organizations statute (RICO), antitrust laws, and state laws pertaining to tortious interference with contract, unfair competition, and more.[7] And commercial (private-to-private) bribery may still violate the FCPA's accounting provisions, the Travel Act, antimoney laundering laws, and other federal or foreign laws. Any type of corrupt payment thus carries a risk of prosecution.[8]

For all of these reasons, it is essential to understand (1) what the FCPA provisions say, (2) how they are applied in practice, and (3) how to comply.

I.   Antibribery

A.   The Law

Call it karma; call it just desserts; call it reaping what you sow. Call it what you will, but know that the FCPA, like so many laws and regulations before and since, was nurtured by pervasive revelations of wrongdoing.[9] As the shock waves of Watergate reverberated across the country in the 1970s, the SEC undertook investigations, during the course of which over 400 U.S. companies admitted to making bribes to foreign officials. This revelation of bribery as a standard business practice prompted Congress to pass the FCPA in 1977, beginning, slowly but definitively, a whole new world for global business.

Who Is Subject to the FCPA? The antibribery provisions apply to "issuers," "domestic concerns," and any "person" that bribes a foreign official.[10] Issuers include companies registered with the SEC or foreign companies with shares on the U.S. stock exchange. Domestic concerns cover virtually any business operating in the United States, including corporations, partnerships, and sole proprietorships. "Persons" can be anybody, including foreign corporate concerns, whose corrupt act occurs in any part within the United States.

Individuals and companies can be liable even if the bribery is perpetrated on behalf of another person or company. Such persons may be liable under agency theories, or for conspiracy to violate the FCPA.

How Is Jurisdiction Exercised? U.S. courts can exercise jurisdiction for FCPA violations over U.S. nationals. For foreign nationals, there is jurisdiction where the alleged violation involved some action in "interstate commerce."[11] This requirement is easily met—it may mean making a telephone call; sending an e-mail, text message, or fax; sending a wire transfer from a U.S. bank; or traveling across state borders, traveling internationally, or traveling to or from the United States.[12]

When Is a Payment Considered Corrupt, or a Bribe? The FCPA applies only to payments intended to induce or influence a foreign official to use his or her position "in order to assist . . . in obtaining or retaining business for or with, or directing business to, any person." This requirement is known as the "business purpose test" and is broadly interpreted.[13] Even where payments do not directly correlate with an economic or business gain, courts are willing to infer a quid pro quo by the nature of the payment.[14]

Moreover, the corrupt act need not actually succeed, so long as the requisite intent is present. Even if the foreign official declines or never receives the payment, the payer may be liable.[15] Executives who authorize others to do their bidding—a "pay whoever you need to but don't tell me about it" mentality—face liability even if such a bribe is not ultimately paid.[16]

What Is a "Foreign Official"? A foreign official can be any employee of a foreign government or department thereof, regardless of rank or title.[17] But it also includes "instrumentalities" of a foreign government as well as public international organizations such as the World Bank, the International Monetary Fund (IMF), and World Trade Organization (WTO).[18]

In the first appellate court case to define the term, the 11th Circuit Court of Appeals held on May 16, 2014, that an instrumentality is "an entity

controlled by the government of a foreign country that performs a function the controlling government treats as its own."[19] The use of the term
"instrumentalities" extends the reach of the FCPA greatly, and may leave
companies unsure whether a partner or client is a foreign official. Many
states own or control companies within another country either wholly or
in part; think of state-owned medical providers, Russian oil companies,
and Chinese extractive industries, for example. Every employee of state-
owned entities, thanks to the FCPA reference to "instrumentalities" of the
foreign government, is considered a foreign official.[20]

When evaluating whether a person or company constitutes an instrumentality, consider the following nonexhaustive list of factors:

1. The government's formal designation of that entity
2. Whether the government has a majority interest in the entity
3. The government's ability to hire and fire the entity's principals
4. The extent to which the entity's profits go to the government, and/or, the
   extent to which the government funds the entity if it fails to break even, and
5. The length of time these indicia have existed[21]

The ownership percentage of the state is the most important factor. Usually, more than 50 percent governmental ownership means the company
is an instrumentality, but the reverse is not necessarily true. The nature of
the state means that even where there is no de jure ownership, de facto
control may necessitate a recategorization. In one case, the DOJ categorized
a company as an instrumentality where the Malaysian ministry of finance,
though a minority owner, nonetheless exercised veto power over important
decisions.[22]

Bribery of all types is inadvisable, but public sector bribery heightens the
risk, so companies should engage in due diligence to properly identify whether
local contacts, clients, or partners are foreign officials or instrumentalities.
The following is a nonexhaustive list of steps to make this determination:

1. Obtain clear information about the owners of the organization, and learn
   whether those owners are government officials, or family or close friends of
   government officials.
2. Review the corporate structure and identify whether the ultimate decision
   maker may be sitting in a government building.
3. Review corporate minutes where available.
4. Interview employees and even past clients or partners of the company to
   understand historical corporate dealings.
5. Do online searches, identify the reputation of the company, and look for
   instances of coordination between the company and the government.

Where a contact is identified as a foreign official, take steps to increase transparency of operations. Clearly document all actions taken with regard to the foreign official, stating the intent behind any payments made, and ensuring that all employees assigned to the foreign official are unblinkingly clear as to their limitations and obligations with respect to bribery.

Exceptions to the FCPA: The FCPA is not violated where a payment is lawful under the written laws of the foreign country. The defendant must affirmatively prove the payment was legal in that country.[23] The mere absence of a law prohibiting bribery is not sufficient. In practice, this defense is infrequently used, as countries rarely permit corrupt payments.[24]

A second defense is the "facilitating payment" defense. "Grease payments," as they are also known, facilitate the performance of a routine governmental action by a foreign official. This is a "narrow exception" that only applies to nondiscretionary acts such as obtaining permits, telephone service, water, or power.[25]

Erroneously relying on the facilitating payment exception poses a prominent danger to companies. Says Boxall: "Your employees and even your board members may hear 'facilitation' payment and think, sure, my $X million bribe to the Kazakhstani government minister facilitated the contract. If you allow facilitation payments at all, ensure your workforce understands the limited nature of the exception and the ways facilitation payments must be documented."[26]

Additionally, in many countries, laws may be *designed* to be broken. Through selective enforcement against those deemed wealthy or likely to pay, a foreign official will ask for a payment to overlook the "violation."[27] This payment violates the FCPA, because the payment is intended to influence the governmental official to engage in an act that is, technically at least, illegal.

Moreover, most countries prohibit facilitation payments, and many anticorruption laws (most prominently the U.K.'s Bribery Act 2010) outlaw facilitation payments wherever they occur.[28] Therefore, this exception should be relied on only in exceptional circumstances, if at all. Many companies find it expedient to prohibit facilitation payments in their entirety.

Companies can rest assured, and employees should be made aware, that a payment made in response to a threat to one's physical safety is *not* considered an FCPA violation. However, importantly, economic coercion (e.g., requiring a payment to gain entry into a market or obtain a contract) is illegal.[29]

B.   Actions Commonly Associated with Corruption and Bribery

This section will discuss some of the common types of bribery. These are areas that should be audited and subject to increased oversight. But, as with every regulatory issue, the work doesn't begin by trying to catch the wrongdoer; it starts with convincing the workforce not to engage in the wrongdoing in the first place.

Remember the fraud triangle from chapter 9—pressure, opportunity, and rationalization to bribe may be present in highly corrupt countries or industries. Consider training on the destructive forces of corruption for local communities, and help reduce the rationalizations. Reduce opportunity by ensuring employees know their actions are subject to oversight and monitoring, and by stressing the civil and criminal penalties for individual wrongdoers and for the company.

Pressure may be the most important driver. Operating in highly corrupt areas is difficult. In reality, it may be impossible for a workforce to get *anything* done without giving a bribe. That's not an overstatement, it's an unfortunate reality. So before entering a new market, ask whether goals can be accomplished without a bribe. Consider the Transparency International's Corruption Perception Index (CPI), but also consider the specific industry involved. Boxall notes that new entrants have no chance where others in the industry are already bribing.[30] As far as officials are concerned, "existing industry players have built up an expectation that this is going to happen, and it's like you, as the official, are an idiot if you don't ask for a bribe," Boxall says.[31] And if they are told no, officials know they can just go to the next company and get their bribe.[32]

If entering a market where corruption is prevalent, managers can reduce the pressure by lowering expectations. They can also communicate that management understands the challenges it will face and expects that it will operate in accordance with company anticorruption policy. Where managers or sales people can't reach their objectives without bribery, the pressure builds to do so. And when one employee gives into bribery and is suddenly rewarded for reaching a target, your entire salesforce is likely to follow suit.

In a recent speech, Dave Senay, CEO of public relations firm Fleishman-Hillard, spoke of the new world of transparency and anticorruption. When asked how to convince U.S. companies to not engage in bribery, Senay's advice was simple: "Don't make a deal with the devil. It's a short-term decision. The going is slower, of course, but when the pieces fall—and they will fall—you'll still be standing."[33]

The following are some of the most common mechanisms used to shield naked bribes. Managers and authorized individuals should be trained to recognize red flags. The workforce should be trained to respond to requests for bribes through delicate refusal and/or reporting to higher channels within the organization. The following high-risk areas should also be a point of focus for monitoring and auditing FCPA risks.

1. Gift Giving and Entertainment: A gift is provided without expectation for reciprocal treatment. But as the more cynical among us would agree, oftentimes such "gifts" are less benevolent, perhaps being used in an effort to ingratiate oneself with a client or prospective partner, for instance. The question is, at what point does a gift become a bribe. The DOJ keeps the standard (if not the analysis) simple: as with any payment, if the gift is intended to improperly influence the official, it is a bribe.[34]

This is true regardless of the size of the gift, though the size may be indicative of the intent behind the gift. For example, in a related context, a California company was found to have made improper payments when it spent $7 million to send select customers from China to "training" seminars in popular resort destinations across the United States. The DOJ took note that, not only did the company have no facilities in the locations chosen, but no training actually took place upon arrival.[35] Along with the enormous price tag, this was clearly no ordinary training.

Past cases have only focused on small gifts where they are part of a systemic scheme of corruption. Ordinarily, paying for coffee or a taxi or such other nominal value items will not result in FCPA charges.[36]

An area of particular risk is in those countries where corruption and a culture of gift giving intermingle. China, with a ranking of 80 on Transparency International's 2013 CPI,[37] is also renowned for its gift-giving culture. This, along with China's market power, makes China a regular feature in FCPA cases.

Policies should be in place to manage these relationships in a manner appropriate to an organization's needs.[38] For operations in countries like China, a particular individual with FCPA training may be appointed to approve any such gifts, and to ensure that the gifts reflect nothing more than respect and goodwill. You don't, Boxall says, want the guy in the field making decisions on everything. Not only might your field person lack knowledge on the FCPA, but he or she probably also has a direct financial incentive to bend (or break) the rules. Don't put your workers in that position.[39]

Compliance policies as to gift giving should include clear, readily available guidelines that cover the processes for gift giving. Organizations may consider requiring express consent prior to making a gift—larger companies may use automated clearance processes—along with clear monetary limits and annual limitations. These policies should be made applicable to all employees, including directors and officers. If an exception is necessary for select employees, that, too, should be documented.[40] DOJ regulators consider proper documentation of gifts as one sign of honest intent.[41]

Boxall offers this suggestion when creating gift-giving policies: keep it in context. Gifts for occasions like birthdays or business dinners are common in the United States as well as abroad, so a blank prohibition when operating abroad probably isn't appropriate any more than it would be when operating in the United States.

Boxall relates the story of a wedding in the Republic of Korea (South Korea). The bride was the daughter of a state-owned entity's CEO, making the CEO a foreign official. In Korea and other parts of Asia, it is traditional to extend wedding invitations to senior business contacts (such as the local general managers of U.S. companies), for those business contacts to decline the invitation, and for them to then offer a modest cash gift (say, $200, or its equivalent in the local currency) as a wedding present. But most Programs flatly prohibit cash payments to a government official. To not do so in this case, however, "is completely and utterly unacceptable. We're not talking about bribery here; we're talking about social acceptability. And yet we couldn't do it all," Boxall says. "The compliance people in the U.S. wouldn't allow us to do it and that risks driving payments underground. Not reporting is the only way to avoid embarrassment for the employee on the ground."[42]

Boxall argues that because the gift was culturally expected, by the very nature of its regularity it wouldn't have the effect of improperly influencing the official, especially if it were very small in proportion to the official's wealth. But if that same cash gift is traditionally $200, and a local U.S. manager gives $100,000, well, now that organization has the official's attention. The moral of this story is that gift giving is a complex, gray area. Companies should consider localizing or tailoring their Programs to retain flexibility amid cultural dissimilarities. Additionally, each company must make decisions as to its own risk tolerance when composing policies and procedures to mitigate risks in this subjective area of law.

2. Charitable Giving and Due Diligence: Just as with gifts, charitable giving is permissible as long as the intent is not to improperly influence a government official. In some cases, individuals abroad may set up sham charities to funnel money for their own purposes. When a company is asked by a foreign official to donate to a charity, it should consider initiating an investigation as to the legitimacy of such charity.[43]

Due diligence investigations should include a review of the organization's ownership, management structure, and operations. Identify whether any owners or managers are governmental officials or close friends or family of governmental officials, such that there may be an improper relationship. Consider requesting key corporate documents, including access to books and records. Interview representatives of the charity to elicit information about the charity's relationship with the government. Review the criminal history of the charity and of individuals to ensure it is a bona fide charity. Ask the charity to certify compliance with your organization's anticorruption policy and provide for the termination of the agreement in the event of a violation.[44]

As red flags are raised, deepen the investigation. If a member of the charity has links to the government, for example, investigate those links. Ascertain whether the conflicted charity official will personally benefit from the contribution. In one case, a relationship between the charity and the government was deemed permissible by the DOJ where both the country's laws and the charity's internal laws prohibited the conflicted employee from receiving compensation from his relationship with the government.[45]

After completing this due diligence, weigh the risks and decide whether it is appropriate to proceed. If so, ongoing monitoring should take place, inclusive of monitoring the use of any funds provided to the charity to ensure that operational goals related to the provision of funds are met.[46]

3. Third-Party Risks: The vast majority of FCPA cases involve conduct by third parties.[47] Third-party agents operating abroad on behalf of a company may therefore present the biggest risk to companies under the FCPA. A company cannot hide behind the actions of an agent; willful ignorance is no defense.[48]

As with charitable giving, as red flags arise, increasing levels of due diligence should take place.[49] Indeed, the DOJ and SEC state that in evaluating the effectiveness of a company's Program, due diligence investigations (or lack thereof) are considered.[50] Areas of inquiry and red flags include where the third party:

1. Has a history of improper payment practices or a criminal history
2. Has a poor business reputation, or has had its contract terminated by other parties for improper conduct
3. Does not have in place an adequate compliance Program or refuses to certify compliance and/or allow audit clauses in contracts
4. Provides information about its services or principals that is not verifiable by data, only anecdotally
5. Provides lavish gifts or hospitality to leads or contacts
6. Is in a different line of business than that for which it has been engaged, lacks experience in the field or industry, or is inadequately staffed to perform the work
7. Has a plan for performing the work that is vague and/or suggests a reliance on contacts or relationships

8. Demands a fee, commission, or volume discount that is unusually high compared to the market rate or is based on a success fee or bonus, or the third party requests an unusual advance payment
9. Submits or offers to submit inflated, inaccurate, or suspicious invoices
10. Requests unusual payment structures, such as cash, cash equivalent, or bearer instrument payments; requests payment to an offshore financial center, a third party (including to a charity), or a shell company.[51]

Boxall relates the story of a Korean company that she suspected was siphoning money to a slush fund using a shell company. According to Boxall:

> [The company] is registered, had a business address, and doesn't have any of the wrong people. On paper there were no red flags. But I had reason to suspect on this one. So I said [to my employees] I want to know if this company exists. And they said, "yeah yeah, it exists, we have their documentation." I said "no, I want you to go around at quarter to 9"—it opened at 9—"and I want you to hang around and see if people are going in and out, if people are arriving. I want to know if there's a real business there." They called me back the next day tail between their legs and said the "office" was a storage facility.[52]

This story is indicative of the need to remain flexible—the above red flags are a helpful starting point—but a good compliance manager knows that there is no rule book when ferreting out clever, often ingenuous wrongdoers.

Where there are red flags, investigate further until concerns are alleviated or wrongdoing is revealed. And in all cases, ongoing monitoring should take place. Verify that work is performed in accordance with the agreement. Anticorruption certifications should be renewed on an annual basis. Also consider including third parties in compliance training.[53]

Successor Liability: Companies also face liability under the theory of successor liability for the actions of companies acquired or with whom the organization has merged.[54] The DOJ warns: "Contracts obtained through bribes may be legally unenforceable, business obtained illegally may be lost when bribe payments are stopped, there may be liability for prior illegal conduct, and the prior corrupt acts may harm the acquiring company's reputation and future business prospects."[55] Consequently, due diligence is again required of these prospective acquisitions. Consider the following nonexhaustive steps prior to acquisition:

1. Review the company's sales and financial data, customer contracts, and third-party and distributor agreements.

2. Perform a risk-based analysis of the company's customer base.
3. Perform an audit of selected transactions engaged in by the company.
4. Ascertain the company's compliance efforts and any corruption issues over the past ten years.[56]

After acquisition, the acquiring company is advised to quickly integrate the acquired company with the acquiring company's compliance Program, inclusive of anticorruption certifications from, communications to, and training with, newly acquired employees and third parties.[57]

Where a company is acquired despite FCPA violations, or where violations are found after acquisition, companies should consider self-reporting. Dun & Bradstreet (D&B), a publicly traded company, acquired a Chinese marketing firm in 2009. In 2012, D&B voluntarily disclosed that the firm may have violated the FCPA.[58] In many cases, such successor companies are able to negotiate Non-Prosecution Agreements (NPA) or Deferred-Prosecution Agreements (DPA) in return for their cooperation with investigators. Whereas companies that fail to disclose predecessor misconduct must fear liability for the duration of the statute of limitations under the FCPA, companies obtaining NPAs or DPAs are able to gain the certainty that they will not be subject to future enforcement actions.[59]

II.   FCPA Accounting Provisions

Though the accounting provisions of the FCPA do not apply only to bribery, enforcement has typically involved misreporting bribe payments.[60] The accounting provisions only apply to those subject to the SEC, or "issuers." There are two components of the accounting provisions: the "books and records" portion and the "internal control" portion.

Under the "books and records" provision, "issuers must make and keep books, records, and accounts that, in reasonable detail, accurately and fairly reflect an issuer's transactions and dispositions of an issuer's assets."[61] Companies commonly mischaracterize bribes in an effort to conceal wrongdoing.

Such mischaracterization may fall under categories including: "Commissions or Royalties; Consulting Fees; Sales and Marketing Expenses; Scientific Incentives or Studies; Travel and Entertainment Expenses; Rebates or Discounts; After Sales Service Fees; Miscellaneous Expenses; Petty Cash Withdrawals; Free Goods; Intercompany Accounts; Supplier/Vendor Payments; Write-offs; or 'Customs Intervention' Payments."[62] These areas merit additional monitoring and should be subject to periodic audits.

Under the "internal controls" provision, "issuers must devise and maintain a system of internal accounting controls sufficient to assure management's control, authority, and responsibility over the firm's assets."[63] This includes creating an environment in which controls are stressed as part of the organization's integrity and ethics commitments, engaging in risk assessments, monitoring and auditing policies and procedures to ensure management directions are carried out, and communicating control policies.[64]

The FCPA is a dangerous creature for organizations. Enforcement is drastically up, and there is no sign of it slowing down. With similar or even stricter regulations proliferating worldwide, global enforcement agencies are increasingly coordinating to undermine corrupt actors. The risks are big, and though admittedly it takes more effort to follow the law than to break it—especially in highly corrupt countries—the short-term benefits of cheating will almost certainly be outweighed by the long-term consequences.

III.   Export Administration Regulations (EAR)

The Export Administration Regulations (EAR) govern (1) restrictions on direct exports from the United States; (2) re-exports of U.S.-origin products, software, and technology from one country outside of the United States to another; and (3) the disclosure of U.S.-origin technology to a non-U.S. national, whether in the United States or abroad.[65] Products, software, and technology that have a primarily commercial use fall under the EAR, while those with a primarily military use typically fall under International Traffic in Arms Regulations (ITAR), discussed below. The EAR is administered by the Department of Commerce's Bureau of Industry and Security (BIS). However, an alphabet soup of agencies exercise jurisdiction over exports, including the DOJ, the Nuclear Regulatory Commission (NRC), the Department of Energy (DOE), and others.

Penalties for noncompliance include civil fines of up to $250,000 per violation or two times the amount of the transaction, whichever is greater. Consequently, civil fees can be enormous for those companies illegally shipping for years. Criminal penalties include up to $1 million in fines per violation and/or 20 years in jail. Administrative penalties include the loss of export privileges, a result that could be devastating to firms reliant on export sales.[66]

Additionally, given that the purpose of these licenses is to protect American security, public sentiment can be unforgiving to violators. Companies that ignore sanction regimes, shipping, for example, to political hot spots such as Syria or Iran, face strong, often emotional recriminations.

A. Does the EAR Apply to You?

Most commercial goods destined for export are subject to the (EAR), but there are a few exceptions.

Exceptions. First, exports are not subject to the EAR if the item is subject to the jurisdiction of another agency,[67] which in turn (and unfortunately for exporters) requires a familiarity with a wide variety of agency regulations. For example, if ITAR applies, then ITAR takes precedence over EAR regulations. Additionally, when exporting items that are before the United States Patent and Trademark Office (USPTO) for pending patent applications, supplements, or amendments, then the USPTO approves exports of such technology, which would otherwise be subject to the EAR.[68]

Second, if exporting technology or software that is publicly available (or which by the transaction at issue will become publicly available), then the EAR also does not apply.[69] A nonexhaustive list of publicly available items includes:

1. Publication of research papers.
2. Documents made available for sale where the cost of the information is at or below the cost of production and distribution.
3. The release of information at an "open" conference. "Open" means: (a) participants are free to take notes, (b) attendance at the conference is available to all interested persons, and, (c) the fee, if any, is reasonably related to costs.[70]

Unless one of the above exceptions applies, organizations are likely subject to the EAR when sending goods from the United States to another country. "Export" is a broadly defined term under the EAR. It includes not only the actual shipment or transmission of items, but also the release of technology or software subject to the EAR.[71] Importantly, an export includes the release of technology either *within the United States or without* to a foreign national.[72]

The "release" of technology is itself broadly defined to include the mere visual inspection of U.S.-origin equipment and facilities, and even oral exchanges of information.[73] If a company located in the United States gives a foreign national employee access to restricted EAR items, a license is therefore required for that individual to access what is now considered an "exported" item.

Companies are also subject to the EAR when re-exporting products from one country outside of the United States to another if those products are of U.S. origin.[74] Even products that are not of U.S. origin are subject to the EAR when the products incorporate U.S.-origin commodities of a minimum threshold (or "de minimus," in EAR parlance) relative to the overall value of the otherwise non-U.S. product.[75] Though 25 percent is usually the de minimus amount, the minimum threshold varies.

B.   Is a License Needed to Export a Particular Good or Service?

Where the EAR does apply, the next step is to determine whether a license is required for the export of the product. Most exports do not require an application to the BIS for a license.[76] Exceptions may negate the licensing requirement, but a license may be required depending on the following:

1. Type of product
2. Location to which the export is being sent
3. End user of the product
4. Ultimate end use of the product
5. Other activities undertaken by the end user

Each of these licensing requirements and exceptions thereto are discussed below.

Type of Product: Items subject to licensing requirements are listed on the BIS's Commerce Control List (CCL). There are ten categories of controlled items, including but not limited to electronics, computers, information security, sensors and lasers, and aerospace and propulsion.[77] The reason(s) for regulating each item is provided within each categorization. These include national security, nuclear proliferation, and more.

The reason for control is important: it is the basis by which to identify whether a restriction applies to an export to a particular country. As a safeguard against mistakes, it is advisable to cross-check the CCL categorization with the manufacturer or another interested party. The BIS also makes representatives available for consultation.

Once the product is classified, cross reference to the Commerce Country Chart to determine whether the country to which you intend to export is controlled for the same reason. Some products require a license regardless of the destination of the item. However, for many items, the license is dependent on the ultimate destination of the product. Hypothetically, then, a license may be required if sending Product A to Bulgaria, but not if the destination is Albania, whereas a license is required for Product B regardless of whether it goes to Bulgaria, Albania, or anywhere else. Therefore, while step one is to identify whether the item is on the CCL and therefore subject to a comprehensive product-based licensing requirement, the next step is to determine whether the EAR requires a license as a result of the recipient country.

Location of Export: The Commerce Country Chart is the next resource that must be consulted. The reason for which an item is controlled is listed horizontally on a table, while countries are listed vertically. Chart users can match the reason for control with the recipient country. If any one of the listed reasons for control of the destination country is the same as that for a product, a license is required absent an exception.

The EAR also covers embargoes to some extent. Countries such as Cuba, Iran, North Korea, Syria, Sudan, and others may have broad or even universal restrictions on exports of any type, regardless of the reason for control for the item at issue.[78] However, the primary agency responsible for regulating embargoes is the Treasury Department's Office of Foreign Assets Control (OFAC). Under OFAC, persons can be held liable merely for facilitating a sale to an embargoed country. "Facilitating" could be broadly construed to include mere referrals of business opportunities, as well as providing financing, guaranteeing a sale, and changing corporate policies to permit a sale. Exporters should review OFAC requirements as well as the EAR when the recipient may be subject to a U.S. embargo.

End User: Certain persons (individuals and organizations) are restricted from receiving exports from the United States. This includes those designated as: proliferators of weapons of mass destruction or supporters thereof, threats to U.S. national security, and specially designated terrorists or terrorist organizations.[79] If a person is so designated, that person will be included on the Entity List.[80]

Additionally, end users may be prohibited from receiving or sending items as a result of administrative penalties for violations under the EAR.[81] These penalties manifest themselves as Denial Orders promulgated to persons whose export privileges are denied.[82]

End Use: The ultimate purpose of your product, or end use, may necessitate a license. The restrictions on end use include, but are not limited to, nuclear, chemical, missile, or biological proliferation; nuclear maritime uses; nuclear, chemical, or biological uses; and aircraft and vessel uses.[83] If an item will be (or may be) used for one of the restricted purposes, then a license is required even if the location and type of item would not ordinarily need a license.

C. Do Any Exceptions Negate the Licensing Requirement?

The following broad exceptions may negate the licensing requirement. However, if a license is required as a result of a Denial Order, prohibited end user, or prohibited end use, the below exceptions do not apply.

Low Value Items: If (a) the item is a shipment of limited value (LVS) and (b) the recipient country is not on a restricted list, then no license is likely required.[84] Low value is defined under the LVS heading for each of the nine categories of controlled items on the ECCN list, and generally falls between a few hundred and a few thousand dollars.[85] Along with the value limit for each individual export, the total annual value of the same export to the same end user may not exceed 12 times the LVS for that ECCN.[86]

So, for simplicity's sake: if the value of a product is one, and the value limit is 10, up to 10 items can be shipped each time without a license. If 11 items are sent in one shipment, a license is required for the shipment. If the same 10 items are shipped more than 12 times to the same recipient within one year, the annual limit is exceeded and the product must be licensed.

Exports to Low-Risk Countries: When identifying an item on the ECCN, remember that the purpose of the licensing restriction is listed. Where (a) the item has a license requirement only for reasons of national security (marked by "NS"), (b) The item's destination is a country not on a restricted list,[87] and (c) the item is identified by "GBS—Yes" on the CCL, then no license is likely required.[88]

Civilian End Users: Where (a) the item has a license requirement *only* for reasons of national security, (b) the item itself is deemed by the EAR for civilian end use (marked by "CIV—Yes" in the ECCN), (c) the item's ultimate destination is a recipient in Country Group D:1 as identified in Supplement No. 1 to 15 CFR §740,[89] and (d) the item is actually being used by a civilian end user for civilian purposes, then no license is likely required.[90]

Technology and Software Under Restriction: Where (a) the item is protected for national security only, (b) the recipient country is not on a restricted list,[91] and (c) the item is identified by "TSR—Yes" on the ECCN, then no license is likely required. To qualify for this exception, an exporter must obtain from the importer a written assurance that states (among other things) that the importer will not export or re-export the technology to a national or country in the restricted group identified in Country Chart D:1 and E:1.[92]

Other Exceptions: Exceptions may also apply for certain computer products; software and operation technology; one-for-one replacement of parts, components, accessories, and attachments; gifts and charitable/humanitarian donations; and more.[93]

D.   Best Practices for Compliance with the EAR

Policies and Procedures: Procedures should be in place to determine the regulatory agency that applies to exports. Where the EAR applies, an organization should determine the category and the licensing requirements (if any), and establish procedures for ongoing monitoring. Classifications may change over time. For instance, restrictions on countries of destination may be added or lifted. Consequently, a company's categorizations should be updated on a regular basis. From identifying the applicable regulation to licensing and ultimately monitoring, each procedure should be written in a step-by-step narrative form.

The Department of Commerce writes in its manual for export compliance: "At each step of the process, you should ask 'What happens next?'" By posing this question, a Task Force can define step-by-step procedures for daily operational implementation for employees that will be involved in your export program."[94]

Identify "gates" through which a transaction must pass before being approved for export or import. "Internal controls may be in the form of second levels of approvals, comparisons of customers against the prohibited persons and entities lists, requirements for collection of specific end-use information, completion of check lists of actions to be taken prior to next steps, etc."[95]

Employees should be trained to understand the importance of self-reporting violations, seeking guidance on questionable actions, and seeking approval for transactions, and be able to provide examples of situations that warrant such steps. Workers intricately involved with export issues should be evaluated, and their financial and other incentives should be based on conformance, or lack thereof, with these policies.

The benefits of having such a Program in place are extensive. They include: cost savings; less potential for audits, fines, and criminal and civil penalties; fewer legal fees; speedier export licenses and quicker recognition of when a license is needed; reduced risk of delay at the border; and an overall more efficient international trade management system.

Identifying Red Flags: Determining whether a product is subject to licensing requirements requires due diligence investigations prior to export. This means, in part, engaging in due diligence with respect to the importer to ascertain the importer's intended end use, possible end users other than the importer, and the ultimate destination of the item. Keep in mind that the importer, knowing that the intended use or end-user is prohibited under U.S. export laws, may attempt to mislead exporting organizations.

The BIS states that employees should be trained to recognize and respond adequately to red flags.[96] Procedures should be in place to ensure that due diligence is completed on each prospective partner or customer. Where red flags rise, procedures should also ensure that such concerns are reported to the relevant party within an organization. Below is a sampling of red flags identified by BIS:

1. The customer or purchasing agent is reluctant to offer information about the end use of a product.
2. The product's capabilities do not fit the buyer's line of business (e.g., a small bakery places an order for sophisticated lasers).
3. The product ordered is incompatible with the technical level of the country to which the product is being shipped (e.g., semiconductor manufacturing equipment would be of little use in a country without an electronics industry).
4. The customer has little or no business background.
5. The customer is willing to pay cash for a very expensive item when the terms of the sale call for financing.
6. The customer is unfamiliar with the product's performance characteristics but still wants the product.
7. Routine installation, training, or maintenance services are declined by the customer.
8. Delivery dates are vague, or deliveries are planned for out-of-the-way destinations.
9. A freight-forwarding firm is listed as the product's final destination.
10. The shipping route is abnormal for the product and destination.
11. Packaging is inconsistent with the stated method of shipment or destination.
12. When questioned, the buyer is evasive or unclear about whether the purchased product is for domestic use, export, or re-export.[97]

Renee Osborne of the Department of Commerce, speaking at a seminar on best practices for EAR compliance Programs, suggested that all stakeholders should have the ability to put a questionable order on hold.[98] Osborne also recommends that clearly defined criteria be put in place to assess whether the hold can ultimately be pulled. For example, once a hold is put in place, an authorized individual trained in the intricacies of EAR compliance may be the only person that can pull the hold. The individual that placed the hold should not be the same person with the authority to remove the hold.

Self-Reporting: As is the case with most regulatory agencies, BIS "strongly encourages" internal reporting when a violation of the EAR is revealed.[99] Though no assurances are given that the violation will not be referred to the DOJ or that aggravating factors will not result in tough fines and sanctions, self-reporting is considered an important mitigating factor.[100]

To self-report, BIS requires that companies follow specific procedures set forth at 15 CFR §764.5. For actual or suspected violations, this includes (but is not limited to) providing a narrative account of the following: the nature of the violation, when and how the violation occurred, and all parties involved in the violation. Subsequently, an investigation should take place into all transactions within the area of suspicion. This review should go back five years from the date of disclosure to BIS.[101]

Record Keeping: Companies are required to retain a wide variety of records relating to exports. Additionally, organizations may find it prudent to retain records above and beyond that required by the EAR. For example, companies should also retain records pertaining to due diligence, to holds, to the release of holds, to licensing decisions, and to ongoing monitoring. All records should be retained in a safe, readily accessible, and clearly indexed location. The following items, among others, are specifically required for retention:

1. Export-control documents submitted to BIS, unless submitted electronically
2. Memoranda, notes, correspondence, and contracts
3. Invitations to bid
4. Books of account and financial records
5. Restrictive trade practices or boycott documents and reports
6. BIS return notices, denial notices, and results of commodity classification requests
7. Other: de minimus calculations, annual reports, end use certificates, export clearance, violations, voluntary self-disclosure records, and subpoenas[102]

Most EAR records should be retained for five years from the latest of:

1. The export from the United States of the item.
2. The re-export of the item, if known to the organization.
3. Any termination of the transaction. For boycott requests, such records should be retained for five years from the date of the receipt of the request.

Additionally, organizations may find it prudent to retain records above and beyond that required by the EAR. For example, companies should also retain records pertaining to due diligence, holds, the release of holds, licensing decisions, and ongoing monitoring.

Policies and procedures should be in place to ensure the consistent retention of such records in an easy-to-access file or database. Monitor and audit to ensure such record-keeping policies are followed by the workforce. Back up all records electronically. Companies may consider designating a records officer to coordinate this process across multiple levels and departments.

Documents required under the EAR must be made available for inspection and for copying to the BIS, customs, or any other U.S. agency.[103] Failure to properly document can bring adverse consequences. Not only could it weaken the organization's case if litigation arises over the question of whether the organization acted legally under the EAR or another law, but noncompliant organizations risk incurring the ire of regulators stymied in their efforts to complete their own investigations.

IV.   Boycotts

The Arab League boycott of Israel was the impetus for antiboycott laws set forth in the EAR.[104] Many countries in the Middle East and Africa require local companies to undertake activities to strengthen or enforce the boycott,[105] but U.S. persons are prohibited from taking certain actions with intent to comply with a foreign boycott. Whether an individual has intent to take part in a foreign boycott is, like so many other sections in the EAR, a broad term. While it may sound easy to avoid taking part in a boycott, a variety of seemingly innocuous activities can subject one to liability.

There are three types of international boycotts:

1. Primary boycotts, where one country refuses to trade with another
2. Secondary boycotts, where one country refuses to trade with anyone who does business with the country being boycotted
3. Tertiary boycotts, where one country refuses to trade with anyone who does business with companies or firms on their "blacklist"

Antiboycott laws do not apply to primary boycotts. The second and third types of boycotts are applicable, however.[106]

Intent to comply with a foreign boycott occurs where intent to comply with a boycott is *part* of the reason for so acting, even if there are also other, entirely legitimate business interests for so acting.[107] For example, Company A receives a boycott questionnaire from boycotting Country Y. The questionnaire asks A whether it has any manufacturing plants located in boycotted Country B. A responds to Y's questionnaire. Writes BIS: "A's responding to Y's questionnaire is deemed to be action with intent to comply with Y's boycott because A knows that the questionnaire is boycott related." Importantly, this is true even if A responds to Y that it does have plants in the boycotted country and even if A has no intent to cease operations in B.[108]

A. Antiboycott Restrictions

Refusals to Do Business: Companies may not refuse to do business in a boycotted country or with a boycotted country's nationals.[109] However, a company is not in violation if the agreement merely states that the U.S. person agrees to abide by the laws of the boycotting country.[110]

Compare the following examples. In the first example, Company A does not send a request for bid to Company B. The reason is that Company B is prohibited from doing business in Country Y. Company A has violated the antiboycott laws of the United States for not including Company B as a result of the boycott.[111]

Instead, Company A should allow Company B to bid. This may seem illogical; after all, it is not even legal in Country Y for B to participate. However, the BIS, by implication, would require that Company B make the decision to not participate in the bid, which Company B is likely to do because it would not be able to meet the requirements for a successful bid. For instance, A may state that one of the conditions for a successful bid is that the bidder be able to provide specified services in Country Y.[112] Because B cannot operate in Country Y, B cannot successfully bid. But A has nonetheless kept the bidding open to Company B and has therefore not supported the boycott.

Discriminatory Actions: U.S. persons may not refuse to employ or otherwise discriminate against any U.S. person on the basis of race, religion, sex, or national origin.[113] For example, Company A is building an office complex in Country Y. Company A does not make offers of employment to U.S. nationals of a certain religion because foreign nationals of that religion are prohibited from working in Country Y. Company A is in violation of this section, and instead should have made such offers of employment.[114] Such offers can, however, be contingent on prospective employees successfully obtaining entry documents into Country Y.[115]

Company A could include a clause in the contract for employment that "no persons who are citizens, residents, or nationals of Country X are to work on this project."[116] This, perhaps surprisingly, is permissible, because the exclusion is not based on race, religion, sex, or national origin.

Furnishing Information about Race, Religion, Sex, or National Origin: U.S. persons may not furnish information about the race, religion, sex, or national origin of U.S. persons.[117] Therefore, persons may not answer questionnaires, for instance, asking the company to state whether any workers are members of a particular religion.[118]

Prohibition against Furnishing Information about Business Relationships with Boycotted Countries or Blacklisted Persons:[119] This information may only be furnished in a "normal business" context. That is, documents made available publicly, such as annual reports, disclosure statements, promotional brochures, and business handbooks would not fall under this restriction.[120]

This exception does *not* apply, however, if the publicly available documents are explicitly requested by the boycotting country or a company thereof for purposes of compliance with the boycott.[121] Moreover, some companies have included information about boycotted countries in their publicly available documents so that the boycotting countries can find the information they seek while the companies do not appear to actually comply with an impermissible request. However, if there is evidence that such information is made publicly available as a method to cover prohibited actions, then in this case, too, intent is inferred and charges may follow.[122]

Other Restrictions: U.S. persons may not implement letters of credit containing prohibitions related to a boycott, and may not provide information about associations with charitable and fraternal organizations that support a boycotted country.[123]

B.   Exceptions to the Prohibited Conduct

Laws of the Boycotting Country: U.S. persons may not refuse on an "across-the-board basis to do business with a boycotted country or a national or resident of a boycotted country."[124] However, it is permissible to agree to follow the laws of the boycotting country with regard to imports, exports, immigration, employment, and shipping.[125] For example, Company A may substitute for another the product parts of Company B, where Company B is a vendor that A typically uses, if B's products are not permitted for importation to Country Y. Moreover, because the provision of services is considered an import, Company A could even agree to not hire nationals of the boycotted country where that is a condition of A's contract, though companies will want to consider possible reputational and ethical damage in so doing. Remember, however, that Company A could not agree for boycott purposes to refuse to work with *all* companies from the boycotted country; instead, this restriction is limited to imports, exports, or shipping.[126]

While Company A can agree to not import from or import to the prohibited country, restrictions on the furnishing of information (as discussed above) related thereto are still applicable. Therefore, Company A cannot, for example, furnish certifications stating that Company A has not imported goods from Company B or the country of Company B.[127]

In complying with such laws, companies may provide certain documentation to the boycotting country. However, such documentation must be stated in positive terms (e.g., "Company A did business with Company C") rather than in negative terms (e.g., "Company A did not do business with Company B or with Country X").

Additionally, residents of the boycotting country, including U.S. residents, may agree to abide by the laws of that country with respect to their activities exclusively within that country.[128]

Unilateral and Specific Selection: In some circumstances, it is permissible to allow the boycotting country, a national thereof, or even a resident of the boycotting country, to make the determination as to carriers, insurers, or suppliers of services or goods within the country on behalf of the company.[129] "Residents" of the boycotting country, incidentally, can even include a U.S. person who is a bona fide[130] resident of the boycotting country. The selection must be "unilateral" and "specific."

A specific selection is stated in the affirmative, rather than in the negative.[131] Thus, a specific selection occurs where boycotting Country Y asks Company A to ship goods using Company B. If, instead, Country Y says Company C may *not* provide goods, this is prohibited as contrary to the specific selection rule.[132]

A unilateral selection means that the decision maker of the boycotting country acts alone in exercising discretion. The U.S. person cannot provide boycott-based assistance to the boycotting country, national, or resident.[133]

C. Reporting

Unless an exception applies, U.S. persons receiving requests to further or support a boycott within this section must report such request to the Department of Commerce.[134] Where the person receiving the request is located in the United States, reports are due by the last day of the month following the calendar quarter in which the request was received.[135] Where the person receiving the request is located outside the United States, reports are due by the last day of the second month following the calendar quarter in which the request was received.[136] Given this short time period, it is essential that employees report violations internally without delay so that managers have sufficient time to act.

Employees should be trained to understand the importance of self-reporting and to understand situations warranting internal reporting. If a company is doing business in the Middle East or North Africa, for example, it is vital that everyone involved in the transactions is aware of the boycott rules and can screen all transactions for potential issues.

V.   International Traffic in Arms Regulations (ITAR)

Items that have both military and civilian uses ("dual use" items) generally fall under the EAR. However, where the use is primarily military, the item is likely subject to the jurisdiction of the State Department's Directorate of Defense Trade Controls (DDTC). ITAR is known for its cumbersome, complex processes,[137] and a detailed explanation of ITAR is beyond the scope of this book. A brief overview is provided so that exporters have a full picture of the export regime.

If an item has a primarily military use, then it is "specifically designed, configured, adapted, or modified for a military application" and does not have a predominately civilian use.[138] What the government considers a military article may be surprising. Military articles include commercial items adapted, modified, or configured for military application. For example, if a screw is modified to fit military vehicles by being made slightly thicker and stronger, it now has a military application.

The DDTC enforces its rules through ITAR. Exports regulated by ITAR are listed on the United States Munitions List. This list includes 21 broad categories, with users making subjective decisions as which category, if any, their item may fit into. Items on the list may not be exported without a DDTC license.[139] Violations of ITAR, including exporting without a license, may subject wrongdoers to fines of up to $1 million and up to 20 years in prison.[140]

Organizations should remain vigilant when dealing with items subject to ITAR. Just as with the EAR, exports include oral or visual disclosure of technical materials, and may include the transfer of technical data to foreign nationals of one's own company, including foreign nationals working in the United States.[141]

Therefore, companies should categorize all materials with military or dual use applications. First, companies should determine whether ITAR, the EAR, or another regulation applies. Then they should decide which restrictions under the regulatory regime apply to their products. If licenses are required for export, it may be advisable to obtain licenses if there are foreign nationals, partners, or contracted parties that will or may access those items. Where licenses are not obtained, limiting access to preapproved persons only is advisable.

Conclusion

Globalization continues to expand the marketplace for U.S. businesses. With this comes opportunities, but as this chapter has shown, it also comes with additional responsibilities. While the trend toward the internationalization of laws began only slowly, recent years—even amid the Great Recession—have shown that governments around the world are joining together to implement new regulations. Many of these, like the FCPA and the U.K.'s Bribery Act 2010, are testing the limits of jurisdiction by reaching across country borders. Organizations should enjoy the advantages of a global economy, but remember that some restraint, and certainly caution, is advisable.

CHAPTER TWELVE

Money Laundering

I. Stages and Impact of Money Laundering

What Is Money Laundering? Money laundering is the process by which funds derived from illegal activities are placed into the financial system in such a manner as to make the funds appear legitimate.[1] Transferring money electronically is traceable, and so criminal transactions often take place using cash. But cash has only limited utility; modern practicalities necessitate the money enter the financial system. In the 1980s, stories of drug czars dropping stacks of cash at their local banks aroused outrage, leading to some of the first effective anti–money laundering (AML) laws. Today, criminals are more sophisticated, and so, financial institutions must work harder to uncover money laundering.

It's not just traditional criminals that are of concern, either. Terrorist organizations often engage in "reverse money laundering"—using legitimate sources of funds and converting the funds for illicit use by terrorists[2]—which has encouraged further scrutiny and regulation. September 11, 2001, further upped the ante with the passage of the USA PATRIOT Act (Patriot Act).

Impact of Money Laundering: Money laundering is an almost unfathomably large trillion-dollar industry. Most estimates put it at 2 to 5 percent of the world's entire GDP.[3] Countries are increasingly cooperating to combat money laundering. With more than 100 countries implementing laws against money laundering,[4] the scope of money laundering laws is only increasing, as is the ability of regulators to more thoroughly enforce this multijurisdictional dilemma.

Stages of Money Laundering: Though the complexity varies greatly, with criminals running the gambit from elementary to sophisticated, most laundering schemes follow three stages:

1. *Placement:* At this stage, launderers place their cash into the financial system. Because the jig is up if the money is known to derive from a criminal source, launderers can find ingenious ways to place their money into the system. Any transaction of more than $10,000 in cash must be reported to federal bank regulators, and so oftentimes cash is deposited in amounts below this threshold. Multiple parties may also deposit the income into multiple bank accounts, and false identifications may be used to further muddle the trail.

Additionally, launderers may use their cash to purchase goods or services, such as jewelry, gold, and luxury goods. These goods can then be returned to the place of purchase for a refund check, with the check then deposited at a financial institution. This distracts the bank from the origin of the funds. Launderers also funnel funds into legitimate businesses by representing the monies as cash receipts, which are then mingled with the legitimate earnings and deposited.

As discussed below, financial institutions, through the imposition of regulatory requirements, bear the burden of policing against these efforts at placement. As noted, institutions must report transactions over $10,000; they must verify customers' identifications and engage in due diligence on customers. Moreover, funds from high-risk customers or transactions demand increased oversight.[5]

2. *Layering:* Layering is the process of moving and manipulating funds so as to conceal their sources and confuse paper trails. This often involves moving funds through multiple accounts, including domestic and international accounts. Layering may be facilitated through wire transfers between institutions, intrabank transfers via accounts owned by the same individual, depositing refund checks from the return of luxury goods, and more.[6] For example, launderers use wire transfers to send funds to banks in jurisdictions that employ bank secrecy laws, so that the receiving bank does not identify the source of the incoming funds. At this point, the launderer can keep the funds in the recipient bank or, since the origin of the funds has been confused, the launderer may then wire the funds back to a more conveniently located bank.

3. *Integration:* After the illicit funds are in the financial system and layered so as to confuse the origin, launderers use this stage to create the appearance of legality through additional transactions such as loans or real estate transactions. By engaging in these transactions, the launderer has a plausible explanation as to the source of funds. This process may occur with inflated business receipts; overvaluing, undervaluing, or creating false invoices; establishing a front company or phony charitable organization, and more.[7]

The Money Laundering Control Act of 1986: The subsequent section discusses the Bank Secrecy Act (BSA) and its application to financial institutions. However, it is not only financial institutions that must devote attention and resources to issues of money laundering. The Money Laundering Control Act of 1986 created liability for individuals who conduct transactions knowing that the funds have been derived through unlawful activities.[8] "Transactions" are not limited to those with financial institutions. Rather, any exchange of money between two parties constitutes a financial transaction that could result in a criminal prosecution. Unlawful activities include extortion, bribery, kidnapping, and the ubiquitous mail and wire fraud, among others.[9] Consequently, any dealings with a figure that obtained funds through unlawful activities could subject an individual or organization to liability—or at least a regulatory investigation—under this section.

Though the standard is actual knowledge that the funds were derived from criminal activities, the most effective way to show that the individual did not possess such knowledge is by pointing toward documentation of background investigations. For those who would purposefully disengage so as to avoid "actual knowledge," willful blindness may also establish liability.[10] Therefore, many of the procedures that financial institutions engage in, especially the due diligence investigations and verification procedures on customers, should also be followed by nonfinancial institutions.

II. The Bank Secrecy Act (BSA) and the USA PATRIOT Act

The Bank Secrecy Act (BSA), supplemented by the USA PATRIOT Act of 2001, is the primary regulatory regime applicable to financial institutions. The BSA broadly defines "financial institutions" to include banks; broker dealers in securities; mutual funds; insurance companies; casinos; dealers in precious metals, jewels and stones; operators of credit card systems; and more.[11] The BSA is regulated by FinCEN, which is a division of the Treasury Department. Banks are also subject to bank regulatory agencies, and these agencies enforce BSA provisions.

This section covers reporting, record keeping, and compliance Program requirements of the BSA. Institutions covered by the BSA are required to verify the identity of their customers. Once so identified, due diligence on those customers is required. Where suspicious activities become known to the institution, a Suspicious Activity Report (SAR) must be filed with FinCEN. Additionally, Currency Transaction Reports (CTR) must be filed for each transaction over $10,000. In order to retain policies and procedures for each of these requirements, institutions are required by law to have a compliance Program in place. Cumulatively, these procedures constitute a BSA/AML (anti–money laundering) program.

A. Customer Identification Program (CIP)

What Is a CIP? Financial institutions must implement a written, board approved CIP program to verify the identity of customers.[12] Though foreign subsidiaries of financial institutions are not required to have such a program,[13] it is advisable to have a program in place at all branches.

The program should, as the name suggests, include the policies and procedures to determine the actual identity of the entity's customers. As noted above, launderers often conceal their identities. To verify identity, banks should obtain documentation from the customer when opening an account. This documentation should include a government-issued identification that includes a name, birth date, address, and social security number or other identification number.[14] For high-risk customers, who are further defined below, additional information may be required. This could include nondocumentary evidence, such as verification of account information, submission of financial statements, and more. Entities must also check all customers' names against specified, federally provided terrorist lists.

The program should define what constitutes a "reasonable belief" in the veracity of an individual's identity. Moreover, the entity should have a clear action plan for responding where identity cannot be identified to a reasonable degree of certainty. This includes the circumstances in which the entity will refuse to open an account or do business with the individual, as well as the threshold for filing a SAR, described below.

As noted above, it is best practice for nonfinancial institutions as well to engage in these background investigations prior to commencing relations with a potential customer or partner so as to avoid liability under the Money Laundering Control Act.

Customer Notice: Customers must be informed of the processes followed to verify identity. This notice can be posted in a visible area of the institution, such as a bank lobby, on a Web site, or on documents provided to the customer. An agency-approved sample notice is as follows:

IMPORTANT INFORMATION ABOUT PROCEDURES FOR OPENING A NEW ACCOUNT—To help the government fight the funding of terrorism and money laundering activities, federal law requires all financial institutions to obtain, verify, and record information that identifies each person who opens an account. What this means for you: When you open an account, we will ask for your name, address, date of birth, and other information that will allow us to identify you. We may also ask to see your driver's license or other identifying documents.[15]

CIP Record Keeping: Entities should retain all CIP records for five years. This includes an original or copy of all records relied on to authenticate identity, as well as a narrative as to the type of document, the ID number, place of issuance, and the date and expiration of issuance. Moreover, retain records of steps taken to determine customer identification and any results therefrom, including discrepancies.[16]

B.   Customer Due Diligence

Once the customer is identified, the entity should engage in a customer risk assessment to determine whether there is a risk for money laundering, terrorism, or other crimes.[17] This investigation should take place when the customer opens an account, periodically thereafter, and also whenever the customer engages in a high-risk event. The FDIC considers this oversight the "cornerstone" of a strong BSA/AML program.

1. Risk Assessment: Many institutions assign risk ratings to customers.[18] Where customer risks are elevated, so, too, should due diligence escalate. Customers may be high risks as a result of the nature of the account being open or used, the customer's history or background, or due to geographic considerations. High risk transactions include:

- electronic funds payment services
- electronic banking
- private banking
- trust and asset management
- monetary instruments
- foreign accounts
- foreign exchange
- services provided to third-party payment processors or senders[19]

High-risk customers include:

- foreign financial institutions
- nonbank financial institutions, such as casinos or dealers in precious metals, stones, or jewels
- senior political figures and their families
- nonresident aliens and accounts of foreign individuals
- foreign corporations and domestic business entities (especially offshore corporations) located in higher-risk geographic locations

- foreign deposit brokers
- cash-intensive businesses, such as restaurants, liquor stores, and parking garages
- nongovernmental organizations and charities
- professional service providers, such as attorneys, accountants, doctors, and real estate brokers.[20]

High-risk locations include:

- Countries supporting terrorism
- Countries categorized as "of primary money laundering concern" by the Secretary of the Treasury or State Department
- Offshore financial centers and domestic risk areas including those areas with high-intensity drug trafficking or financial crimes areas.[21]

2. Due Diligence Actions: Increased due diligence should take place for high-risk customers. Additionally, an otherwise low-risk customer may become a higher-risk customer where high-risk activities are involved or where the customer deviates from normal or expected activities. Where such risks are heightened, institutions may consider obtaining the following, prior to engaging in business or as soon as the risk becomes known:

a. Information about the purpose of the account or transaction so as to better ascertain the legitimacy of funds.
b. The proximity of the customer's residence to the entity. Where customers travel long distances, it may be in an effort to conceal the origin of funds or to access what are perceived as institutions with lax oversight.
c. The name of all individuals with ownership or control over the account.
d. A description of the customer's primary occupation and whether the customer is likely to engage in high-risk transactions on a regular basis. If the customer indicates that he will not engage in what the entity considers high-risk transactions and subsequently does engage in a high-risk transaction, especial notice should be taken.
e. References from banks that have worked with the customer.
f. Description of the customer's business operation, including anticipated volume of currency and total sales and a list of major customers and suppliers.[22]

Beyond the above steps for high-risk customers, the Patriot Act specifies that where U.S. financial institutions hold private banking accounts of non-U.S. persons, policies and procedures to detect and report money laundering must be in place. Specifically, this requires verifying the identity of the nominal and beneficial owners of an account; documentation showing the source of funds; and enhanced scrutiny of accounts and transactions by senior foreign political figures and their families.[23]

Additionally, financial institutions are prohibited from establishing, maintaining, administering, or managing a correspondent account in the United States for or on behalf of a foreign shell bank. A foreign shell bank is defined as a foreign bank without a physical presence in any country.[24]

Lastly, as with customer identification verifications, all business entities should engage in this sort of background investigation prior to commencing relations with a potential customer or partner so as to avoid liability under the Money Laundering Control Act. Many of the red flags discussed below should also be considered by nonfinancial entities.

C.   Suspicious Activity Reporting

This section examines SARs, including how and when to file these reports, and best practices for identifying suspicious activity.

1. Filing a Suspicious Activity Report: Whenever an institution detects known or suspected criminal violations of a federal law, or a suspicious transaction related to money-laundering activities or a violation of the BSA, an SAR must be filed with the Treasury Department. Specifically, reports must be filed for:

a. Transactions aggregating $5,000 or more that involve potential money laundering, suspected terrorist financing activities, or violations of the BSA. If a financial institution insider is involved in the suspicious transaction(s), the SAR must be filed at any transaction amount. An institution must file a report of money laundering suspicions where the institution is aware that funds are derived from illegal activities or are being used to conceal funds derived from illegal activities.[25] Additionally, due diligence may reveal that the transaction has no apparent relation to the customer's business or to an otherwise lawful purpose.[26]

b. Other suspected criminal activity requires filing an SAR if the transactions aggregate $5,000 or more and a suspect can be identified. If the financial institution is unable to identify a suspect, but believes it was an actual or potential victim of a criminal violation, then an SAR must be filed for transactions aggregating $25,000 or more.

c. Even if these thresholds are not met, institutions may voluntarily file an SAR. Additionally, for suspicious activities involving transactions over $10,000, institutions are reminded to also file a CTR, discussed below.

2. Red Flags: Red flags may arise from customer identification, customer due diligence, or other activities of the customer or another party. The

FDIC has identified the following red flags, among others, which warrant additional investigation by the entity and which may require filing an SAR.[27]

a. A customer, after being informed that a CTR will be filed, abruptly discontinues the transaction.
b. Customer refuses or is reluctant to provide information or identification.
c. Repeat or recurring transactions below the reportable threshold, where such transactions appear designed to avoid reporting requirements.
d. Transactions are unexpectedly conducted in even dollar amounts.
e. Transactions inconsistent with the customer's business, occupation, or income level.
f. Unusually large transactions between a small, remote institution and a large bank.
g. Significant exchanges of small denomination bills for large denomination bills.
h. Frequent cash shipments with no apparent business reason.
i. Suspicious movement of funds out of one financial institution, into another financial institution, and back into the first financial institution. This can be indicative of the layering stage of money laundering.
j. The individual does not have a local residential or business address and there is no apparent legitimate reason for opening an account with the bank.
k. The individual deposits cash and then immediately requests a wire transfer or cash shipment.
l. Early redemption of certificates of deposit results in penalties and loss of interest. This may also expedite the placement stage, and therefore should raise questions as to the basis for such a willingness to take a loss.
m. Wire transfers of funds to jurisdictions with bank secrecy laws.
n. Frequent wire-transfer activity, high-volume transfers with low account balances, and wires with similar dollar amounts that are not justified by the nature of the customer's business.[28]

3. SAR Compliance Policies and Procedures: Institutions should have policies and procedures to identify and respond to suspicious activities. These include:

Identification of unusual activity:

- Employees should be trained to ensure that suspicious activity is identified and reported. Policies and procedures should support this.[29]
- Law enforcement inquiries, such as a grand jury subpoena, may indicate wrongdoing or suspicion of wrongdoing by a customer.[30] These inquiries may lead the institution to review the customer's account.
- Most entities are advised to have in place a monitoring system that tracks transactions of a certain type, such as those involving large amounts of cash, or

those sourced to or from foreign jurisdictions.[31] Monitoring transactions of this sort facilitates the identification of red flags.

Managing alerts to unusual activity:

- Institutions should identify the individual or department charged with investigating suspicious activities. A system to elevate more serious issues to higher levels within the organization should be in place.[32]
- An individual or department should be authorized to make the decision as to whether or not to file an SAR. The documentation supporting this decision, whether affirmative or negative, should be retained.[33] Where an SAR is filed, the board must be notified of the contents of the SAR filing, unless a board member is a suspect identified in the SAR.[34]

Filing an SAR: The following items must be provided in the SAR within 30 days after detection of the incident (or up to 60 days if additional time is needed to identify a suspect):

- Information about the suspect, including name, social security number or TIN, and account number
- The type of suspicious activity, including the date range
- The dollar amount involved and any losses to the institution[35]

D.   Currency Transaction Reports (CTR)

This section examines currency transaction reports, including when and how reports should be filed, and exemptions from filing.

1. When to File Reports: Institutions must file reports with the Treasury Department for each currency transaction over $10,000.[36] A "currency transaction" is the physical transfer of currency from one person to another, and includes deposits, withdrawals, exchanges or transfers of currency, or other payments. Multiple transactions by the same person that total more than $10,000 in any one business day are treated as a single transaction.[37]

2. Filing Requirements: Institutions must include the name, address, SSN or TIN, and date of birth of the person conducting the transaction. Additionally, institutions must specify the documentation used to verify the identity of the individual, the account number, the amount and the type of transaction, and the name and contact information of an authorized representative of the institution.[38] Physical forms should be filed within 15 days of the reportable transaction and electronic filings within 25 days.[39]

3. Exemptions: Certain persons may be exempt from CTR filings. These include banks, government agencies and departments, and listed entities. Customers that regularly withdraw more than $10,000 for payroll purposes may be exempt from reports pertaining to their withdrawals only if the customer: (a) has maintained an account with the institution for at least 12 months, (b) regularly makes transactions exceeding $10,000, and (c) is incorporated or organized in the United States.[40]

Additionally, commercial enterprises may be entirely exempt if the enterprise meets the requirements set forth in the previous paragraph for cash withdrawal customers and also if: (a) the enterprise is not engaged in a high risk business, (b) has maintained an account with the institution for at least 12 months, (c) regularly makes transactions exceeding $10,000, and (d) is incorporated or organized in the United States. High-risk businesses include money service businesses; dealers or charterers in motor and other vehicles; investment advisers or bankers; professionals practicing law, medicine, or accountancy; real estate brokers; pawn brokers; gaming entities; trade union entities; and others.[41]

Prior to granting an exemption, an authorized compliance manager should review and approve the exemption.[42]

E.   Other

This section examines obligations for persons with foreign bank accounts and handling requests for information from law enforcement agencies.

1. Foreign Bank Accounts: Each person who has a financial interest in or authority over any financial accounts maintained in a foreign country must report the relationships to the IRS annually if the aggregate value of the accounts exceeds $10,000 at any point during the calendar year.[43]

2. Requests for Information: Law enforcement agencies may send a request for information to the Treasury Department, which in turn can require institutions to verify whether a person has an account or has engaged in transactions with the institution.[44] These requests can only relate to money laundering suspects or terrorist activities.[45] Institutions have two weeks to respond to these requests.[46] Such requests must be kept confidential from the individual to whom the request pertains. If information on an individual is found within the institution's records, the institution should consider further internal investigations to determine whether an SAR should be filed along with the response to the requesting party.[47]

F. BSA/AML Compliance Program

Financial institutions must have written and board-approved compliance Programs. Four procedures are necessary to establish an adequate Program.

1. Internal Controls: A system of policies and procedures should ensure conformity with each of the above requirements under the BSA. See the above sections for specific details. Generally speaking, however, a risk assessment should precede the implementation of internal controls. This assessment should first identify the presence and regularity of high-risk areas (see section II, above), and second, analyze these risks.[48] Once institutions have a comprehensive understanding of the extent and nature of their risks, only then can specific internal controls mitigate those risks.

2. Periodic Audits: Entities are required to audit their compliance Programs. This can be conducted by an internal audit department, outside auditors, or consultants. The department responsible for day-to-day activities of the compliance Program should not, however, conduct the audit.

The audit should include a review of all policies and procedures to ensure conformity with the BSA. Additionally, the auditor(s) should review the specific actions taken by the entity when assessing and managing high-risk transactions.[49]

A risk assessment should also occur during the audit. This should take place not less than every 12 to 18 months, or more often if the nature of the institution's activities or customers dramatically enhances the risk profile.[50]

3. BSA/AML Manager: Institutions are required to authorize an individual or team with day-to-day authority for coordinating and monitoring BSA compliance. The senior authority responsible for BSA compliance should have such authority and resources to make and enforce policies.[51]

4. Employee Training: As noted, employees should be trained to recognize red flags. But this is not the full extent of training. Employees should be trained to conform with any BSA requirements that fall within the purview of the employees. This includes new employee orientation. Specifically, training should cover:

a. The institution's policies and procedures
b. Training on the three stages of money laundering
c. Identification of red flags
d. Identification and examples of suspicious activities
e. Overview and importance of customer due diligence (CDD) and customer identification program (CIP) procedures and requirements.[52]

The most common violations under the BSA are (1) failure to adequately identify and report large cash transactions, (2) failure to report suspicious activities, (3) failure to identify and verify customer identity, and (4) failure to maintain proper documentation of transactions.[53] Therefore, these issues should receive particular training attention.

Conclusion

Money laundering has taken on increased importance in the years following 9/11. Like so many other regulations covered in this book, the international developments are most striking. Financial institutions carry the heaviest burden, but all organizations must remain diligent to verify that monies exchanged derive only from legitimate sources. The procedures taken will vary with the facts of the case. As with all investigations, uncertainty is all too often the only certainty. But the above steps provide a starting point for examining relationships with a watchful eye.

CHAPTER THIRTEEN

Health Care Concerns and Data Privacy

I. The Family and Medical Leave Act

A. Coverage

The Family and Medical Leave Act (FMLA) is a "leave entitlement law." It allows "covered employees" of "covered employers" to take up to 12 weeks "leave" in a 12-month period in certain instances. The FMLA is a federal law, and must therefore be considered in conjunction with relevant state laws. Moreover, the FMLA commonly arises from serious illnesses of the employee, and so it also may overlap with the Americans with Disabilities Act (ADA), which is discussed further in chapter 13.

Leave is covered by the FMLA in the following instances:

1. The birth of a child and/or to care for a newborn child within one year of birth
2. The adoption of a child or foster child and to care for the newly placed child within one year of placement
3. A serious health condition of self, spouse, child, or parent
4a. Any qualifying exigency arising out of the fact that the employee's spouse, son, daughter, or parent is a covered military member on "covered active duty" *or*
4b. To care for a covered service member with a serious injury or illness if the eligible employee is the service member's spouse, son, daughter, parent, or next of kin (for which 27 workweeks of leave over a 12-month period may be granted).

The FMLA only requires that "covered employers" offer leave to their "covered employees."

What Is a Covered Employer? A covered employer is any organization that employs, within the United States or a territory thereof, 50 or more employees for at least 20 (nonconsecutive) weeks of the year.[1] Public agencies are covered employers without regard to the number of individuals employed, though special rules may cover federal employees.[2]

What Is a Covered Employee? A covered employee has worked:

1. for a covered employer for at least 12 months in the United States or a territory thereof;
2. at a location where there are at least 50 employees of the employer within a 75-mile radius; and
3. at least 1,250 hours in the 12 months prior to the start of leave.[3]

A covered employee need not have worked 12 consecutive months of employment in the United States or one of its territories. In fact, all time worked is counted toward the 12 months unless the employee took a greater than seven-year break since the last time he or she worked for the employer.[4] Where the employer denies that the employee worked at least 1,250 hours, the employer bears the burden of proof that the employee has not worked the requisite hours.[5] Consequently, and as set forth below, documentation of hours and of the basis for any FMLA denials is required by the FMLA.

B. "Leave" under the FMLA

If the individual is a covered employee working for a covered employer, the employee may be eligible for leave under the following circumstances:

1. Birth of a Child and to Care for a Newborn Child within One Year of Birth: Parents are entitled to leave within 12 months of a child's birth, and this is regardless of whether the child has a serious health condition.[6] Note that this leave (and leave for the adoption or care of a child or foster child) is provided for both the mother and father without prejudice as to gender.[7] However, if both mother and father work for the same employer, then the employer may limit the spouses to 12 weeks leave between the two, as long as the leave is for the birth or care of a healthy child, and not as a result of a serious health condition as described below.

2. Adoption of a Child or Foster Child and to Care for the Newly Placed Child within One Year of Placement: Just as with the birth of a child, parents of an adopted child or foster child may take time to care for the child within 12 months of placement.[8] Additionally, leave may be taken prior to the placement, in order to attend court appearances, doctor visits, attorney meetings, and more.[9]

3. Serious Health Condition of Self, Spouse, Child, or Parent: A serious health condition is an illness, injury, impairment, or physical or mental condition that involves: (a) inpatient care[10] or (b) continuing treatment[11] by a health care provider. The FMLA states: "Ordinarily, unless complications arise, the common cold, the flu, ear aches, upset stomach, minor ulcers, headaches other than migraine, routine dental or orthodontia problems, periodontal disease, etc., are examples of conditions that do not meet the definition of a serious health condition and do not qualify for FMLA leave."[12]

Leave may be taken to care for a child under 18 with a serious health condition. However, for children 18 or older, the child must have a serious health condition caused by a physical or mental disability that causes the child to be incapable of self-care.[13] Where leave is allowed for a parent under this section or the subsections 4a or 4b, below, in-laws do not qualify as parents.[14]

4a. Any Qualifying Exigency Arising out of the Fact that the Employee's Spouse, Child, or Parent Is a Covered Military Member on "Covered Active Duty": A covered military member is a regular or reserve in the military deployed to a foreign country. Exigencies entitling an employee to leave include but are not limited to:

- If less than seven days' notice is provided prior to deployment, the spouse, child, or parent of the military member may take up to seven days' leave from the date of notification
- To attend official military events and activities, such as ceremonies
- For issues pertaining to child care and school activities of the military member's child
- In order to make financial and legal arrangements to address the military member's absence
- To spend time with the military member while on short-term, temporary R&R.[15]

or

4b. To Care for a Covered Service Member with a Serious Injury or Illness if the Eligible Employee Is the Service Member's Spouse, Child, Parent, or Next of Kin (Military Caregiver Leave): This leave may be taken where the service member suffered an injury or illness in the line of duty while on active duty (or aggravated an existing injury), which rendered the member unable to perform his military duties. For veterans, such eligibility may also arise (among other scenarios) where the veteran meets certain disability requisites set by the VA or where a physical or mental condition impairs the veteran's ability to secure gainful employment.[16]

Unlike the other conditions for leave, in these circumstances leave may total 26 weeks over 12 months.

C. Rights of the Employee While on Leave

1. Twelve Weeks Leave: Except for military caregiver leave, a maximum of 12 weeks leave is allowed under the FMLA over a 12-month period. In some cases, this leave may be taken intermittently, that is, in separate blocks of time, though arising out of a single qualifying reason.[17] The permissible increments of leave are measured by the amounts of time that the employer uses to account for other forms of leave. If the employer measures leave in 15-minute increments, therefore, then those taking intermittent leave can take leave in 15-minute blocks. And lest employers attempt to evade the spirit of the law by measuring leave in daily or weekly increments, the FMLA states that the maximum measuring block for intermittent leave is one hour.[18]

Intermittent leave creates enormous headaches for employers, both in maintaining day-to-day operations and in tracking the leave in as little as 15-minute increments. Organizations should have plans in place to shift employees and responsibilities on short notice, and methods (such as electronic documentation systems) by which employees can conveniently provide notice of even those shortest of FMLA leaves.

Leave may also be taken through a reduced leave schedule in which an employee's usual workload is reduced, either to fewer hours per day or fewer days per week.[19]

Intermittent or reduced leave may be taken where one's own serious health condition or that of a spouse, parent, or child can best be accommodated by the intermittent or reduced leave. Additionally, where periodic treatment is required (such as for cancer treatments), and where chronic health conditions periodically incapacitate the employee or her family member, employees may opt for intermittent or reduced leave.[20] However, when leave is taken after the birth of a healthy child or the placement of a healthy child through adoption or foster care, intermittent or reduced leave is only permissible if the employer agrees.[21]

Where intermittent or reduced leave is taken, the employer may transfer the employee to an alternative position for which the employee is qualified in order to better accommodate the recurring periods of leave.[22] Such transfer must offer equivalent pay and benefits, may not be done to discourage or pressure the worker from taking the leave, and must not work a "hardship" on the employee.[23] Hardships may include a desk worker being reassigned to perform manual labor, a day-shift employee being reassigned to a "graveyard shift," or an employee being transfered to a geographically distant office or branch.[24] Upon return, the employee should be reinstated to his or her original job or its equivalent.[25]

Employers should tread cautiously when considering such transfers. Along with ensuring and documenting that all of the above requirements are met, employers should also consider implications with regard to any collective bargaining agreements, federal laws (including the ADA), and state laws.[26]

2. Pay: FMLA leave is unpaid. However, employees may choose to use employer-provided paid leave in conjunction with FMLA leave. Even if the employee decides against using paid leave, the employer can require that accumulated paid leave be used. Where paid leave is used, it does count toward the 12 weeks of FMLA leave.[27]

3. Reinstatement: Upon return from FMLA leave, employees are entitled to return to the position held when leave began, or to an equivalent position. An equivalent position means "virtually identical as to pay, benefits, working conditions, privileges, perquisites, and status."[28]

Reinstatement is required even if the employer restructured the organization or division to accommodate the employee's leave, and even if the employee's position has been filled.[29] However, reinstatement is not required if the employer can show that the employee would not have been retained even if FMLA leave had not been taken.[30] If an employee is laid off while on leave, all obligations pursuant to FMLA leave cease, including health care benefits, though collective bargaining or contractual obligations may persist.[31]

This is, of course, a risk-fraught approach. Examples where this may reasonably occur include where the employee's entire division or sector is laid off, or where the employee was hired for a particular (and now completed) job or for a limited term. Additionally, employers are not required to continue to offer the same hours or overtime benefits to a returned employee, but again, only if the employer can show that the shift has been eliminated or overtime has decreased irrespective of the FMLA leave.[32]

An additional exception applies for "key employees," or those employees that receive the top 10 percent of salary within a 75-mile radius of their place of work. Restoration to the position may be denied if the employer determines that the *restoration* (not the leave itself) will cause "substantial and grievous economic injury to the operations of the employer." However, restoration can only be denied if, upon the employee's providing notice of leave, the employer provides the employee with notice that her position may not be subject to reinstatement. Further, the employer must subsequently inform the employee that her position will not be reinstated as soon as the employer makes that determination, and ideally prior to the commencement of FMLA leave. The notice of denial must state the employer's basis for such denial.[33]

4. Benefits: Employees are entitled to retain pre-existing benefits under employee group health plans.[34] The employee is responsible for continuing to make whatever premium payments were being made prior to taking leave.[35]

No benefits under a health plan need be offered by the employer where:

a. The employee purchases the insurance, no contributions are made by the employer, and participation by the employee is voluntary
b. The employer's sole function is to collect premiums through payroll deductions and remit to the insurer
c. The employer receives no consideration or compensation
d. The premium does not increase in the event the employment relationship terminates.[36]

5. The Chill Theory: Employers may not unreasonably interfere with an employee's leave. In *Terwilliger v. Howard Memorial Hospital,*[37] the court found an unreasonable interference, or a "chilling effect" on the plaintiff's FMLA rights, where the employer called the employee too frequently while on leave.

D. Obligations of the Employee

1. Notice: The ultimate decision as to whether an employee qualifies for FMLA leave lies with the employer. However, the employee also has an obligation to provide notice of a request for FMLA leave to the employer. The employee need not use the words "FMLA" in the request, but merely must provide enough information to put the employer on notice that FMLA leave is at issue.[38]

Where the leave is foreseeable, then notice must be provided to the employer at least 30 days in advance of the leave.[39] Where unforeseeable, notice should be provided "as soon as practicable," and practicality is dependent on the specific circumstances at issue.[40]

Importantly, the FMLA allows employers to require conformity with certain employer policies in providing notice.[41] Employers should consider requiring employees to provide notice in writing, and may consider requiring that the notice set forth the reasons for the requested leave, the expected duration of the leave, and the anticipated start of leave, as well as the person or department to whom the request should be directed.

Especially for unforeseeable and intermittent leave, which may result in little notice to organizations, employers face hurdles in retaining continuity of operations. Therefore, clear processes for providing notice should be in place. Employers should ensure that employees know how to provide notice, and are able to do so without facing bureaucratic delays or uncertainty. An individual or department may be authorized to handle all such notices, and should, in turn, follow procedures for notifying relevant parties within the organization of pending leave. Improper notice may be a basis for denying or delaying FMLA leave, but only if all notice requirements are set forth in writing (see Section E, below).[42]

2. Certification: In many cases, employers require that employees provide a certification that affirms the basis for the requested leave. This could be a doctor's certification affirming a serious injury or illness; a birth certificate affirming that a spouse, child, or parent are in fact related; or military records of an alleged covered military member. Employers can also require a certification that an employee is fit to return to work, as long as the leave was initiated due to the employee's own serious health condition, which made the employee unable to perform the job.[43]

When obtaining health certifications, employers can provide a list of the employee's essential duties so that the medical professional can state whether the employee is able to perform his or her tasks.[44] Ordinarily, such requests for certification should be provided upon notice of desired FMLA leave by the employer or within five days.[45] However, certifications may subsequently be requested if the duration of the leave calls the stated basis for the leave into question. The employee should make a best effort to obtain the certification within 15 days of the employer's request.

Employers should maintain at all times a list of all employees' essential duties, so that any employee requesting leave can be provided the certification form within a maximum of five days of the request for leave. If a health professional denies that an employee is able to perform essential job functions as described by the employer, the employee may assert that the employer outlined essential duties specifically so as to avoid a positive certification. Therefore, an essential duties description prepared prior to the request for leave has the important added benefit of establishing objectivity, and thereby bolstering the employers' foundation for denial.

The employer should provide notice in an employee handbook or other guidance if costs of obtaining certifications are to be borne by the employee.[46]

E. Obligations of Employer

1. FMLA Notice: FMLA-covered employers must post notice in a visible location on their premises explaining (a) the FMLA provisions and (b) procedures for filing complaints with the Wage and Hour Division of the DOL. Electronic notice is acceptable as long as it actually reaches employees. Moreover, covered employers with eligible employees should provide notice in employee handbooks, or in other written guidance provided upon hiring. The DOL has provided a prototype of this notice, WH1420, available at http://www.dol.gov/whd/publications/.

2. Rights and Responsibilities Notice: Written notice must be given to all employees stating:

a. That leave may be counted toward one's 12 weeks of annual FMLA leave.
b. The certification requirements of the employer.
c. Whether the employee has the right to substitute paid leave, and whether the employer will *require* the use of paid leave.
d. The requirements for employees, if any, to continue making premium payments for health benefits.
e. An employee's status as a key employee, if applicable, and consequences and conditions for denying reinstatement.
f. That the employee has the right to continued health coverage.
g. The consequences to the employee of failing to return to work if the employer made premium health care payments during FMLA leave. A prototype of this notice, WH-381, is available at http://www.dol.gov/whd/publications/.

Additional notices may be provided along with this notice. Employers may, for instance, wish to require that employees provide periodic updates on their status and their intent to return to work. Additionally, employers may require that notice of an employee's desire to take FMLA leave be provided in writing, rather than merely verbally; notice may also be provided of the person or department to whom FMLA leave requests should be directed.

3. Notice of FMLA Eligibility: As stated above, employees have an obligation to provide notice to employers of requested FMLA leave. However, employers also have an obligation to follow up with the employee where the employer is put on notice that the employee has a qualifying medical condition. A mere change in employee behavior may suffice. To relate a personal anecdote: in one instance an employee was fired after behaving bizarrely in the office. It turned out the employee had a brain tumor. He sued the employer and won.

The employer must notify the employee of eligibility for leave within five business days of notice of a need for leave. If FMLA eligibility is denied by the employer, then employers must state the basis for such denial (e.g., less than 1,250 hours worked, less than 12 months' employment, etc.). Form WH-381, available at http://www.dol.gov/whd/publications/, is a DOL form that can be used to provide notifications under this section.[47]

Five days is a short amount of time to make this decision, and precious time must not be wasted deciding how to act. Instead, the review process must begin immediately. An individual or department may be authorized to make this eligibility decision, and such person(s) should have access to databases showing whether the employee has been with the organization for 12 months, has worked 1,250 hours over a 12-month period, and works within a 75-mile radius of 50 or more employees.

Additionally, procedures for verifying the basis for the leave should be in place, such as obtaining certifications. Ideally, employees should know what information to provide to verify their request for leave so that all the employer must do upon notice is verify the authenticity of such records.

4. Record Keeping: For a period of not less than three years, employers should retain records pertaining to any FMLA activities and obligations. All records must be made available to DOL representatives for copying and inspection, upon request. As stated elsewhere herein, record keeping may best be centralized, though all employees that handle records should understand their obligations to retain such records or to forward them to the authorized individual within the organization. All FMLA records should be retained, and the FMLA explicitly requires the retention of the following:

a. Payroll and identifying employee data, including name, address, and occupation; rate or basis of pay and terms of compensation; daily and weekly hours worked per pay period; additions to or deductions from wages; and total compensation paid
b. Dates and, if taken in less than daily increments, hours of FMLA leave
c. Copies of employee notices of leave, if in writing, and copies of all written notices given to employees as required under FMLA
d. Any documents (including written and electronic records) describing employee benefits or employer policies and practices regarding the taking of paid and unpaid leave
e. Premium payments of employee benefits
f. Records of any dispute between the employer and an eligible employee regarding designation of leave as FMLA leave, including any written statement from the employer or employee of the reasons for the designation and for the disagreement

g. Records and documents relating to certifications, recertifications, or medical histories of employees or employees' family members created for purposes of FMLA. These must be held as confidential medical records in separate files/ records from the usual personnel files.

If employees are exempt from FLSA minimum wage and overtime requirements, then no record of actual hours worked is required as long as the employer presumes FMLA eligibility for all employees with the employer for at least 12 months.

Conclusion

There are gray areas under FMLA, as with all regulations. Perhaps the greatest complication in this area is its possible overlap with other laws, such as ADA and state-specific laws. But, by and large, the rules to follow under FMLA are transparent, and organizations acting cautiously, respectfully toward their employees, and diligently retaining FMLA records greatly minimize the risk of violation.

II.   The Health Insurance Portability and Accountability Act (HIPAA)

A. Overview

What Is the Scope of HIPAA? HIPAA, or the Health Insurance Portability and Accountability Act of 1996, has three primary implications. First, HIPAA provisions facilitate transfers, or "portability," of employee health insurance from one employer to another. Second, HIPPA attempts to reduce Medicare fraud. Third, it regulates the privacy and security of users' health information, known as protected health information (PHI). It is this privacy issue that is most broadly relevant—particularly for businesses that may hold PHI of their employees—and it is privacy and security which are the primary focus of this section.

Entities covered by HIPAA include health care providers, health care clearinghouses,[48] and health plans[49] (collectively, "covered entities" or "CEs"). Privacy and security provisions may also apply to non–health care businesses or, in the parlance of HIPAA, "business associates." This is something of a novelty. Before 2009, businesses were only liable under the privacy and security provisions if a health care provider extended a contract to a business (known as a business associate agreement) requiring that the business abide by the HIPAA standards to which the health care provider itself was liable. However, amendments to HIPAA in the form of

HITECH (the Health Information Technology for Economic and Clinical Health Act) not only strengthened privacy and security provisions, but also explicitly made these provisions applicable to businesses conducting transactions containing PHI for another business or health care provider (hereafter Entity), most likely a covered Entity.[50]

What Is PHI? Protected Health Information (PHI) is medical information in which individuals are personally identifiable.[51] This can include information identifying both an individual and his or her medical condition, such as a name, social security number, address, license number, telephone number, photograph, unique identifying code, or some combination of this information. Such identifying information may manifest itself in any form, including by oral communication, in writing, or electronically. To qualify as PHI, the information must also relate to past, present, or future medical care, treatment, or payment for care. Information that does not identify an individual is not PHI, and is *not* subject to the below HIPAA regulations.

Individuals own, and retain, certain rights pertaining to their PHI. These privacy rights include the right to receive notice as to the purposes for which their PHI will be used, to amend PHI, to request an accounting of the release of their PHI, and to restrict the use of their PHI. These are discussed in more detail below.

Holders of PHI also have an obligation to protect the confidentiality and safety of the PHI, which constitute the security obligations discussed below.

B. Privacy

Using and Disclosing PHI: The privacy provisions of HIPAA and HITECH limit PHI holders' right to release PHI to other entities or persons. The procedures that Entities must follow depend on the recipient of the PHI and the purpose for the release. In some cases, authorization from the individual to release PHI is required.

No authorization is required for Entities to release PHI to the individual whose information is contained therein, as long as no other individuals' PHI is included in the records or information.[52] Additionally, Entities may release information as permitted by law, such as for purposes of court proceedings or answering valid subpoenas; situations pertaining to public health activities; disclosures about actual or possible victims of abuse, neglect, or domestic violence; for purposes of law enforcement; and to avert serious threats to health or safety.[53] Entities also have discretion to release PHI for purposes of treatment, payment, or health care operations for the individual.[54]

The release of information for other purposes requires the individual's authorization. Releases of this sort may be for purposes of marketing, research, media releases, sales, and more.[55]

Authorization for Release: An authorization for the release of PHI should include:

1. The specific description of the information to be used or disclosed
2. The name of the person(s) authorized to make the requested use or disclosure
3. The name of other person(s) to whom the Entity may make the requested use or disclosure
4. A description of the purpose for which the information will be used
5. An expiration date or expiration event limiting the duration of the authorization's validity
6. The PHI holder's signature
7. An indication that remuneration is involved where PHI is sold, such as in the case of a release for purposes of marketing or the sale of PHI to pharmaceutical companies
8. Notice to the individual of the right to revoke the authorization in writing and, unless stated elsewhere, the exceptions to the right to revoke and a description of how to revoke
9. An indication that, in most cases, the Entity may not make the individual's treatment, payment, enrollment, or eligibility for any benefit from the Entity contingent on the individual agreeing to the authorization for release[56]

Authorizations for release are invalid where:

1. The expiration has passed
2. The authorization is not completely filled out
3. The authorization is revoked
4. Any material information is known by the Entity to be false[57]

Subject to limited exceptions, a written revocation of an authorization is effective any time before the Entity has taken action in reliance on the authorization.[58] All language within the authorization should be set forth in plain language that is easily understood by an ordinary person.[59] All valid authorizations should be retained by the Entity,[60] as discussed further below.

Notice of Privacy Practices for PHI: Entities must provide notice to all individuals whose PHI the Entity holds. This notice may be provided upon the receipt of PHI, or upon hiring the individual.[61] All notices should include a header that says: "THIS NOTICE DESCRIBES HOW

MEDICAL INFORMATION ABOUT YOU MAY BE USED AND DIS-CLOSED AND HOW YOU CAN GET ACCESS TO THIS INFORMATION. PLEASE REVIEW IT CAREFULLY."[62]

The notice should also include:

1. A description and example of the types of uses and disclosures that may be made for (a) treatment, (b) payment, and (c) health care operations
2. A description of other purposes for which releases may occur without authorization
3. A statement that all other uses will be made only with the individual's written authorization, and a statement that the individual may revoke an authorization
4. A statement providing notice of the individual's rights with respect to PHI, such as the right to request restrictions on its use (and the Entity's right to deny such requests, subject to limited exceptions), the right to inspect and make copies of the individual's own PHI, the right to amend PHI, the right to receive an accounting of disclosures, the right to a paper copy of electronic PHI records, and the right to receive confidential communications of PHI[63]

Requests for copies of PHI must be responded to in a timely manner and in no more than 30 days.[64] Entities must provide the individual access to his or her PHI in whatever medium the individual requests (e.g., electronically or via hard copy).[65] Entities may provide reasonable fees for the reproduction and labor costs of producing PHI.[66]

Right to an Accounting of PHI Disclosures: Within 60 days of the request, Entities must provide an "accounting" of all disclosures of an individual's PHI over the previous six years.[67] Among other limited exceptions, such an accounting is not required where the disclosure was:

1. For purposes of treatment, payment, or health care operations
2. To the individual
3. Pursuant to an authorization granted by the individual
4. For purposes of national security, intelligence, or to law enforcement officials[68]

For each disclosure within the six-year time frame, include:

1. The date, name of the Entity or person receiving the PHI, and, if known, the address
2. A description of the PHI disclosed
3. A statement of purpose of the disclosure[69]

C. Security

Securing PHI: While privacy provisions relate to maintaining the confidentiality of patient data, security pertains to the methods, strategies, tools, and processes used to ensure privacy. To secure PHI, Entities must protect against threats or hazards to the security or integrity of patient data, and they must protect against reasonably anticipated uses or disclosures that are not permitted.[70]

To accomplish these protections, safeguards must be in place. The specific protections will vary depending on the size, complexity, and capability of the Entity.[71] Additionally, the costs of security measures, technical capabilities, and the probability and criticality of potential risks are also factors.[72] This risk assessment is one of the most important aspects to gauge in designing your security program. When securing electronic PHI, organizations should consult the detailed guidance provided by the National Institute of Standards and Technology.[73] Whatever the safeguards identified, the security program should be paired with an extensive compliance Program with policies and procedures to avoid security breaches.

Systemic Protections: Entities must prevent, detect, contain, and correct security violations.[74] To better prevent ever-changing risks, periodic risk assessments should take place.[75] In the data security realm, new methods for incursion are a constant threat. Therefore, along with risk assessments, Entities should periodically update security and change passwords.[76] Moreover, passwords should be strong and kept confidential. Procedures should also be in place to guard against, detect, and report malicious software, and to monitor log-in attempts and report discrepancies.[77] Where security incidents occur, policies to react to the violation and thereby mitigate harmful effects while avoiding future incidents should also be in place.[78] Moreover, procedures should be delineated by which employees can report actual or suspected security incidents.

Security protection means, in part, preparing for the unknown. This can be almost anything—a hacking event, theft, even an act of nature. Whatever the event, an articulated plan to respond to emergencies should be in place.[79] Organizations should know how information will be protected and accessed in case of fire, vandalism, system failure, or any other damage to the system holding PHI or the facility housing the system.

Physical protections should accompany digital protections. Entities should outline which employees are able to access the facilities and systems in which PHI is housed. Procedures should control and validate those who are authorized to access the system.[80] In some circumstances, locks on doors, security officers, passcodes, and the like may be advisable.

Organizations can protect against unauthorized access by having automatic log-off systems, and by implementing encryption and decryption devices.[81] If information is released, be it accidentally or purposefully, encrypting the data helps to avoid the release of PHI and therefore may prevent a breach. Moreover, security mechanisms should be able to recognize whether PHI has been altered or destroyed in an unauthorized manner.[82]

It can be a challenge to find a balance between security of PHI and convenience of access. But adequate policies help ensure compliance with each of the above regulations. Moreover, the proper storage of PHI is essential. This may require restricting employees from openly discussing PHI, given that disclosures can occur verbally. Moreover, Entities should take a consistent approach to safely dispose of PHI (such as the shredding of hard copies and digital deletion for electronic copies).

HIPAA states that employees who fail to abide by the company's policies should be sanctioned.[83] As discussed elsewhere herein, the carrot-and-stick approach is optimum, and so incentives to uphold security and privacy integrity should also be in place.

What Is a Breach? A breach occurs when PHI is acquired, accessed, used, or disclosed in a manner not permitted *and* that compromises the security or privacy of the PHI.[84] Data breaches commonly occur through hacking; improper disposal of PHI; loss of electronic devices; theft of laptops, hard disks, and portable electronic devices; and unauthorized access. Note that a breach ordinarily does not occur if an employee, acting within the scope of employment, unintentionally accesses PHI but does not further release, use, or disclose it.[85]

Procedures in the Event of a Breach: Where a breach occurs, the Entity must contact the individual whose PHI was revealed. In certain circumstances, the Entity may also be required to contact media outlets and the secretary of HHS.

1. Individual: Where PHI has been, or is reasonably believed to have been, subject to a breach, the Entity must contact the individual without delay, and no more than 60 days after the discovery of the breach or after discovery should have occurred through reasonable diligence.[86] The notification must state, in plain language:

a. What happened
b. The date of discovery of the breach
c. The information breached (e.g, names, social security numbers, addresses, etc.)
d. Steps that the Entity has taken to protect PHI
e. What the Entity is doing about it, such as investigating, mitigating actions, and protecting from future breaches[87]

Additionally, the individual should receive contact information, including a toll-free number and, where appropriate an e-mail, physical address, or Web site to visit.[88] The individual should be notified by mail unless the Entity is expressly granted permission to contact via e-mail.[89] Where the breach is severe, however, the Entity may consider ensuring the message is received by the employee by also reaching out via e-mail, by phone, or in person, if appropriate. If unable to reach the individual for 10 days, then the Entity must post information regarding the breach on its Web site or in major media for a period of 90 days.[90]

2. Media: "Prominent media" within the state or jurisdiction must be notified within 60 days if more than 500 individuals within the state or jurisdiction are affected.[91] The same information as is required for the individual notice must be provided to the media.

3. Secretary of HHS: The secretary of HHS must be notified if more than 500 people are affected. The secretary will then post a notice on the HHS Web site.[92] For all breaches involving fewer than 500 people, Entities need not report immediately, but all breaches must be reported to the secretary of HHS on an annualized basis.[93]

Given these notification requirements, as well as employee dissatisfaction, breaches may result in significant reputational and financial burdens on Entities. It is only natural, then, that Entities may be tempted to avoid categorizing an incident as a "breach." Certainly, there may be ambiguity as to whether a breach has occurred. But Entities should take caution—the burden is on the Entity to prove that an incident was not a breach, and therefore that notice was not required.[94] Similarly, if a breach did occur, the burden is on the Entity to prove that all notices were properly given.[95] Therefore, at each step of the process, clear documentation, including the rationale behind decisions, should be set forth by each decision maker within the organization.

Compliance and Penalties: HIPAA subjects Entities to a "tiered culpability" structure, which gauges the degree to which the Entity was culpable. In essence, this evaluates whether the Entity was merely negligent or something worse. It also considers whether the violation was corrected within a 30-day period. A history of compliance, attempts to correct noncompliance, and responses to complaints are also considered.[96] For the worst violations under HIPAA, Entities face fines "in excess of $1.5 million."[97]

Entities are subject to strict time limitations under HIPAA, including: 30 days to provide copies to requesting employees, 60 days to report breaches, 60 days to provide accountings of disclosures, and 30 days to remedy violations and thereby mitigate monetary penalties. Moreover, Entities are expected to operate effectively at times of great misinformation or misunderstanding, such as in the immediate aftermath of natural disasters, thefts, and security breaches. Such responsiveness will not come intuitively. Instead, policies should clearly delineate the step-by-step process to be taken in each such contingency. These policies should filter down to all responsible employees. Real-world training, in which such calamities are simulated and responses practiced, should take place on a recurring basis.

Conclusion

The chapters in this book have frequently sourced the history of a particular regulation, often originating from public outrage. It may be that the world is in the midst of this history-making epoch as to data privacy. Ongoing concerns over data protection and numerous scandals at some of the world's largest corporations have brought the issue to the legislative forefront. The day may soon come in which federal law implements data privacy polices—indeed, European Union (EU) data privacy laws provide a ready-made shell for legislators. Those organizations that have already been acting to comply with data privacy protections under HIPAA will be most prepared to make a smooth and timely transition.

CHAPTER FOURTEEN

Fair Labor Standards Act

The Fair Labor Standards Act (FLSA) was passed in 1938 amid the economic horrors of the Great Depression.[1] The economy had been shrinking, and new hiring stalled as employers instead put working hours on the backs of fewer employees. This allowed those employers to save on the fixed costs associated with each employee, such as training and any benefits that might have been offered. The FLSA requires, inter alia, the payment of overtime wages. This made it costly to offer more hours to existing employees, which during the Depression was intended to provide the economic impetus to avoid paying overtime by instead hiring new employees. Though management griped, and the issue is far too complex and muddled to say how much of an effect this policy had on the eventual easing of the Depression, the fact is the law remains today one of America's labor law pillars.

Along with overtime wage requirements, the FLSA also sets a minimum wage requirement and limits the employment of children. The FLSA applies to all employees who work for employers with annual revenues of at least $500,000.[2] Individuals are also covered "if their work regularly involves them in commerce between States ('interstate commerce')."[3] With over 130 million American workers covered by the FLSA, most employees are covered by one or both of these inclusionary elements.[4]

This section sets forth minimum wage requirements, overtime pay, and child labor limitations, along with record-keeping requirements and best practices for FLSA compliance.

I. Minimum Wage

Employers subject to the FLSA are required to pay employees at least $7.25 per hour (as of January 2015).[5] Employers must also look to state laws, which may set higher rates than are required under Federal law. Alaska, Arizona,

California, Colorado, Connecticut, Delaware, District of Columbia, Florida, Illinois, Maine, Massachusetts, Michigan, Minnesota, Missouri, Montana, Nevada, New Jersey, New Mexico, New York, Ohio, Oregon, Rhode Island, Vermont, Washington, all have minimum wages above $7.25.[6] States cannot set a minimum wage below $7.25.

Employers may violate the minimum wage standard by improperly billing an employee's hours. For instance, employers may improperly consider employees "off the clock" when in fact the FLSA dictates workable hours. For more on calculating payable hours, see Section IV, below.

Moreover, employers cannot pay different wages to employees on the basis of gender. Consequently, employees doing equal work for jobs that require equal skill, effort, and responsibility must be paid the same wage.[7] The only exception to this rule is where disparate payments are the result of a seniority system, merit system, system in which earnings are set by quantity or quality of production, or some other reasonable differential.[8] Where employers are in violation of this rule, no employee may have wages lowered to conform to the opposite-sex employee's wage; instead, the lower-paid employee's wages must be raised to conform to the higher-paid opposite-sex employee.[9]

II. Child Labor

A. Overview

It should come as no surprise that "oppressive" child labor is prohibited. What may come as a surprise is that oppressive child labor means, with certain exceptions, the employment of anyone less than 16 years of age. Oppressive child labor also means the employment of children between the ages of 16 to 18 in any occupation that is particularly hazardous for the employment of children or detrimental to the health or well-being of that child, as determined by the Secretary of Labor.

However, employing 14- to 16-year-olds may be acceptable if it does not interfere with the schooling, health, or well-being of the child.[10] This means the child must work around school hours or on weekends and breaks. When school is not in session, children should not work more than 40 hours in any one week, or more than eight hours in any given day. On days when school is in session, children aged 14 to 16 should not work more than 18 hours in any one week, or more than three hours in any one day. Moreover, children shall not work before 7:00 a.m. or after 7:00 p.m., except from June 1 through Labor Day, when the evening hour extends until 9:00 p.m.

No child under 18 may work in an occupation deemed harmful to the health or well-being of the child. Such occupations include employment in manufacturing, mining, or occupations in workrooms where goods are manufactured; work in engine rooms or equipment areas; occupations involving the operation of power-driven machinery; and sales of most goods or services.[11] Employers can consult with DOL representatives to help ascertain whether a particular occupation is detrimental to the health or well-being of prospective child workers. Additionally, employers should consult state-specific laws to determine whether prohibitions on the employment of children apply.

B. Compliance

FLSA child labor prohibitions are commonly violated by miscalculating the number of hours a child has worked, thereby exceeding the work thresholds. Properly documenting hours worked is examined below in Section IV.

Another area of particular concern is the unwitting employment of a child. For instance, a child may present false identification or foreign nationals may have difficulty verifying birth dates. The secretary of labor offers employers a sort of safe harbor against this risk. If the employer has any reason to doubt the birth date of a worker, a DOL certificate can be obtained that affirms the young employee's birth date and employability. When the DOL has such a certificate on file, the employer will not be considered to be in violation of the "no oppressive child labor" prohibition regarding the age of the child, assuming compliance in all other areas.

Employers should follow DOL-specified directions to obtain such a certificate. However, the general rule is that employers, or the worker seeking to obtain employment, should send documentary evidence of birth to the DOL.[12] This is traditionally a birth certificate, passport, or a document that shows both a date of arrival in the United States and a birth date.

Employers are advised to obtain such certificates when a prospective employee appears particularly young, especially when a young worker's birth date cannot be verified to a high degree of certainty. Employers who employ a large number of young workers should be especially careful. At minimum, employers of young workers should engage in due diligence to verify dates of birth, and should have procedures for determining when red flags merit further actions.

III.   Overtime

A.   Overview

Notwithstanding children, there is no federal limit as to how many hours employees may work in any given week. However, employers must pay at least one and a half times the employee's regular rate of pay for each hour worked over 40 hours in any given week.[13] If an employer is in violation of the FLSA, an overtime violation is the most likely culprit. Back wages associated with overtime violations accounted for 88 percent of all FLSA back wages collected and 93 percent of all workers due FLSA back wages in 2008.[14]

An employee's "regular rate" includes all remuneration but not gifts, expense reimbursements, or payments made for short periods such as vacation, holiday, and illness.[15]

Though state law may require otherwise, federal law does not require overtime based on the number of hours worked in any day—such as more than 8 or 10 hours—nor is extra pay due for weekend or holiday work.

B.   Compliance

There are three basic reasons overtime provisions are so commonly violated.[16] One reason is inadequate record-keeping practices. Another reason pertains to misconceptions about what is compensable work time. These problems are analyzed in Section IV, below. But the other primary reason is that employees look for loopholes.

Some employers set hourly rates artificially with the intent of making the time-and-a-half rate low, and then pay bonuses to make up the difference in the low hourly pay. However, the regular rate of pay includes bonuses ("all remuneration"), and so this attempt comes to naught.

Similarly, employers cannot vary the rate of pay depending on hours worked. For instance, an employer who knows overtime is often required during summer months may specify in contracts that summer wages are lower than the rest of the year. This is prohibited, as the hourly rate paid for identical work must be standard.[17]

Employers may also try to provide a fixed annual salary to employees, rather than compensate on an hourly pay scale, so as to avoid overtime pay. With the exception of those exempt employees set forth in Section VI, this, too, is prohibited.[18]

Further, employers may not average hours worked across workweeks to determine overtime under this section. An employee who works 30 hours one week and 50 hours the next is due overtime in the second week, despite the fact that the hours worked average 40 over the two-week period.[19] Moreover, all overtime must be paid, even if the employee was not asked to work the overtime.

This section only provides some of the most common schemes. The DOL has overturned much more complex schemes than these. So employers beware (and, especially, beware of the tricks your supervisors may use unbeknownst to you): the DOL has decades of cumulative experience, and it knows how to spot a trick from a mile away.

IV.   The Challenge of Accurate Record Keeping: What Is "Time Worked"?

Correctly recording hours worked is foundational to compliance with this section. If hours worked are underrecorded, employers may be in violation of minimum wage requirements, in violation of overtime compensation, and/or in violation of child labor time limits. While determining whether time qualifies as compensable work may seem obvious, difficulties arise at the boundaries.

On Duty versus On Call: Employees who are on duty but not actually performing work are "on the clock." Think of a movie production. A cameraman may have dead time while waiting for a late actor's arrival. But as long as the cameraman is not free to pursue his own devices, he is on duty. This is true even if the employee is allowed to leave the premises.[20] Employees are only "off the clock" if they are told they can leave and return at a specified time,[21] with an interval sufficient to enable the employees to use their time effectively for their own purposes. To use an extreme example, if there is a slight delay at a work facility, employees cannot be told to go home for 15 minutes in order to get them off the clock.

Similarly, on-call workers are on the clock if they are required to remain on the employer's premises or so close to the premises as to be unable to use their time effectively. However, an on-call employee who is able to leave the premises but can be recalled via phone or e-mail is not on the clock.[22]

Rest Period versus Meal Time: Rest periods of five minutes to no more than 20 minutes are standard and, if provided, constitute paid working time. With one exception, the FLSA does not require the provision of rest periods, only the payment for those rest periods if they are offered.[23] Note that California, Colorado, Kentucky, Minnesota, Nevada, Oregon, and Washington do require paid rest periods for all employees.[24] If rest periods are offered, employers cannot force employees to substitute idle times (on duty but not performing work) as their rest periods.[25]

Just as rest periods are not required by the FLSA, neither are meal breaks required. However, 20 states, plus Guam and Puerto Rico, do require meal breaks.[26]

Under the FLSA, a "bona fide meal period" is not compensable. These are rest periods of 30 minutes or more in which the employee is completely relieved from duty to eat a meal. An employee is not relieved of duties if required to perform any duties while eating. This means that if employees are required to sit at their desks, perhaps to greet visitors or answer phones, they are on duty even if no visitors come and the phone stays quiet.[27]

Herein lies the problem: Some of a company's more devoted employees may wish to work at their desks. Others may return inside of 30 minutes. In both cases, those employees would be entitled to pay. Employers have a few options to deal with this.

If corporate policy is to provide noncompensable lunch breaks for employees, then employers may consider *requiring* that employees leave their work space and take at least 30 minutes for their meals.[28] A better option is for timekeeping systems to prohibit log-ins before the 30 minutes have expired, and use supervisors to ensure no work is done off the clock. This can be tricky, not to say awkward, in practice. The alternative is to decide whether employees are paid for meal breaks on a case-by-case basis—a challenge in and of itself. For all of these approaches, employers may require employee attestations in which the employee states whether any work was done during the unpaid break. If so, the employee may be paid but the employer will make clear this is a violation of policy. The attestation is also valuable documentation in the event the employee later claims he or she was cheated out of due pay.[29]

This might seem like small change, and not something to worry about. After all, an employee who eats at his or her desk is only entitled to 30 minutes of pay—maybe as little as $3.25 for a minimum-wage worker. But multiply this by 5 days a week, and then 50 weeks a year. Multiply that number by however many employees participate in this practice. Then add to the mix a plaintiff's attorney that, if successful, will recover *all* of his attorney's fees with as much as two times the amount of lost pay as back wages for the employees. The reality is that employers face enormous liability arising from simple meal breaks.[30]

To avoid this risk, some employers may decide to simply "buck up" and provide paid meal leaves. If that option is chosen, employers not only eliminate this particular risk, but also gain the benefit of their employees' goodwill. For those employers who are determined to permit only unpaid meal times, training managers to understand and comply with the above issues is essential.[31]

Employee Training: Ensure that supervisors understand how these requirements work in practice. Oftentimes, supervisors will understandably refuse to pay for unauthorized overtime, or "working" lunch breaks, particularly where the employee was actually forbidden from working during that time. Alternatively, supervisors may try to cut corners to meet budgetary goals or impress upper management. Supervisors should understand their limits, and should understand how to encourage compliance with internal policies, short of docking pay in violation of the FLSA.

Nonexempt employees should also be trained with a focus on properly recording their hours worked. It should be clarified that they are not expected to (indeed, not permitted to) work without pay. For example, some employers have payroll integrity policies that forbid falsifying time records and working off the clock.[32] Employers should provide ways in which employees can report violations—such as a supervisor's demand that they work overtime without adequate compensation—free of retaliation. In the event there is a violation, such training will help show a good faith attempt at compliance, which reduces the likelihood of being forced to pay double the back pay.[33]

Along with education and training, organizations must develop policies and procedures to ensure compliance with these provisions. Each organization will take a different approach—do you punish employees who return from lunch early? Do you allow overtime? Do you have children under 18 working at your facility? These are fact-specific questions that should be responsive to each organization's own business practices, strategy, and employee culture. Whatever policies are ultimately implemented, employers should propagate those written policies to employees and supervisors alike, and include during training sessions a review of those policies.

V.　Record Keeping

The DOL has authority to review an employer's records.[34] For each employee, employers must retain a record showing:

1. Name in full
2. Home address
3. Date of birth if under 19
4. Sex and occupation in which employed
5. Time of day and day of week (e.g., Monday) on which the employee's work-week begins

6. Regular hourly rate of pay for any workweek in which overtime compensation is due, and the amount and nature of each payment that is excluded from the "regular rate" (e.g., employee reimbursements, gifts, etc.)
7. Hours worked each workday and total hours worked each workweek
8. Total daily or weekly straight-time earnings or wages due for hours worked during the workday or workweek, exclusive of premium overtime compensation
9. Total premium pay for overtime hours
10. Total additions to or deductions from wages paid each pay period
11. Total wages paid each pay period
12. Date of payment and the pay period covered by payment

Additionally, where employees make retroactive payments, such as after discovering a timekeeping error, further record-keeping requirements apply.[35]

Payroll records and most other records should be retained for three years. Some records need only be retained for a minimum of two years.[36]

VI. Exempt Employees

Exempt employees are not subject to the minimum wage and overtime requirements. Here, mischaracterizing an employee as exempt is the primary risk facing employees. While it is possible that a mischaracterization will result in minimum wage violations, the most common issues pertain to violations of the overtime provisions.

The exemption applies to "bona fide" executives, administrative workers, professionals, outside salespersons, and computer-oriented workers.[37] An employee's title or position is not enough to make that employee exempt. Instead, employees are exempt if they perform specific duties and receive a minimum level of compensation, as specified below.

A. Types of Exempt Employees

Bona Fide Executive.
Compensation: At least $455 per week
The primary duties of the employee must be the management of the organization or a department or subdivision thereof, in which the employee regularly directs the work of two or more full-time[38] employees; and "who has the authority to hire or fire other employees or whose suggestions and recommendations as to the hiring, firing, advancement, promotion, or other change of status of other employees are given particular weight."[39]

Alternatively, executives include those with at least a 20 percent equity interest in the organization in which the employee is employed and in which the employee is "actively engaged in its management."[40]

Administrative Employee.

Compensation: At least $455 per week

The primary duties of the employee must be the "performance of office or non-manual work directly related to the management or general business operations of the employer or the employer's customers." The primary duties must also include "the exercise of discretion and independent judgment with respect to matters of significance."[41] Merely working in an office, rather than on a production or sales floor, is not enough.[42]

Whether one exercises "independent judgment and discretion as to matters of significance" is often at the heart of the determination. The DOL provides examples. These include, but are not limited to:

- authority to formulate, affect, interpret, or implement management policies or operating practices
- carrying out major assignments in conducting operations of the business
- authority to commit the employer in matters of significant financial impact
- ability to waive or deviate from established policies and procedures without approval
- authority to negotiate and bind the company on significant matters
- providing consultation or expert advice to management
- involvement in planning long- or short-term business objectives
- investigating and resolving matters of significance on behalf of management
- representing the company in handling complaints, arbitrating disputes, or resolving grievances.[43]

Examples of administrative workers include insurance adjusters, financial services employees, executive assistants, HR managers, purchasing agents, academic instructors, and project managers. [44]

Professional Employees.

Compensation: At least $455 per week.

The primary duties of the employee must include "the performance of work: Requiring knowledge of an advanced type in a field of science or learning customarily acquired by a prolonged course of specialized intellectual instruction; *or* Requiring invention, imagination, originality or talent in a recognized field of artistic or creative endeavor."[45]

The "knowledge of an advanced type" requirement restricts this exemption to those professions in which specialized training—such as law school for lawyers—is the standard requirement for employment in the profession. However, the use of the word "customarily" is to signal that not every employee within the said profession need have such academic credentials. For example, a lawyer who did not go to law school and a chemist without a chemistry degree may still qualify as professionals.[46]

Examples of exempt professional workers with this "knowledge of an advanced type" include, among others, medical technicians, nurses, dental hygienists, physician assistants, accountants, lawyers, chefs, paralegals, and practitioners of medicine.[47]

The second type of exempt professional is one involved in "creative endeavors." Creativity means something original, as distinguished from "work which can be produced by a person with general manual or intellectual ability and training."

Examples of creative professionals include actors, musicians, composers, conductors, and essayists, among others.[48]

Computer Employees.

Compensation: Computer employees may be eligible as professionals, in which case compensation must be at least $455 per week.

If, however, the employee does not qualify as a professionally exempt employee, then a cornucopia of duties—including programming, design, analysis, and more—may qualify that employee as a computer-exempt employee.[49] To so qualify, payment must also be at least $27.63 per hour.

Outside Sales Employees.

Compensation: No minimum salary is set for outside sales employees.[50]

These employees' primary duties must be making sales and obtaining orders or contracts, and doing so while regularly engaged at a place other than the employer's place of business.[51] Indeed, the sale may not take place at any fixed place of the employer or employee, but must instead occur at the customer's place of business, a mutually agreed-upon meeting place, or at the customer's home.[52] Therefore, sales people who primarily work through the use of mail, telephone, or Internet are not exempt salespeople.[53]

Highly Compensated Employees.

Employees whose total annual compensation is at least $100,000 are exempt from this section as long as they ordinarily perform any one or more of the exempt duties of an executive, administrator, or professional employee. Thus, this exception would apply where the highly compensated worker does not primarily perform the duties of any one exempt worker but instead regularly performs some combination of exempt duties.

B. Compliance

Mischaracterizations: The mischaracterization of employees' positions often leads to a false sense of compliance. Employers may label workers as exempt in order to avoid overtime payments. Title inflation also contributes to the problem, in which workers are given highfalutin titles that do not necessarily correlate to work performed.[54] But, as stated above, titles, while perhaps instructive, are insufficient determinations of exempt status.

Too many employees merely engage in a cursory analysis.[55] What is needed is an analysis in which the employee's duties are carefully considered to ensure conformance with the above requirements. Such duties should then be codified to reflect the responsibilities for all such persons in that position. It should be ensured that the individual auditing the job classification is not the same person who initially created the classification system.[56] This individual has an incentive to paper over issues so as to avoid criticism. To increase the likelihood of correctly classifying an employee, consider performance evaluations in which the activities and responsibilities that support the exempt status are specifically considered.[57] This thereby serves as a built-in, continuous audit. When completing the employee evaluation and when auditing job classifications, all records and documents relating to those efforts should be retained as evidence of best efforts to comply.[58]

In many cases, employees completing such audits find mistakes. By alerting the employee, the organization risks inviting the very lawsuit that the audit was meant to avoid. Some commentators therefore suggest contacting the DOL at this point and self-reporting.[59] The DOL has the authority, as individuals do not, to negotiate a comprehensive settlement.[60] Others may decide to simply go straight to the employee. Though the employee could still opt to bring a lawsuit, by admitting the mistake and paying back wages employers can lessen the incentive to bring a lawsuit.[61]

In any event, once a mistake is found, it is not going anywhere. Failing to correct the issue simply invites the assertion of malicious underpayment, thereby increasing possible penalties. Equity and business alike would thus compel organizations to deal with these issues upon discovery.

To determine the method of resolution, employees uncovering such mistakes may consider consulting an FLSA attorney. Additionally, the DOL offers an anonymous telephone line by which employers can seek guidance as to the repercussions of a self-report.

Improper Deductions: Employers must pay exempt employees their full salary for any given week in which work is performed. Employers may lose the exemption if there are improper deductions from salary of otherwise exempt employees.[62] Improper deductions would include reducing pay for working a partial day or reducing pay for inferior work performance.

2004 FLSA revisions provide a "safe harbor" for employers that:

i.   Clearly communicate a policy prohibiting improper deductions and including a complaint mechanism
ii. Reimburse employees for any improper deductions
iii. Make a good faith commitment to comply in the future
iv. Do not willfully violate the policy by continuing the improper deductions after receiving employee complaints[63]

Under certain conditions, deductions *may* be permissible for missing entire days of work, to conform to unpaid leave grants under the FMLA, and in accordance with sickness policies.[64] Consequently, any salary deductions should be vetted for permissibility, and periodic audits should review past deductions to ensure conformity with the rules.

Conclusion

Everyone from lowest-level employees to highest officers should understand obligations under FLSA. If workers understand why they are being asked to comply with procedures for lunch breaks, for example, they are more likely to do so. Similarly, if supervisors understand that payroll deductions and unpaid overtime should not be in their arsenal of disciplinary tools, they too are more likely to remain both compliant and effective in their positions. Lastly, tone at the top is no less important in the area of labor law than in any other area of compliance. Indeed, showing a commitment to pay employees what they are due is an opportunity to communicate an organization's culture of integrity and ethics.

CHAPTER FIFTEEN

The Environmental Protection Act and Amnesty Provisions

Organizations are subject to a complex matrix of environmental laws and regulations. The EPA enforces more than 30 statutes, has a staff of 17,000 employees, and, with a $55.9 billion budget, it is the federal government's largest regulatory agency.[1] Moreover, environmental laws vary greatly between states. The federal government sets standards for environmental compliance. However, most states are authorized to carry out the over 4,500 rules issued by the EPA.[2] States also often exceed the standards set forth by the federal government.[3]

Certain organizations and industries are subject to more environmental compliance risks than others. Heavy manufacturers, power plants, and chemical plants are clear examples. Determining which laws apply to each organization requires identifying and consulting with the regulatory agency implementing federal law in the states in which the organization operates, as well as ensuring compliance with any municipal environmental laws. In Idaho, Massachusetts, New Hampshire, Washington, D.C., and Puerto Rico, no state or local agency is authorized to enforce EPA statutes, and therefore federal regulators are the authorized individuals. However, state promulgated rules may still apply. Consulting with the relevant regulators is essential for determining an organization's legal obligations. Additionally, industry trade manuals and association groups are often helpful sources of information regarding environmental compliance.

This chapter examines the major environmental regulations—the Clean Air Act (CAA) and the Clean Water Act (CWA)—as well as amnesty provisions related to violations of EPA regulations.

I.   Clean Air Act (CAA)

The CAA was passed amid public outrage at horrific, crippling, and even deadly scenes of pollution. In 1963, the CAA established funding for the study and cleanup of air pollution. A much stronger version of this act was passed in 1970, the year of the EPA's birth. In 1990, the CAA was again expanded.[4]

The CAA is complex and voluminous. In 1970, the law consisted of 50 pages. With the 1990 amendments, it expanded to 800 pages, with 538 specific requirements for new rules, standards, and reports.[5] Broadly speaking, however, the CAA requires the EPA to set national standards for air pollutants.

To do this, the EPA distinguishes between attainment areas, where the air is cleaner than the primary standard calls for, and nonattainment areas, which are below standard. In nonattainment areas, the EPA works with states to develop State Implementation Plans (SIP) to reduce air pollutants to the required level. The states then use a permit system to ensure that polluting sources meet the levels required.[6]

The EPA describes the permit system as follows:

> Operating permits include information on which pollutants are being released, how much may be released, and what kinds of steps the source's owner or operator is required to take to reduce the pollution. Permits must include plans to measure and report the air pollution emitted. Operating permits are especially useful for businesses covered by more than one part of the Clean Air Act and additional state or local requirements, since information about all of a source's air pollution is in one place.[7]

Whether an organization needs a permit depends, in part, on whether it operates in a nonattainment area. Organizations may seek advice from state regulators to determine their obligations. If a permit is required, organizations must follow specific directions to obtain the permit.[8]

The most prominent of the standards to control pollution apply to what are known as "criteria pollutants." These consist of six heavily regulated substances, including carbon monoxide, nitrogen dioxide, sulfur dioxide, ozone molecules, particulate matter, and lead. Private businesses emit 47 percent of all criteria pollutants.[9] For each pollutant, the EPA sets a standard for the maximum permissible concentration of the substance.[10] Therefore, as a first step, organizations should determine whether they release these substances in any amount in the course of operations.

Carbon monoxide may be produced by fuels such as gasoline. Nitrogen dioxide comes mainly from vehicle exhaust and fuel combustion.[11] Sulfur dioxide comes from the burning of fossil fuels, and two-thirds of sulfur dioxide is emitted by electric utilities burning coal and oil.[12] Ozone molecules are indirectly emitted by compounds, including petroleum fuels, solvents, paints, adhesives, pesticides and waxes.[13] One-half of all ozone molecules are emitted by private industry.[14] Particulate matters come from coal-burning power plants, as well as diesel exhausts. Of the pollutants, particulates pose the greatest risk of adverse health effects.[15] Organizations should therefore devote special attention to determining whether they discharge particulate matter and, if so, to managing that discharge. Lead, the last of the criteria pollutants and the least-prevalent today, is primarily discharged by lead smelters and battery plants.[16]

Beyond these criteria pollutants, the EPA regulates 650 other air toxics. Twenty percent of such discharges are released by electric utilities, oil refineries, chemical plants, steel mills, and paper plants. Vehicles discharge 41 percent.[17]

II. Clean Water Act (CWA)

The Federal Water Pollution Control Act, the predecessor to the CAA, became law in 1948. But in 1969, the Cuyahoga River, just outside of Cleveland, burned. With it burned the righteous indignation of a population watching as its waterways became ever more polluted. Songs were written about the flaming waters, *Time* covered the story, and, once again, the public was inflamed to demand action. Amendments to the act in 1972 saw the birth of the CWA, and the gradual, if incomplete, cleansing of the country's waters.

The CWA requires a permit where there is the release of a polluted factory discharge, otherwise known as an effluent, into a U.S. waterway.[18] This permit is administered by the National Pollution Discharge Elimination System (NPDES) permit program, and it regulates effluents from a single point source, that is, the point where the discharge originates from a single location. The permit is required only if the pollutant directly enters the "waters of the United States." For pollutants entering indirectly, such as through publicly owned treatment works (POTWs), the National Pretreatment Program sets its own standards.

What Is a Pollutant? The term "pollutant" is defined very broadly by the NPDES regulations and case law and includes any type of industrial, municipal, and agricultural waste discharged into water. For regulatory purposes, pollutants have been grouped into three categories.

Conventional pollutants[19] include:

- five-day biochemical oxygen demand (BOD)
- total suspended solids (TSS)
- pH
- fecal coliform
- oil and grease (O&G)

Toxic/priority pollutants[20] include:

- metals
- man-made organic compounds

Nonconventional pollutants are all other pollutants, and include:

- ammonia
- nitrogen
- phosphorus
- chemical oxygen demand (COD)
- whole effluent toxicity (WET)

What Are "Waters of the United States"? The EPA interprets waters of the United States broadly to include all waters within federal jurisdiction. The definition consists of virtually all surface waters in the United States, including navigable waters and tributaries thereof, interstate waters, and most intrastate lakes, rivers, and streams.[21]

Obligations of Permittees: NPDES permittees must comply with self-monitoring requirements that are periodically subject to verification by inspectors.[22] State regulators typically enforce the NPDES provisions on behalf of the EPA.[23] Record keeping is central to compliance with the NPDES and the permit will specify the types of records that must be retained. These records may include, among others, documentation of sampling and analysis data, monitoring records, laboratory records, facility-operating records, treatment-plant records, management records, pretreatment records, and risk-management plans.[24] Where records are erroneous or appear incomplete, investigators have cause to engage in a more in-depth investigation.[25] Broadly stated, records should be current, up-to-date, and should evidence compliance with the permit conditions.[26]

Additionally, policies and procedures should reflect the requirements under the NPDES permit. The EPA says that an operations manual is "the most important" part of the inspector's review of policies and procedures.[27]

Inspectors will consider "the abilities and limitations of the operating staff" when evaluating NPDES compliance.[28] Consequently, the organization should train appropriate members of its workforce to comply with

NPDES standards. Investigators may consider whether there is an adequate number of staff to fulfill its mission. They may also look for relevant certifications to determine whether staff is qualified for its role. Whether training takes place for new staff, new operators, or new supervisors, and whether continuing training takes place, are relevant factors as well.[29]

Lastly, the EPA, in effect, reviews the tone at the top. Investigators are advised to consider whether management is a motivating force; whether supervisors have managerial support; and whether training operations are encouraged and supported by management; as well as job security, promotional opportunities, and the work environment generally.[30] The EPA apparently recognizes that these indirect factors, including employee morale, affect overall staff compliance.

Nonpoint effluent, or runoff that enters the water from various locations, is essentially uncontrolled. Nonetheless, the EPA has discretion to regulate any source of water pollution under the CWA.[31] Accordingly, any organization that pollutes is potentially subject to EPA oversight, and should take steps to comply with any standards set by the EPA under the CAA, the CWA, or any other statutes enforced by the EPA, the states, or municipalities.

III. Amnesty

Perhaps it is this complexity of environmental law that resulted in the federal government's administration of an extensive amnesty program. But it may also reflect the severity of punishments under the EPA along with heavy enforcement. The EPA amnesty program is formally known as "Incentives for Self-Policing: Discovery, Disclosure, Correction and Prevention of Violations." Informally, the program is referred to as the "Audit Policy." Though most states enforce environmental policies on behalf of the EPA, many states have similar penalty-mitigation policies in these federally authorized or approved programs.[32]

Additionally, small businesses may apply for amnesty under the more liberal Small Business Regulatory Enforcement Fairness Act (SBREFA). A small business is an entity that employs 100 or fewer individuals.[33] Amnesty requirements under SBREFA are less stringent and easier to apply for.[34] Therefore, small businesses may consider self-reporting through this mechanism rather than through the Audit Policy.

For both amnesty provisions, the "incentives" to self-police and ultimately to self-report include the potential for a "substantial reduction" or even elimination of civil penalties. Moreover, for those qualifying under the Policy, the EPA is unlikely to recommend criminal prosecution to the

DOJ for potential criminal violations.[35] The EPA may, however, recommend the prosecution of culpable individuals when those individuals are involved with (or willfully blind to) violations, engage in a cover-up, or otherwise condone noncompliant activities.[36]

Lastly, the Audit Policy "restates EPA's long-standing policy" that, where audits are voluntarily undertaken by organizations, the EPA will not request those audit reports, nor use the reports against organizations. However, those reports (and much other pertinent information) are fair game if the EPA already has independent evidence of a violation.[37]

Organizations must meet nine conditions to qualify for a 100 percent reduction of the gravity-based penalties[38] otherwise applicable to a violation. Where the first condition is not met but the other eight conditions are met, organizations are eligible for a 75% reduction of those gravity-based penalties.[39] Moreover, criminal prosecution will not be recommended where conditions two through nine are met, "as long as its self-policing, discovery and disclosure were conducted in good faith and the entity adopts a systematic approach to preventing recurrence of the violation."[40]

Systematic Discovery through Environmental Audits or Due Diligence: The first condition under the Audit Policy is the systematic discovery of violations through "an environmental audit or a compliance management system that reflects the entity's due diligence in preventing, detecting and correcting violations."[41] As with any regulatory issue, not all violations will be discovered through audits. However, the burden is on the organization to document its due diligence activities.

Where a violation is discovered by means other than an audit, the organization should be able to show how its Program led to the revelation.[42] For example, if an individual uncovers a violation, the organization may point to systematic training that taught the individual to recognize red flags and provided the mechanism to report up the organizational chain. The EPA is explicit that the factors of an effective Program set forth by the FSGO are illustrative of whether due diligence is sufficient.[43]

These factors include sufficient record keeping, which means up-to-date information, the retention of all records required to comply with the organization's regulatory obligations, and any records pertaining to testing for compliance and maintenance of systems or machinery.[44] Organizations' policies and procedures, especially for highly regulated companies and permit holders under the CWA or CAA, should be formalized and should directly refer to the companies' standards established to remain compliant. Policies may also refer to process and quality controls, preventative maintenance, and more.[45] The organization should be sufficiently staffed to uphold all compliance requirements to which the organization is held, with adequate training to ensure all relevant staff understands its responsibilities.[46]

Voluntary Discovery: A violation must be discovered by the internal processes of the organization, rather than in response to an investigation or claim. Stated differently, the organization will not be eligible for the Audit Policy if the investigation and discovery occur only after outside parties have initiated their own investigation, or otherwise indicated to the organization that an investigation is pending. Nor is the Audit Policy available if a regulator required the organization to undertake an audit of its activities.

Some violations, once discovered, must be reported to regulators due to health and safety concerns. But just because the decision to *report* is mandatory does not mean that the organization fails to meet the voluntary discovery requirement. "Voluntary discovery" refers to the actions taken to uncover the violation, even if, once found, reporting the violation is mandatory, rather than voluntary.[47]

What constitutes a "voluntary discovery" is more liberally interpreted under the small business policy.[48] For example, small businesses remain eligible for SBREFA if a violation is discovered in coordination with government-sponsored on-site compliance assistance activities.[49]

Prompt Disclosure: After the revelation of the violation, organizations must self-report within 21 days, unless the statute or regulation at issue specifies a shorter reporting period. For instance, the unpermitted release of hazardous substances must be reported immediately.[50] If the organization suspects that its investigation will not be complete within the 21-day deadline, then it should seek an extension from the appropriate EPA office *prior* to the deadline.[51]

The 21-day period begins when the violation or potential violation is discovered. A discovery occurs when an employee or agent has what an objective, similarly informed individual would consider a reasonable basis for believing the violation did or may have occurred, or is occurring.[52]

Disclosure should be made to the relevant EPA regional office. Where the violation implicates multiple regional offices, organizations are advised to report directly to EPA headquarters.[53]

Discovery and Disclosure Independent of the Government or a Third-Party Plaintiff: The organization itself must discover the violation. Thus, amnesty is unavailable if a government investigator, or a plaintiff's attorney who is engaged in discovery, uncovers a violation. Indeed, the violation must be discovered before another party likely would have identified the problem through its own investigative work or from other information at hand. Thus, an organization cannot suddenly "uncover" violations once an investigation or legal discovery commences, or after a citizens group gives notice of intent to sue, even if those investigations have not yet led to the revelation of violations.[54]

If, however, a multiple-facility operation is under investigation at one of its facilities, the EPA may still grant credit if violations are subsequently discovered by the organization at different facilities than the one under investigation.[55]

Correction and Remediation: The harm caused by violations must be remediated within 60 days from the date of discovery, or as soon as possible if 60 days is unreasonable.[56] If the organization requires more than 60 days, it must provide notice in writing to the agency prior to the 60-day deadline.[57] Upon remediation, the organization must certify in writing to the appropriate authorities that the harm was corrected.[58]

Under SBREFA, organizations have 90 days to correct the violation. However, if 90 days is unreasonable, small businesses may submit a written schedule certifying the process to correct the violation within 180 days.[59] Small businesses have 360 days to correct violations involving pollution-prevention modifications.[60]

Prevent Recurrence: After discovery, notification, and remediation, the organization must act to prevent a recurrence of the violation. The organization should analyze the causes of the violation and take steps to ensure the violation is a one-time-only misdeed. This may include improvements to the audit system, increased training, or stricter oversight.[61]

No Repeat Violations: Amnesty is unavailable if the same or a similar violation occurred within the same facility in the past three years. Where the organization has multiple facilities, no identical or similar violations may have occurred at any one of its other facilities within the preceding five years. A "violation" has previously occurred under the Audit Policy where the act is subject to federal, state, or local judicial or administrative orders, consent agreements, convictions, or plea agreements, as well as any act for which the organization previously received a penalty reduction. Stated otherwise, a violation has occurred previously if the organization knew of its noncompliance from previous experience and therefore missed its opportunity to remedy the problem.[62]

Other Violations Excluded: Where the violation resulted in serious actual harm to the environment or presented serious and imminent risks to the public health, amnesty is unavailable. However, as of the time of this writing, the EPA has never invoked this clause to deny amnesty for a disclosure, suggesting that the standard for a serious violation is very high.[63]

Cooperation: Following discovery and reporting, the organization must fully cooperate with the EPA. This includes the affirmative duty to provide requested information to the EPA, including such information as is required to determine the applicability of this Audit Policy. It also forbids destroying or tampering with evidence pertaining to the violation.[64]

Conclusion

Complying with the environmental laws of the United States is no easy task. Organizations must look to a bevy of federal, state, and municipal laws. The precise obligations of organizations are likely to vary. This variation is dependent on the type of permit obtained, if any, and the amount and type of pollution borne by the organization. But complying with environmental law is not so different from compliance with any other area of the law. It requires understanding one's obligations, putting strict standards and procedures in place to conform to those obligations, and training one's workforce to perform in accordance with those standards and procedures.

CHAPTER SIXTEEN

Antitrust Compliance

Repeatedly throughout this book the origin of laws has been attributed to public scandals, the arousal of popular anger, and the eventual action of Congress to legislate. Antitrust law is not different. The story is just older.

In 1890, the first of the U.S. antitrust laws was passed in the wake of industrialists' ever-increasing market power. Perhaps the best known "trust bust" was of John D. Rockefeller's Standard Oil Company. The company was broken up into separate companies which eventually became competitors, as intended by the antitrust law. The continuing influence of Standard Oil's successor companies (ExxonMobil, Socony, Chevron, Amoco and many others) bear witness to the lengths to which Standard Oil—famously depicted as an octopus strangling all other life forms—had grown.

The premise behind antitrust laws is that when companies obtain the market power like that of a Standard Oil, customers quite literally pay the price as a result of the lack of competition.[1] Michael Keating, vice-president and associate general counsel–litigation and product safety for Emerson Electric Company, says: "By preserving a competitive economy, the free enterprise system can best deliver quality products and services to the consuming public. Antitrust laws seek to accomplish this goal by preventing the unfair abuse of market power."[2] But antitrust laws do not prohibit companies from growing large, or even from monopolizing. Instead, the prohibition applies to *unreasonable* restraints of trade.[3]

Industries in which market power is centralized with a few companies or one company are susceptible to antitrust actions. Government contractors and, more generally, any companies that bid on contracts for products or services, operate in high-risk areas. Moreover, high-value mergers and acquisitions receive additional scrutiny. Nonetheless, cases have been brought against a wide range of industries.[4]

Keating warns that "penalties for violation of this complex body of laws are vast and significant, ranging from imprisonment and fines, court injunctions, Federal Trade Commission (FTC) orders limiting a company or individual's freedom of action, divestiture of a business (or a portion thereof), treble damages, disgorgement of profits, and the imposition of costs and attorneys' fees."[5] Companies are subject to civil penalties and criminal penalties, which may be brought by the DOJ, FTC, state attorney generals (AGs), or private parties. The DOJ traditionally handles criminal antitrust suits, in which companies face fines of $100 million or up to twice the gain or loss involved, and individuals face up to 10 years in prison.[6] Most states have their own antitrust laws but, additionally, state AGs are authorized to bring federal suits on behalf of injured consumers within their own states.[7] Private parties also may sue on their own behalf, and with the opportunity to recover treble damages, private parties are provided a golden opportunity to assert antitrust violations.[8]

Because antitrust investigations most commonly originate from complaints received by consumers or those within the organization,[9] compliance policies to prevent and detect violations are essential. This is all the more true given amnesty provisions that, if specified conditions are met, will provide amnesty to the first (and only the first) company that reports an antitrust violation among competitors.[10]

There are three primary federal antitrust acts in the United States: (1) the Sherman Act of 1890, used against Rockefeller's Standard Oil; (2) the Federal Trade Commission (FTC) Act; and, (3) the Clayton Act.[11] The Supreme Court has held that all violations of the Sherman Act also violate the FTC Act, thereby subjecting companies and individuals to a separate set of risks. Additionally, most states have their own antitrust laws.

Although beyond the purview of this writing, antitrust is now entrenched in the global litigation arena as well, with laws promulgated by foreign governments and the European Union.[12] These are generally known as competition laws. Consequently, companies with global operations must take a stand to prevent antitrust violations in all of their global forms.

I. Sherman Act

The Sherman Antitrust Act is the "principal law" evincing the United States' commitment to an unrestrained free market.[13] Section one of the act prohibits "every contract, combination or conspiracy in restraint of trade," and section two prohibits "any monopolization, attempted monopolization, and conspiracy or combination to monopolize."[14] Whereas section two contemplates unilateral actions, section one applies to agreements with other parties. However, section one violations can occur without written agreements, such as oral or even implicit agreements.

Not all restraints of trade are illegal. The litmus test is whether the restraint is unreasonable. However, agreements to fix prices, divide markets, or rig bids are by definition unreasonable, and thus "per se" illegal. This means that no argument may be made that the restraint is reasonable and thus legal. Notwithstanding per se illegal agreements, all other agreements are subject to the "rule of reason" test, in which the analysis is whether the agreement in question increases the ability to raise prices or reduce output, quality, or services beyond that which would prevail in the absence of the agreement.[15]

Section one restraints of trade may be "vertical" or "horizontal." A horizontal restraint takes place between actual or potential customers.[16] Vertical restraints take place between firms at different levels of a supply chain, such as that of a manufacturer and supplier.[17]

A.   Horizontal Restraints: Dealing with Customers

Competitors often (legitimately) interact with one another through trade associations, joint ventures, standard setting organizations, and more. Typically, these do not result in antitrust violations. However, these interactions present risk. "Facets of the competitive landscape such as price, service, product features, discounts, and credit terms are all to be arrived at through the independent bargaining process and not through the landscape of collusive behavior among competitors," Keating says. "Two simple rules will help ensure compliance with this complex area of law that governs our relationship with a competitor: act unilaterally, and act independently."[18]

Prohibited arrangements between competitors include price-fixing, bid rigging, market division and customer allocation, group boycotts, and agreements to restrict advertisements, among others.

1. Price-fixing: Companies are required to set their own prices.[19] Price-fixing occurs when competitors jointly agree to raise, lower, or stabilize prices or terms. Examples of price-fixing include those agreements to:

a. establish or adhere to price discounts
b. hold prices firm
c. eliminate or reduce discounts
d. adopt a standard formula for computing prices
e. maintain price differentials between different types, sizes, or quantities of product

f. adhere to a minimum fee or price schedule
g. fix credit terms
h. not advertise prices[20]

2. Bid Rigging: Bid rigging may occur when a business that is awarded a contract by successfully soliciting a competitive bid coordinates its bid with competitors.[21] Bid-rigging conspiracies include:

a. *Bid Suppression*: A competitor who would otherwise bid refrains from bidding so that the designated winning competitor's bid is accepted.
b. *Complementary Bidding*: Competitors submit inflated bids or bids with special terms that will be rejected, but give the appearance of a competitive bid.
c. *Bid Rotation*: Conspirators submit bids but take turns as the low bidder.
d. *Subcontracting*: Competitors who agree not to bid or to submit a losing bid are given subcontracts or supply contracts from the winning bidder.[22]

3. Market Division and Customer Allocation: This manifests itself in competitors dividing sales territories or assigning customers to one another.[23] This is, in essence, an agreement to limit competition.

4. Group Boycotts: Ordinarily, companies may individually agree to not do business with another firm. However, violations may occur where competitors agree to not do business with targeted individuals or businesses, especially if the competitors possess market power.[24] Boycotts may also be designed to prevent new entrants from gaining access to the market.[25]

B. Vertical Dealings

Vertical dealings may include agreements between manufacturers and suppliers or manufacturers and dealers, as well as any other actors at different levels of the supply chain.[26] Vertical restraints are not per se illegal and, Keating says, "are governed by more subtle prohibitions than exist between competitors."[27] These restraints are analyzed by balancing legitimate benefits and justifications against harmful competitive effects.[28] Vertical arrangements include manufacturer-imposed requirements, exclusive dealings or requirements contracts, and refusals to supply.

1. Manufacturer-Imposed Requirements: Manufacturers may restrict a buyer from selling the product above or below a certain price, or they may limit the territory in which the product may be sold or the customers to whom the buyer can sell. These requirements are all legal, just as long as they are reasonable. For instance, in order to ensure a market for its goods, manufacturers may require that buyers set a ceiling (or a floor) on the prices they will charge. However, antitrust issues may arise if *all* manufacturers in a given area jointly agree to force their buyers to abide by that ceiling (or floor). Such a step is simply an indirect form of price-fixing. Similarly, suppliers or dealers of the manufacturer may unreasonably act together to induce or coerce a manufacturer to implement such restraints.[29] And, says Keating, "While a manufacturer can suggest minimum resale prices, no coercive pressure can be brought to bear."[30]

2. Exclusive Dealings or Requirements: This agreement prevents the buyer of goods from selling the products of a different manufacturer. Alternatively, it may prevent the manufacturer from buying the inputs of a different supplier. These are quite common and, ordinarily, are legal. Such agreements allow merchants to specialize in a certain area and provide an incentive to train salespeople on the particular product—think of a Nike shoe store or a GM dealership. Such an agreement may be paired with a price floor for the product, so that customers don't take a "free ride" on the higher level of knowledge at the specialty store and then purchase the product more cheaply elsewhere.[31] However, such agreements can be used in an anticompetitive manner. For example, if a dominant actor requires all of its customers to only sell its own products, then exclusive contracts may be used to deny a competitor access to the market by limiting that competitor's access to retailers.[32]

3. Refusal to Supply: As noted above, businesses generally have the right to choose with whom they do business. However, a refusal to supply may be illegal if the purpose is to acquire or maintain a monopoly, or if done in coordination with competitors to retain market positions.[33]

C.   Single Firm Conduct: Monopolization

Section two of the Sherman Act applies to monopolies and attempted monopolization of a market. A monopoly exists when only one firm controls the market for a product or service.[34] It is not illegal to have a monopoly, but the organization must legitimately form and maintain the monopoly. Examples of legitimate monopolies include those where products or services are unique, and where companies obtain a monopolistic position through prudent, even aggressive, business decisions. Illegal monopolies are those in which the market power is obtained not because of a superior product or service, but because of the unreasonable suppression of competition.[35] Examples of illegal actions include exclusive supply or purchase agreements; bundling, in which the sale of two products is tied together; predatory or below-cost pricing; and refusals to deal.

1. Exclusive Agreements: Agreements to use a single manufacturer, supplier, or dealer may be unlawful where that party possesses monopoly power. In that case, the contract could impede new firms from entering the market or existing firms from expanding their presence.[36] For instance, if Company A produces a product that requires Good X, and Company A requires every supplier of Good X to agree to only sell to Company A, then Company B is unable to enter the market since no suppliers are able to provide it with Good X. This is a restraint on new entrants. Because the premise of antitrust laws is that competition increases quality and lowers prices, such actions may be illegal.

2. Bundling: A company may monopolize one market and, conditional to the purchase of that monopolized product or service, require its customers to buy a second product in a competitive market along with the first product. Customers may not want the second product, but if they want or need the first, monopolized product, they have no choice. This act of tying a product or service to another is referred to as bundling, and it may occur as a method by which a dominant company attempts to gain market share in other markets, in order to harm the existing competitors in that market and raise its revenues while ostensibly keeping its prices the same. Whether tying is permissible depends on whether the bundle restricts competition without providing benefits to consumers.[37]

3. Predatory Pricing: Predatory pricing occurs where a dominant company lowers its prices, not in order to legitimately obtain business, but rather to force out its competitors. This may occur if, for instance, the selling price is below the cost of production. A large company or a highly diversified company may be able to retain losses for a period of time sufficient to oust its competitors. Subsequently, the now-dominant company raises its prices to monopolistic levels, thereby harming the consumer in the long run. The U.S. Supreme Court is skeptical of such claims, believing that price dumping of this sort rarely occurs in practice.[38] However, antidumping laws, which operate on a similar premise as predatory pricing restrictions, are liberally enforced in many parts of the world against foreign companies. This area thus merits close examination by those companies operating abroad.

4. Refusal to Deal: If a monopolistic company refuses to do business for purposes of retaining or strengthening its market position, or for purposes of strengthening its position in another market, then section two of the Sherman Act may be violated. The FTC cites one leading refusal-to-deal case:

> in a case from the 1950's, the only newspaper in a town refused to carry advertisements from companies that were also running ads on a local radio

station. The newspaper monitored the radio ads and terminated its ad contracts with any business that ran ads on the radio. The Supreme Court found that the newspaper's refusal to deal with businesses using the radio station strengthened its dominant position in the local advertising market and threatened to eliminate the radio station as a competitor.[39]

II. The FTC Act

Section 5 of the FTC Act bans "unfair methods of competition" and "unfair or deceptive acts or practices." An act or practice is unfair where it: (1) does or is likely to cause substantial injury to consumers, (2) cannot be reasonably avoided by consumers, and (3) is not outweighed by benefits to consumers or to competition.[40] Acts are deceptive where: (1) a representation, omission, or practice does or may mislead the consumer; (2) the consumer's interpretation is reasonable; and (3) the misleading representation, omission, or practice is likely to affect a consumer's decision to purchase or use a product or service.[41] Because a violation of the Sherman Act is by definition an unfair method of competition or an unfair act or practice, a violation of the Sherman Act is also a violation of the FTC Act.[42]

The FTC Act also reaches other unfair practices that may not be covered by the other antitrust acts, and therefore the FTC Act serves as a catchall of sorts.[43] For example, the FTC vigorously enforces restrictions on false or deceptive advertising.[44] The premise is that truthful advertising protects and empowers consumers to make choices in the marketplace.

III. The Clayton Act

The Clayton Antitrust Act of 1914 expanded antitrust restrictions to address those practices which the Sherman Act did not reach. Most prominent is section seven, which prohibits mergers and acquisitions that "may be substantially to lessen competition, or to tend to create a monopoly."[45]

Most mergers and acquisitions present no competitive issues. Merger and acquisition concerns arise when the proposed merger is likely to create or enhance market power or facilitate the exercise of market power. This primarily takes place when two direct competitors are considering a merger, and especially when each of those competitors holds a substantial amount of market power.[46]

The Hart-Scott-Rodino Antitrust Improvements Act of 1976 amended the Clayton Act by requiring that parties planning large mergers and acquisitions file premerger notifications and await government approval.[47] If the waiting period expires or is terminated by the government, the parties are free to close their deal.[48]

The Clayton Act was also amended with the Robinson-Patman Act of 1936. This Act bans discriminatory prices, services, and allowances in dealings between merchants.[49] This was enacted to offset dominant sellers from price cutting and thereby harming other sellers, and dominant buyers from demanding lower prices than smaller buyers could demand.

Global Enforcement: A Growing Menace?

One unsettled and potentially contentious area of antitrust action is the breadth of competitive conduct that can be regulated by U.S. antitrust laws. Specifically, what is the extent of extraterritorial application of U.S. antitrust law, i.e., does U.S. antitrust law govern the business conduct of foreign actors? In a carefully watched case,[50] the Department of Justice (DOJ) has recently argued to the 7th Circuit that the Foreign Trade Antitrust Improvements Act (FTAIA) allows damages to be obtained for improper extraterritorial conduct. The DOJ reasoned that FTAIA is in line with the well-established principle of the Sherman Act that foreign commerce conduct having a domestic effect is actionable and compensable. However, in 2014 the Seventh Circuit issued an opinion authored by Judge Posner that since 99 percent of the product at issue, LCD panels, were made by the foreign subsidiaries of the U.S. parent (Motorola), the injury was only derivative and so not compensable. Nonetheless, this is likely to be an unsettled area until addressed by the U.S. Supreme Court.

—Michael Keating[51]

IV. Antitrust Compliance: Preventing and Detecting Violations

A. Training and Structuring the Program

Training employees in antitrust provisions may reduce the risk of violations occurring and will increase the likelihood of detecting violations. Antitrust training may not be applicable for all parties within an organization. Of particular note are managers, salespeople, and anyone else who may interact with competitors.

If only a subset of employees present significant antitrust risks, companies may consider creating an antitrust handbook to supplement the Code of Conduct. By separating the antitrust provisions from the universal employee handbook, the handbook itself can remain sufficiently concise to reach its intended audience. The supplement can then focus in detail on antitrust concerns. This supplement should provide examples of the types of situations that present antitrust concerns. The examples provided should conform as closely as possible to the specific types of environments in which the employees will operate. Ideally, the examples will be based on real situations, either from the company or from others within the company's industry.

Trade association meetings and other competitor gatherings are an especial risk. Even employees that ordinarily would not present antitrust risks should be trained to recognize antitrust violations. This may be done within the antitrust handbook, or through a handout and training that identifies the risks that arise at competitor gatherings of this sort. Companies may consider prohibiting their employees from attending dinners or frequenting bars in which only competitors are present. Alternatively, they may also request that employees document their interactions with competitors. There are a lot of occasions where legitimate issues are discussed, and employees must ensure that the conversation doesn't devolve to inappropriate topic areas. Employees should be warned against discussing with competitors their customers, bids, prices, discounts, sales, costs, territories, profit margins, market shares, and confidential information.

Most employees know that bid rigging and price-fixing is illegal.[52] But they may not understand that things like market division, customer division, or boycotts could be illegal. Training forces employees to think beyond their own immediate desires for success and to consider the implications of their actions. Such actions should focus on the severity of punishments for antitrust violations. Most antitrust violations go right to the top of the organization (since managers most often are in a position to engage in the prohibited conduct with competitors).[53] Reviewing the very real risk of jail time and personal fines of up to $1 million may signal to employees that the short-term personal benefits are outweighed by the long-term repercussions.[54]

As is stressed throughout this book, organizations should develop tailored training and compliance Programs. Companies with substantial market power, for example, will have greater antitrust concerns than small companies in a highly competitive industry. Organizations should parse the red flags, examples of which are identified in section C, below, to identify those which reflect the specific risks of the organization and the employees to that the training is directed.

The structure of the antitrust compliance Program will vary in accordance with the company's needs. Some companies may consider centralized compliance Programs. This may be ideal if antitrust risks are relatively uniform throughout the organization. But decentralized Programs may be best for those with highly diversified operations—such as those that sell a variety of products or services. Moreover, as stated above, the globalization of antitrust is in full swing, so decentralized Programs by region may best account for the variety of worldwide risks.[55]

Regardless of whether the structure is centralized or decentralized, those tasked with creating and implementing the antitrust Program should bring some combination of legal and business expertise. Antitrust is a complex area of law, so a legal professional is a virtual prerequisite. But business professionals can and should play a role.

First, the business professional can provide guidance as to the company's risk tolerance. Some compliance Programs attempt to protect against every risk, and, in turn, either overwhelm the compliance department or cause confused employees to disregard the rules. Intensive compliance precautions may be appropriate for certain companies, but others will prefer flexibility or view the risks as minor enough to take fewer precautions.

Second, the business professional should educate the legal professional as to the specific areas of operation of the company. Antitrust risks are broad, and not every risk applies to every company. In order to identify antitrust risks and set forth those risks in training and handbooks, the lawyer or compliance professional must understand the intricacies of how the business operates.

Moreover, while it is almost always the case that compliance departments should have sufficient authority and resources to investigate even top-level officials, this is especially the case with antitrust given the propensity for wrongdoing to extend right up to the C-suite.[56]

B. Audits

Training increases the likelihood of scaring off wrongdoers and of helping honest employees recognize and report the wrongdoing. But training may not always prevent wrongdoing, in part because the majority of antitrust wrongdoers are likely to know they are breaking the law.[57]

Audits can be used to help uncover antitrust concerns. Audits can take place upon receiving an unconfirmed report of suspicious activities, or they may take place on a periodic basis in high-risk divisions or areas of operation. These types of audits screen for unusual patterns that would not ordinarily occur without collusion.[58]

Screens look for mathematical anomalies.[59] This may include market shares that are unusually stable or unusually high relative to other divisions within a firm, unusually high margins, and the submission of bids that use round numbers (e.g., 100, 5,000) in mathematically improbable ratios.[60] Evidence also suggests that the prices of collusive firms are less variable than in natural market conditions.[61] Whereas firms acting independently are responsive to changes in their own costs and likely pass those costs or savings to buyers, collusive firms tend to retain relatively static prices.[62]

Benford's Law is one screen organizations may rely upon. This law says that given any *naturally* occurring set of numbers, such as the length of a river, a population of a city, or the cost of a meal, certain patterns arise.[63] One would expect that the proportion of numbers beginning with a different digit (1, 2, 3, etc.) would all be approximately one-ninth. However, the distribution is front loaded—the number one appears about 30 percent of the time; two about 18 percent of the time, less often still for three, and so on all the way through to the number nine, which appears only about 5 percent of the time.[64]

This counterintuitive pattern has been shown to exist across a wide variety of numeric patterns.[65] Therefore, screeners can use this rule to compare bids or other prices that are the suspected result of collusion, and not natural pricing. If the number distribution does not conform to Benford's Law—for example, each digit appears with approximately equal frequency—red flags should arise. Of course, this does not mean that there is collusion, but it may necessitate further inquiries.

Benford's Law is a particularly beneficial source of audit. It is applicable to a wide variety of audits, not just antitrust risks. For instance, the law may help reveal employees who consistently submit falsified or inflated travel expenses.[66]

C. Red Flags

The following are red flags that imply the need for further inquiry. As mentioned, this may mean screening of the areas of inquiry to identify numerical or other anomalies, and it may also include interviewing suspected participants or witnesses.

1. *Red Flags in Bidding*

i.   The same company always wins a particular procurement. This may be more suspicious if one or more companies continually submit unsuccessful bids.

ii. Each company seems to take a turn as the successful bidder.

iii. Some bids are much higher than published price lists, previous bids by the same firms, or engineering cost estimates.

iv. A company appears to be bidding substantially higher on some bids than on other bids, with no apparent cost differences to account for the disparity.

v. Bid prices drop whenever a new or infrequent bidder submits a bid.

vi. A successful bidder subcontracts work to competitors that submitted unsuccessful bids on the same project.

vi. A company that is unable to perform the requirements nonetheless submits a bid.

vii. Multiple companies submit bids with identical typographical or other errors.[67]

2. Red Flags of Price-Fixing

i. Prices are identical for long periods, a condition of especial concern where prices historically differed.

ii. Price increases do not appear to be supported by increased costs.

iii. Discounts are eliminated without a market-based explanation.

iv. Vendors charge local customers higher prices than distant customers.[68]

3. Other Red Flags

i. Advanced knowledge of a competitor's prices

ii. A statement that a customer or geographic territory "belongs" to a competitor

iii. Statements that a bid was "complementary" or a "cover" bid

iv. Any statement indicating prices or bids have been discussed with competitors[69]

4. Conditions Favorable to Collusion

i. Few competitors, or a select few competitors, who possess a large market share.

ii. Other products are not easily substituted for the product, thereby giving increased power to those within the industry.

iii. It is easier to reach illicit agreements on standardized products than on products that have variations in design, quality, services, etc.

iv. Repetitive purchases may increase the chance of collusion, as the vendors may become familiar with one another.

v. Collusion is more likely if the competitors know each other well through social connections, trade associations, legitimate business contacts, or shifting employment from one company to another.

vi. Bidders who congregate in the same building or town to submit their bids have the opportunity for last-minute communications before submission of the bid.[70]

While the roots of antitrust laws reach deep, its relevance remains fresh. This is true for virtually every industry. The public bears little sympathy for collusion among businesses, making this prime picking for aggressive prosecutors. Enforcement continues at the state, federal, and, increasingly, at the global level, and those failing to adapt do so at their own peril.

Notes

Chapter One: Why Doing the Right Thing Matters

1. "PwC's State of Compliance 2013 Survey Reveals Growing Importance of Compliance Role in a Transnational Business Environment," PricewaterhouseCoopers LLP, last modified June 26, 2013, http://www.pwc.com/us/en/press-releases /state-of-compliance-survey-press-release.jhtml.

2. "Best Business Jobs: Compliance Officer," *US News and World Report*, accessed May 17, 2014, http://money.usnews.com/careers/best-jobs/compliance-officer? utm_source=CS290212&utm_medium=newsletter&utm_campaign=compliance& utm_source=Corporate+Secretary&utm_campaign=66e38c4be9-CS290212&utm _medium=email.

3. Tom Tyler, John Dienhart, and Terry Thomas, "The Ethical Commitment to Compliance: Building Value-Based Cultures," *Cal. Mgmt. Rev.* 50, no. 2 (Feb. 2008): 31–51.

4. Nick Ciancio, "The Seven Pillars of an Effective Ethics and Compliance Program," *Healthcare Compliance Ass'n* 42 (July 2007).

5. Securities and Exchange Commission, "Final Rule: Compliance Programs of Investment Companies and Investment Advisers," last modified December 17, 2003, http://www.sec.gov/rules/final/ia-2204.htm.

6. Staff of the U.S. Securities and Exchange Commission, "2013 Annual Report to Congress on the Dodd-Frank Whistleblower Program," accessed May 20, 2014, http://www.sec.gov/whistleblower/reportspubs/annual-reports/annual-report-2013 .pdf.

7. Thomas A. Marcinko, "The New FAR Codes of Conduct and Compliance Program Provisions," *Contract Mgmt.*, July 2008, http://www.ncmahq.org/files /articles/cm0708_18–29.pdf.

8. Federal Contractor Misconduct Database, accessed May 17, 2014, http:// www.contractormisconduct.org/.

9. Department of Justice press release, "Marubeni Corporation Agrees to Plead Guilty to Foreign Bribery Charges and to Pay an $88 Million Fine," March 19, 2014, http://www.justice.gov/opa/pr/2014/March/14-crm-290.html.

10. Department of Justice press release, "Siemens AG and Three Subsidiaries Plead Guilty to Foreign Corrupt Practices Act Violations and Agree to Pay $450 Million in Combined Criminal Fines," December 15, 2008, http://www.justice.gov/opa/pr/2008/December/08-crm-1105.html.

11. Department of Justice press release, "Bridgestone Corp. Agrees to Plead Guilty to Price Fixing on Automobile Parts Installed in U.S. Cars," February 13, 2014, http://www.justice.gov/atr/public/press_releases/2014/303743.htm.

12. Department of Justice press release, "Johnson & Johnson to Pay More Than $2.2 Billion to Resolve Criminal and Civil Investigations," November 4, 2013, http://www.justice.gov/opa/pr/2013/November/13-ag-1170.html.

13. Department of Justice press release, "Justice Department Reaches $335 Million Settlement to Resolve Allegations of Lending Discrimination by Countrywide Financial Corporation," December 21, 2011, http://www.justice.gov/opa/pr/2011/December/11-ag-1694.html.

14. Department of Justice press release, "BP Products to Pay Nearly $180 Million to Settle Clean Air Violations at Texas City Refinery," February 19, 2009, http://www.justice.gov/opa/pr/2009/February/09-enrd-140.html.

15. Department of Justice press release, "Justice Department Announces Criminal Charge Against Toyota Motor Corporation and Deferred Prosecution Agreement with $1.2 Billion Financial Penalty," March 19, 2014, http://www.justice.gov/opa/pr/2014/March/14-ag-286.html.

16. Phillip A. Wellner, "Effective Compliance Programs and Corporate Criminal Prosecutions," *Cardozo L. Rev.* 27, no. 497 (Oct. 2005): 505.

17. Patricia Harned, Jeff Knox, and J. Paul McNulty (ed. transcript), "What an Effective Compliance Program Should Look Like," *J. L. Econ & Pol'y* 9, no. 375 (Spring 2013): 383.

18. Ibid., 385.

19. Ibid.

20. Ibid.

21. Ibid.

22. Ibid.

23. Ibid., 386.

24. United States Sentencing Commission (USSC), *2010 Federal Sentencing Guidelines Manual,* "Chapter 8—Sentencing of Organization," §8B2.1(a)(2), 504.

25. "The Federal Sentencing Guidelines for Organizations at Twenty Years," Ethics Resource Center, 2012, http://www.ethics.org/files/u5/fsgo-report2012.pdf.

26. Ibid., 8.

27. Ibid., 13.

28. Ibid., 14.

29. Harned, "Effective Compliance Programs," 389.

30. Ibid.

31. Silverman, *Compliance Management,* 235.

32. Harned "Effective Compliance Programs," 389.

33. Ibid.

34. Dan Currell and Tracy Davis Bradley, "Finding and Fixing Corporate Misconduct," *Risk Management* 57, no. 3 (Apr. 2010): 56.

35. John MacKessy, "Knowledge of Good and Evil: A Brief History of Compliance," *The Finance Professionals' Post*, New York Society of Security Analysts, May 26, 2010, http://post.nyssa.org/nyssa-news/2010/05/a-brief-history-of-com pliance.html.

36. Joan T. A. Gabel, Nancy R. Mansfield, and Susan M. Houghton, "Letter vs. Spirit: The Evolution of Compliance into Ethics," *American Bus. L. J.*, 46, no. 3 (2009): 453–486.

37. Charles J. Walsh and Alissa Pyrich, "Corporate Compliance Programs as a Defense to Criminal Liability: Can a Corporation Save Its Soul," *Rutgers L. Rev.* 47 (1994): 605.

38. MacKessy, "Knowledge of Good and Evil."

39. Gabel, "Letter vs. Spirit," 453–486.

40. Report to Congressional Committees, GAO/GGD-97–18, "Bank and Thrift Regulation: Implementation of FDICIA's Prompt Regulatory Action Provisions," November 1996, http://www.gpo.gov/fdsys/pkg/GAOREPORTS-GGD-97–18 /html/GAOREPORTS-GGD-97–18.htm.

41. MacKessy, "Knowledge of Good and Evil."

42. FINRA, "FINRA Rules: FINRA Manual," last modified December 15, 2008, http://finra.complinet.com/en/display/display_viewall.html?rbid=2403&element _id=607&record_id=609&filtered_tag=.

43. Gabel, "Letter vs. Spirit," 453–486.

44. Paula Desio, "An Overview of the Organizational Guidelines," United States Sentencing Commission, accessed May 17, 2014, http://www.ussc.gov/sites/default /files/pdf/training/organizational-guidelines/ORGOVERVIEW.pdf.

45. Department of Justice memorandum, "Bringing Criminal Charges Against Corporations," June 16, 1999, http://www.justice.gov/criminal/fraud/documents /reports/1999/charging-corps.pdf.

46. Department of Justice memorandum, "Principles of Federal Prosecution of Business Organizations," January 20, 2003, http://www.americanbar.org /content/dam/aba/migrated/poladv/priorities/privilegewaiver/2003jan20_privwaiv _dojthomp.authcheckdam.pdf.

47. Leslie E. Lenn, "Sarbanes-Oxley Act 2002 (SOX)—10 Years Later," *J. of Legal Issues and Cases in Bus.*, 2 (May 2013): 1–14

48. Securities and Exchange Commission, "The Laws That Govern the Securities Industry: Sarbanes-Oxley Act of 2002," accessed May 19, 2014, https://www .sec.gov/about/laws.shtml#sox2002.

49. Securities and Exchange Commission, "17 CFR Parts 228, 229 and 249: Finale rule; request for comment," last modified January 24, 2003, http://www .sec.gov/rules/final/33–8177.htm.

50. Tyler, "Ethical Commitment to Compliance," 31–51.

51. Department of the Treasury, "The Financial Crisis Response in Chart," April 2012, http://www.treasury.gov/resource-center/data-chart-enter/Documents/20120413_FinancialCrisisResponse.pdf.

52. Paul Kiel and Dan Nguyen, "The Bailout Tracker," *ProPublica*, last modified June 16, 2014, https://projects.propublica.org/bailout/.

53. USSC, *Federal Sentencing Guidelines*, § 8B2.1(a).

54. Ibid., § 8B2.1(b).

55. Martin T. Biegelman and Daniel R. Biegelman, *Building a World-Class Compliance Program: Best Practices and Strategies for Success* (Hoboken, NJ: John Wiley & Sons, 2008), 9.

56. USSC, *Federal Sentencing Guidelines*, §8C2.5.

57. Ibid.

58. Sarbanes-Oxley Act of 2002, Pub. L. No. 107–204, 116 Stat. 745 (2002), https://www.sec.gov/about/laws/soa2002.pdf.

59. Ibid.

60. Ibid.

61. Biegelman, *Building a World-Class Compliance Program*, 9.

62. Ibid.

63. Ibid.

64. Dodd-Frank Wall Street Reform and Consumer Protection Act, H.R. 4173 (2010), https://www.sec.gov/about/laws/wallstreetreform-cpa.pdf.

65. Ibid.

66. Consumer Financial Protection Bureau, "About Us," last modified April 9, 2014, http://www.consumerfinance.gov/the-bureau/

67. Department of the Treasury, "Financial Stability Oversight Council," last modified April 25, 2013, http://www.treasury.gov/initiatives/fsoc/pages/home.aspx.

68. Department of the Treasury, "Federal Insurance Office," last modified June 17, 2013, http://www.treasury.gov/about/organizational-structure/offices/Pages/Federal-Insurance.aspx.

69. Office of the Comptroller of the Currency, "Volcker Rule," March 25, 2014, http://www.occ.gov/news-issuances/bulletins/2014/bulletin-2014–9.html.

70. Public Company Accounting Oversight Board (PCAOB), "PCAOB Statement upon Signing of the Dodd-Frank Wall Street Reform and Consumer Protection Act," July 21, 2010, http://pcaobus.org/News/Releases/Pages/07212010_DoddFrankAct.aspx.

71. Staff of the SEC, "2013 Annual Report to Congress."

Chapter Two: Dealing with Ethical Challenges

1. Kara Bhala, Seven Pillars Institute for Global Finance and Ethics, e-mail message to author, June 17, 2014.

2. Norman Oliver Brown, *Hermes the Thief: The Evolution of a Myth* (Steiner-Books, 1990).

3. Dennis J. Moberg and Mark A. Seabright, "The Development of Moral Imagination," *Bus. Ethics Quarterly* (2000): 845–884.

4. Brown, *Hermes the Thief*.

5. Dave Smith, "Foxconn Riot: Largest Apple Supplier Suffers Another Violent Outbreak," *Int'l Bus. Times*, September 24, 2013.

6. Caspar Rose and Steen Thomsen, "The Impact of Corporate Reputation on Performance: Some Danish Evidence," *European Management Journal* 22, no. 2 (2004): 201–210.

7. C. B. Bhattacharya, Sankar Sen, and Daniel Korschun, "Using Corporate Social Responsibility to Win the War for Talent," *MIT Sloan Management Review* 49 (2012).

8. Ethical Funds, "Investing in a Better World," accessed May 30, 2014, http://www.ethicalfunds.com/Pages/SRI/Socially-Responsible-Investing.aspx.

9. Kenneth Keniston, "Morals and Ethics," *The American Scholar* (1965): 628–632.

10. P. Christie et al., "A Cross-cultural Comparison of Ethical Attitudes of Business Managers: India, Korea and the United States," *J. of Business Ethics* 46, no. 3 (2003): 263–287.

11. Dean McFarlin and Paul D. Sweeney, *International Management: Strategic Opportunities & Cultural Challenges* (Routledge, 2014).

12. Ethical Funds, "Investing in a Better World."

13. Donelson R. Forsyth, "Judging the Morality of Business Practices: The Influence of Personal Moral Philosophies," *J. of Bus. Ethics* 11, no. 5–6 (1992): 461–470.

14. Ibid.

15. Jeremy Bentham, "An Introduction to the Principles of Morals and Legislation," accessed May 30, 2014, http://www.utilitarianism.com/bentham.htm.

16. Ibid.

17. Kara Bhala, Seven Pillars Institute for Global Finance and Ethics, e-mail message to author, June 17, 2014.

18. Thomas M. Jones, Will Felps, and Gregory A. Bigley, "Ethical Theory and Stakeholder-Related Decisions: The Role of Stakeholder Culture," *Academy of Mgmt. Rev.* 32, no. 1 (2007): 137–155.

19. Donelson, "Judging the Morality."

20. Heehs, *The Lives of Sri Aurobindo*, 281.

21. E. Arries, "Virtue Ethics: An Approach to Moral Dilemmas in Nursing," *Curationis* 28, no. 3 (2005): 64–72.

22. Forsyth, "Judging the Morality of Business Practices," *J. of Bus. Ethics* 11.

23. "Universal Values—Peace, Freedom, Social Progress, Equal Rights, Human Dignity—Acutely Needed, Secretary-General Says at Tubingen University, Germany," UN News Centers, December 12, 2003, http://www.un.org/News/Press/docs/2003/sgsm9076.doc.htm.

24. F. Joseph Warin, Michael S. Diamant, and Jill M. Pfenning, "FCPA Compliance in China and the Gifts and Hospitality Challenge," *Virginia L. & Bus. Rev.* 5, no. 1, 60–61.

25. Fred Burton and Scott Stewart, "Crossing the Cultural Divide," *Business Spectator*, January 19, 2008.

26. Thomas Donaldson and Lee E. Preston, "The Stakeholder Theory of the Corporation: Concepts, Evidence, and Implications," *Academy of Mgmt. Rev.* 20, no. 1 (1995): 65–91.

Chapter Three: Corporate Governance, Corporate Responsibility, and the Environment

1. SOX-Online, "Sarbanes-Oxley Essential Information," accessed June 27, 2014, http://www.sox-online.com/basics.html.

2. Organisation for the Economic Co-operation and Development, "Corporate Governance and the Financial Crisis: Key Findings and Main Messages," June 2009, http://www.oecd.org/daf/ca/corporategovernanceprinciples/43056196.pdf.

3. U.S. Securities and Exchange Commission, "Corporate Governance Issues, Including Executive Compensation Disclosure and Related SRO Rules," last modified October 28, 2013, http://www.sec.gov/spotlight/dodd-frank/corporate governance.shtml.

4. European Central Bank, "Glossary," Annual Report: 2004, ECB, Frankfurt, "last modified July 13, 2005, http://stats.oecd.org/glossary/detail.asp?ID=6778.

5. "Report of the Committee on the Financial Aspects of Corporate Governance," Committee on the Financial Aspects of Corporate Governance and Gee and Co. Ltd. (1992), accessed June 27, 2014, http://www.ecgi.org/codes/documents/cadbury.pdf; Sarbanes-Oxley Act of 2002 (Ch. 1, n. 61).

6. "Report of the Committee."

7. "Report of the Committee"; Sarbanes-Oxley Act of 2002.

8. "Report of the Committee."

9. Sarbanes-Oxley Act of 2002.

10. "Report of the Committee"; Sarbanes-Oxley Act of 2002.

11. "Report of the Committee."

12. Ibid.

13. Sarbanes-Oxley Act of 2002.

14. "Report of the Committee."

15. Ibid.

16. "Report of the Committee"; Sarbanes-Oxley Act of 2002.

17. Jüergen Schneider and Siu-yeung Chan, "A Comparison of Corporate Governance Systems in Four Countries" (BRC Working Papers, Business Research Centre, School of Business, Hong Kong Baptist University, Hong Kong, 2001), accessed June 29, 2014, http://ied.hkbu.edu.hk/publications/wp/WP200108.pdf.

18. Bhala 2014.

19. Bernard S. Black, "The Principal Fiduciary Duties of Boards of Directors," presented at Third Asian Roundtable on Corporate Governance, Singapore, April 4, 2001, http://www.oecd.org/daf/ca/corporategovernanceprinciples/1872 746.pdf.

20. Ron Gieseke, in discussion with author, June 2014.

21. Ibid.

22. Business Round Table, "Principles of Corporate Governance 2012," accessed June 29, 2014, http://businessroundtable.org/sites/default/files/BRT _Principles_of_Corporate_Governance_-2012_Formatted_Final.pdf.

23. Gieseke, discussion.

24. Ibid.

25. Ibid.

26. Ibid.

27. Ibid.

28. KPMG, "The Role of the Audit Committee," accessed June 28, 2014, https://www.kpmg.com/RU/en/topics/Audit-Committee-Institute/Publications/ Documents/toolkit/1_The%20role%20of%20the%20audit%20committee_eng .pdf.

29. Business Round Table, "Principles."

30. Deloitte Center for Corporate Governance, "Nominating/Corporate Governance Committee," accessed June 28, 2014, http://www.corpgov.deloitte.com /site/us/nominating-corporate-governance-committee/;jsessionid=h1CNTtnpJLv3 J2HLBxThl8jx1pyPnx2N7wHlGZvvvhxX2qpHq2Sd!-1791547501!NONE.

31. Business Round Table, "Principles."

32. Gieseke, discussion.

33. Deloitte, "Nominating/Corporate Governance Committee."

34. Gieseke, discussion.

35. Ibid.

36. Ibid.

37. Ibid.

38. Ibid.

39. Michael Izza, "Is 'Comply or Explain' Fit for Purpose?," ICAEW, Communities, December 10, 2013, http://www.ion.icaew.com/MoorgatePlace/post /Is—comply-or-explain—fit-for-purpose—.

40. M. Nedelchev, "Good Practices in Corporate Governance: One-Size-Fits-All vs. Comply-or-Explain," *Int'l J. of Bus. Admin.* 4, no. 6 (2013): 75.

41. Robert Costanza et al., "The Value of the World's Ecosystem Services and Natural Capital," *Nature* 387 (1997).

42. Wesley Cragg, "Business Ethics and Stakeholder Theory," *Bus. Ethics Qtly.* (2002): 113–142.

43. Ibid.

44. John Elkington, *Cannibals with Forks: The Triple Bottom Line of 21st Century Business* (Capstone Publishing, 1999).

45. Helen Borland, "Conceptualising Global Strategic Sustainability and Corporate Transformational Change," *Int'l Marketing Rev.* 26, no. 4/5 (2009): 554–572.

46. Paul Shrivastava, "The Role of Corporations in Achieving Ecological Sustainability," *Academy of Mgmt Rev.* 20, no. 4 (1995): 936–960.

47. Thomas Trautmann, Volker H. Hoffmann, and Malte Schneider, "A Taxonomy for Regulatory Uncertainty–Application to Flexible Mechanisms of the Kyoto Protocol," in Proceedings of the Inter. 2006.

48. J. A. Plaza-Úbeda, J. Burgos-Jiménez, D. A. Vazquez, and C. Liston-Heyes, "The 'Win–Win' Paradigm and Stakeholder Integration," *Bus. Strategy and the Environment* 18, no. 8 (2009): 487–499.

49. M. V. Russo, and P. A. Fouts, "A Resource-Based Perspective on Corporate Environmental Performance and Profitability," *Academy of Mgmt. J.* 40(3) (1997): 534–559.

50. Nitish Singh, Carri Tolmei, and Yung-Hwal Park, "Green Firm Specific Advantages for Enhancing Environmental and Economic Performance," Proceedings of Academy of International Business (AIB), Washington, DC, 2012.

51. Global Reporting Initiative, accessed July 2, 2014, https://www.globalreporting.org/Pages/default.aspx.

52. ISO, "ISO 26000—Social Responsibility," accessed July 2, 2014, http://www.iso.org/iso/iso26000.

53. CDP, "Guidance for Responding Companies—Climate Change Program," accessed July 2, 2014, https://www.cdp.net/en-US/Pages/guidance.aspx.

54. United Nations Global Compact, "Overview of the UN Global Compact," last modified April 22, 2013, http://www.unglobalcompact.org/AboutTheGC/index.html.

55. Organisation for the Economic Co-operation and Development, "OECD Guidelines for Mulitnational Enterprises," 2011 ed., accessed July 2, 2014, http://www.oecd.org/daf/inv/mne/48004323.pdf.

56. "Dow Jones Sustainability Indices," accessed July 2, 2014, http://www.sustainability-indices.com/.

57. Assurance and verification guidance can be found in ISO 14064 standards, ISO 26000 standards, AA1000 Assurance Standards, Stakeholder Engagement Standards (AA1000SES), and SAE 3000.

Chapter Four: Risk Assessment and Structuring the Program

1. Silverman, *Compliance Management*, 231 (Ch. 1, n. 26).

2. USSC, *Federal Sentencing Guidelines*, §8B2.1(c) (Ch. 1, n. 24).

3. Jamie Crawford, "Pentagon Document Lays Out Battle Plan against Zombies," CNN, May 16, 2014, http://edition.cnn.com/2014/05/16/politics/pentagon-zombie-apocalypse/.

4. USSC, *Federal Sentencing Guidelines*, §8B2.1, Comm. 7(A)(ii).

5. Silverman, *Compliance Management*, 231.

6. Ibid., 274.

7. Greg Young et al., "Managing Reputational Risk," *Strategic Finance*, Nov. 2010, 37.

8. Silverman, *Compliance Management*, 37.

9. Ibid., 37.

10. Ibid., 68.

11. Rosalyn Ben-Chitrit and Angela Mattie, "The Federal False Claims Act and Qui Tam Actions: What Every Healthcare Manager Should Know," *J. of Legal, Ethical and Reg. Issues* 12 no. 2, (Nov. 2009): 65.

12. Myler, CRM, "Information Compliance Initiative" 60 (Ch. 4, n. 19).

13. Silverman, *Compliance Management*, 160–161.

14. Ibid., 189.

15. Silverman, *Compliance Management*, 230.

16. USSC, *Federal Sentencing Guidelines*, §8B2.1, Comm. 7(B).

17. Ori Ben-Chorin and Timothy P. Hedley, "Auditing and Monitoring Activities Help Uncover Fraud and Assess Control Effectiveness," *The CPA J.*, 71 (June 2011).

18. Silverman, *Compliance Management*, 222.

19. Chorin et al., "Auditing and Monitoring Activities," 69.

20. USSC, *Federal Sentencing Guidelines*, §8B2.1(b)(2)(A-C) (Ch. 1, n. 24).

21. Ibid, §8B2.1, Comm. 1.

22. 698 A.2d 959 (Del. Ch. 1996)

23. Ibid., 970.

24. Silverman, *Compliance Management*, 82.

25. USSC, *Federal Sentencing Guidelines*, §8A1.2, Comm. 3(b).

26. Ibid., §8A1.2, Comm. 3(b).

27. Ibid., §8B2.1, Comm. 3.

28. Ibid., §8B2.1(b)(3).

29. Ibid., §8B2.1, Comm. 4(b).

30. Ibid., §8C2.5(f)(3)(A-B).

31. Ibid., §8A1.2, Comm. 3(J).

32. An individual with operational responsibility is one who has day-to-day authority over the Program, such as a compliance officer. This is not to be confused with a high-level employee, who must ensure that the organization has an effective Program but need not necessarily be involved with the operational aspects of the program on a day-to-day basis. *See generally* ibid., §8B2.1(b)(2)(C).

33. Ibid., §8C2.5(f)(3)(C).

34. This is yet another reason why the manager of a compliance Program must be able to bypass possible bad actors in top management through the extension of a direct line to the board of directors.

35. Silverman, *Compliance Management*, 107.

36. Ibid.

37. Ibid.

38. Ibid.

39. Ibid., 138.

40. Ibid.

41. Ibid., 56.

42. Ibid., 118.

43. Ibid., 118–119.

44. Ibid., 128 (citing to the *Guidelines*).

45. Jonathan Stempel, "U.S. Judge Says Wal-Mart Should Face Lawsuit over Alleged Mexico Bribery," Reuters, May 9, 2014, http://www.reuters.com/article /2014/05/09/us-walmart-mexico-lawsuit-idUSBREA480F620140509.

46. David Barstow and Alejandra Xanic von Bertrab, "The Bribery Aisle: How Wal-Mart Got Its Way in Mexico," *New York Times*, Dec. 17, 2012, http://www .nytimes.com/2012/12/18/business/walmart-bribes-teotihuacan.html?_r=0.

47. Ibid.

48. Stempel, "Wal-Mart Should Face Lawsuit."

49. Ibid., 142.

50. Ibid.

Chapter Five: Elements of a Compliance Program

1. USSC, *Federal Sentencing Guidelines*, §8B2.1, Commentary 2(A) (Ch. 1, n. 24).

2. Ibid., §8B2.1, Comm. 2(C)(ii–iii).

3. For purposes of the FSGO, a small firm is one with less than 200 employees, a large firm is one with 200 or more employees. *See* ibid., §8C2.1, Comm. 1.

4. Ibid., §8B2.1, Comm. 2(C)(ii).

5. Ibid.

6. Ibid., §8B2.1, Comm. 2(C)(iii).

7. Ibid.

8. Wellner, "Effective Compliance Programs," 515 (Ch. 1, n. 16).

9. Ibid., at §8B2.1, Comm. 2(C)(iii).

10. Levine, in discussion with the author, April 2014.

11. See *In re Abbott Laboratories Derivative Shareholders Action*, 325 F.3d 795 (7th Cir. 2003).

12. Silverman, *Compliance Management*, 67 (Ch. 1, n. 26).

13. Ibid., 154.

14. Aley Raza in e-mail to author, May 29, 2014.

15. Amiram Gill, "Corporate Governance as Social Responsibility: A Research Agenda," *Berkeley J. Int'l L.* 26, no. 452 (2008): 466.

16. Silverman, *Compliance Management*, 68.

17. Colgate-Palmolive, "Code of Conduct: Living Our Values," accessed June 24, 2014, http://www.colgate.com/Colgate/US/Corp_v2/LivingOurValues/Code OfConduct/PDFs/2012-Code-of-Conduct-English.pdf (Eng. ed.).

18. CH2M HILL, "Employee Ethics and Business Conduct Principles," last modified November 2010, http://www.ch2m.com/corporate/about_us/procurement/assets/BCA.pdf.

19. General Electric, "Company Code of Conduct," accessed June 24, 2014, http://www.sec.gov/Archives/edgar/data/1262449/000119312508061906/dex142.htm.

20. Ellie Myler, CRM, "Minimizing Risk Through a Corporate Information Compliance Initiative," *The Information Mgmt J.* 59 (Jan/Feb 2008).

21. Colgate-Palmolive, "Code of Conduct" See also CH2M HILL, "Employee Ethics and Business."

22. *See* Silverman, *Compliance Management*, 69; *See also* Colgate-Palmolive, "Code of Conduct," 5; CH2M HILL, "Employee Ethics and Business," 2.

23. *See* Colgate-Palmolive, "Code of Conduct," 22; *See also* CH2M HILL, "Employee Ethics and Business," 18.

24. USSC, *Federal Sentencing Guidelines*, §8B2.1(5)(C).

25. Silverman, *Compliance Management*, 160.

26. Jeroen Tetteroo in e-mail to author, June 26, 2014.

27. Tetteroo in e-mail to author, July 21, 2014.

28. CH2M HILL, "Employee Ethics and Business," ii.

29. Harned et al., "Effective Compliance Program," 382 (Ch. 1, n. 17).

30. USSC, *Federal Sentencing Guidelines*, §8B2.1, Commentary 2(C)(ii).

31. CH2M HILL, "Employee Ethics and Business," 14; Colgate-Palmolive, "Code of Conduct," 5.

32. Wellner, "Effective Compliance Programs," 513.

33. Silverman, *Compliance Management*, 64.

34. Id. at 56 (emphasis added).

35. Diana E. Murphy, "The Federal Sentencing Guidelines for Organizations: A Decade of Promoting Compliance and Ethics," *Inter. Amer. L. Rev.* 87, no. 697 (2002): 714–715 (citing to Stephen Cohen, "Compliance, Corporate Governance, and Ethics: The New Regime" 2 (Mar. 2001) (unpublished manuscript presented at American Assoc. of Prof. & Practical Ethics, on file with the USSC).

36. Silverman, *Compliance Management*, 64.

37. Silverman, *Compliance Management*, 18 (writing that companies must review the laws of a "staggering" "plethora" of oversight agencies, including "comptrollers, inspectors general, internal auditors, ombudsmen, executive regulatory bodies (e.g., the budget office and the procurement office), and specialist regulatory bodies and functions (e.g., water compliance specialists and policies boards). The growth in the number of federal agencies with compliance responsibilities has been significant."

38. Currell and Bradley, "Fixing Corporate Misconduct," 34 (Ch. 1, n. 35).

39. Ben-Chitrit and Mattie, "The Federal False Claims Act and Qui Tam Actions," 58 (Ch. 4 n. 11).

40. Muel Kaptein, "Why Good People Sometimes Do Bad Things: 52 Reflections on Ethics at Work" (2012): 39, http:ssrn.com/abstract=2117396.

41. Ibid.

42. Ibid.

43. Ibid., 47.

44. Ibid.

45. Ibid.

46. Ibid., 155.

47. Ibid., 83.

48. Ibid., 82.

49. Ibid., 83.

50. Ibid., 83.

51. Ibid., 84.

52. Ibid., 154.

53. Ibid., 56.

54. Ibid., 60.

55. A Practice Aid for Records Retention, AICPA Information Technology Section, 2012, http://www.aicpa.org/InterestAreas/InformationTechnology/Resources/BusinessIntelligence/DownloadableDocuments/Records_Retention_Mktg.pdf.

56. Kaptein, "Why Good People Sometimes Do Bad Things," 60.

57. Ibid., 62.

58. Ben-Chorin et al., "Auditing and Monitoring Activities," 70 (Ch. 4, n. 17).

59. Ibid.

60. Ibid.

61. Ben-Chitrit et al., "The Federal False Claims Act," 65.

Chapter Six: Oversight and a Culture of Compliance

1. USSC, *Federal Sentencing Guidelines*, §8B2.1(a)(2) (Ch. 1, n. 24).

2. Silverman, *Compliance Management*, 85 (Ch. 1, n. 26).

3. Wellner, "Effective Compliance Programs," 518 (Ch. 1, n. 16).

4. Ibid.

5. Harned et al., "Effective Compliance Program," 388 (Ch. 1, n. 17).

6. Wellner, "Effective Compliance Programs," 518.

7. Stanley Milgram, "Behavior Study of Obedience," *J. of Abnormal and Social Psychology* 67 no.4 (1963): 372.

8. Ibid., 373.

9. Ibid., 373–374.

10. Ibid., 373.

11. Ibid.

12. Ibid.

13. Ibid.

14. Ibid., 374.

15. Ibid., 373.

16. Ibid.

17. Ibid., 376.

18. Ibid., 375.

19. Kaptein, "Why Good People Sometimes Do Bad Things," 65 (Ch. 5, n. 42).

20. Ibid.

21. Milgram, "Behavior Study of Obedience," 371.

22. Kaptein, "Why Good People Sometimes Do Bad Things," 7–8.

23. Ibid., 60.

24. Ibid.

25. Ibid., 24.

26. Murphy, "The Federal Sentencing Guidelines," 716 (Ch. 5, n. 37).

27. Richard H. Girgenti and Timothy P. Hedley, *Managing the Risk of Fraud and Misconduct: Meeting the Challenges of a Global, Regulated and Digital Environment,* 102 (McGraw Hill, 2011) (citing to Michael Siconolfi, Laurie P. Cohen, and Kevin G. Salwen, "SEC Probes Collusion by Trader—Subpoenas Will Seek Price Fixing Evidence in Treasury Market," *Wall Street Journal,* August 27, 1991, C1).

28. Charles H. Le Grand, "Building a Culture of Compliance," *IBS America, Inc.* (2005).

29. Ibid.

30. Ibid.

31. Ibid.

32. Robert Rosenthal and Lenore Jacobson, *Pygmalion in the Classroom: Teacher Expectation and Pupils' Intellectual Development* (New York: Holt, Rinehart & Winston 1968): 16.

33. Kaptein, "Why Good People Sometimes Do Bad Things," 23 (Ch. 5 n. 42).

34. Rosenthal et al., *Pygmalion in the Classroom,* 20.

35. Kaptein, "Why Good People Sometimes Do Bad Things," 24.

36. Ibid., 90.

37. Ibid., 89.

38. Ibid.

39. Steven D. Levitt and Stephen J. Dubner, *Freakonomics: A Rogue Economist Explores the Hidden Side of Everything,* 45 (New York: HarperCollins Publishers, 2005).

Chapter Seven: Education and Training

1. Levine, discussion.

2. Silverman, *Compliance Management,* 60 (Ch. 1, n. 26).

3. Ibid., 167.

4. Ibid., 165–166

5. Ibid., 228

6. Ibid., 230.

7. Ibid., 167.

8. USSC, *Federal Sentencing Guidelines,* §8B2.1(b)(4)(A) (Ch. 1, n. 24).

9. Silverman, *Compliance Management,* 166.

10. Ben-Chorin and Hedley, "Auditing and Monitoring Activities," 68 (Ch. 4, n. 17).

11. Silverman, *Compliance Management,* 168.

12. Kaptein, "Why Good People Sometimes Do Bad Things," 27 (Ch. 5, n. 42).

13. Ibid,

14. Ibid., 39.

15. Ibid.

16. Ibid., 93.

17. Ibid., 93–94.

18. Ibid., 95.

19. Elizabeth C. Peterson, "SEC Compliance Best Practices," 2011 ed. Leading Lawyers on Managing Risks, Building and Maintaining Compliance Programs, and Understanding New Legislation Navigating the Thorny Path of Corporate Compliance in the Wake of Dodd Frank," 9 (April 2011).

20. Ibid.

21. Ben-Chitrit et al., "The Federal False Claims Act," 60 (Ch. 4, n. 11).

22. Silverman, *Compliance Management*, 170.

23. Ibid., 170–171.

24. Ibid., 173.

25. Ibid.

26. Ibid. 163

27. Ibid.

Chapter Eight: Identifying and Investigating Fraud and Other Wrongdoing

1. Mark Whitacre in discussion with authors, March 4, 2014.

2. Ibid.

3. Ibid.

4. Levitt et al., *Freakonomics*, 41 (Ch. 6, n. 39)

5. Ibid., 42

6. Ibid., 42

7. Ibid., 43.

8. Ibid., 44.

9. Casazza, in discussion with author.

10. Kaptein, "Why Good People Sometimes Do Bad Things," 127 (Ch. 5, n. 42).

11. Ibid., 52.

12. Girgenti et al., *Managing the Risk of Fraud and Misconduct*, 3 (Ch. 6, n. 27).

13. "Secretary Stole £ 4.4 million," MailOnline, accessed June 25, 2014, http://www.dailymail.co.uk/news/article-300688/Secretary-stole-4-4-million.html.

14. Ibid.

15. Ibid.

16. Ibid.

17. Ibid.

18. Kaptein, "Why Good People Sometimes Do Bad Things," 97.

19. Casazza, in discussion with author.

20. Girgenti et al., *Managing the Risk of Fraud and Misconduct*, 5.

21. Ibid., 5.

22. Ibid., 9–10.
23. Ibid., 9.
24. Ibid., 11.
25. Ibid., 11.
26. Ibid., 11.
27. Ibid., 15.
28. "Secretary Stole £4.4 million," MailOnline, http://www.dailymail.co.uk /news/article-300688/Secretary-stole-4–4-million.html.
29. Ibid.
30. Girgenti et al., *Managing the Risk of Fraud and Misconduct*, 22.
31. Ibid., 23.
32. Ibid., 24.
33. Ibid., 25.
34. Ibid., 28–29.
35. Ibid., 25.
36. Ibid., 27.
37. Ibid., 27.
38. Ibid., 30.
39. Ibid., 31.
40. Ibid., 31.
41. Jonathan Stempel, "U.S. Judge Says Wal-Mart Should Face Lawsuit over Alleged Bribery," Reuters, http://www.reuters.com/article/2014/05/09/us-walmart -mexico-lawsuit-idUSBREA480F620140509.
42. Ibid., 21.

Chapter Nine: Identification, Investigation, and Enforcement

1. Mathieu Bouville, *Whistle-Blowing and Morality*, J. of Bus. Ethics 81 (2008): 579.
2. This includes the Clean Water Act, the Resource Conservation and Recovery Act, and the Occupational Safety and Health Act.
3. "2014 Annual Report to Congress on the Dodd-Frank Whistlblower Program," U.S. Securities and Exchange Commission, accessed December 4, 2014, http://www.sec.gov/about/offices/owb/annual-report-2014.pdf.
4. Harned et al., "Effective Compliance Program," 387 (Ch. 1, n. 17).
5. Association of Certified Fraud Examiners (ACFE), "Report to the Nations on Occupational Fraud and Abuse: 2012 Global Fraud Study," 17, accessed June 25, 2014, http://www.acfe.com/uploadedFiles/ACFE_Website/Content/rttn /2012-report-to-nations.pdf.
6. Ben-Chitrit et al., "The Federal False Claims Act," 60 (Ch. 4, n. 11) (citing to N. Getnick and L. A. Skillen, "The Fundamentals of Qui Tam," Int'l Ass'n of Defense Counsel 2003 Mid-Year Meeting (February 2003).
7. Ibid.
8. Ibid., 123.

9. Ibid.

10. Gieseke, discussion.

11. Ibid.

12. Ibid.

13. Ibid.

14. Ibid.

15. USSC, *Federal Sentencing Guidelines*, §8B2.1(5)(C) (Ch. 1, n. 24).

16. Silverman, *Compliance Management*, 176 (Ch. 1, n. 26).

17. Ibid., 190

18. Ben-Chitrit et al., "The Federal False Claims Act," 60 (citing to UPS, *UPS Code of Conduct*, last modified January 1, 2012, http://www.ups.com/content /corp/code_conduct.html.

19. Peterson, "SEC Compliance Best Practices," 9 (Ch. 7, n. 22).

20. Silverman, *Compliance Management,* 176 (citing to Dr. Stuart Gilman of Ethics Resource Center to the Advisory Group on Federal Sentencing Guidelines for Organizations in 2002).

21. Ben-Chitrit et al., "The Federal False Claims Act," 63.

22. Ibid.

23. Silverman, *Compliance Management* 176 (citing to Dr. Stuart Gilman of Ethics Resource Center to the Advisory Group on Federal Sentencing Guidelines for Organizations in 2002).

24. D. Robin, "Toward an Applied Meaning for Ethics in Business," *J. of Bus. Ethics* 89 (2009): 147.

25. Kaptein, "Why Good People Sometimes Do Bad Things," 151 (Ch. 5, n. 42).

26. General Electric, "Company Code of Conduct," 12 (Ch. 5, n. 21).

27. Peterson, "SEC Compliance Best Practices," 9.

28. Joyce Rothschild and Terrence D. Miethe, *Whistle-Blower Disclosures and Management Retaliation: The Battle to Control Information about Organization Corruption*, July 31, 2009, 119, http://www.uk.sagepub.com/fineman/Reading%20On /Chapter%2012d%20-%20Rothschild%20and%20Miethe.pdf.

29. Silverman, *Compliance Management*, 194.

30. Ibid., 192.

31. Tanina Rostain, "The Emergence of 'Law Consultants,'" *Fordham L. Rev.* 75 no. 1397 (2006): 1412 http://ir.lawnet.fordham.edu/cgi/viewcontent.cgi?article =4228&context=flr.

32. Ibid.

33. Ibid.

34. Ibid.

35. Ben-Chitrit et al., "The Federal False Claims Act," 60.

36. Ibid.

37. Casazza, e-mail to author, May 24, 2014.

38. Ibid.

39. Cassaza, e-mail to author.

40. Ibid.

41. Silverman, *Compliance Management*, 176 (citing to Dr. Stuart Gilman of Ethics Resource Center to the Advisory Group on Federal Sentencing Guidelines for Organizations in 2002).

42. Ibid.

43. Ibid.

44. Harned et al., "Effective Compliance Program," 11.

45. Ibid., 195 (as recounted by the National Center for preventive Law's recount of one organization's approach

46. USSC, *Federal Sentencing Guidelines*, §8B2.1, Comm. 5.

47. Kaptein, "Why Good People Sometimes Do Bad Things," 157.

48. Ibid., 155.

49. Silverman, *Compliance Management*, 69.

50. USSC, *Federal Sentencing Guidelines*, §8B2.1, Comm. 6.

51. Ibid., §8C2.5(f)(2).

52. Ibid., §8C2.5, Comm. 10.

53. Ibid., §8C2.5, Comm. 13.

54. Ibid.

55. Silverman, *Compliance Management*, 116.

56. USSC, *Federal Sentencing Guidelines*, §8C2.5(g).

57. Ibid., §8C2.5, Comm. 15.

58. Ibid., §8B2.1(6).

59. Ibid.

Chapter Ten: Compliance Program Evaluation

1. Ben-Chorin et al., "Auditing and Monitoring Activities," 69 (Ch. 4, n. 17).

2. Ibid., 272.

3. Bor-Yi Tsay, "Designing an Internal Control Assessment Program Using COSO's Guidance on Monitoring," *The CPA J.*, 55 (May 2010).

4. Ben-Chorin et al., "Auditing and Monitoring Activities," 68.

5. Silverman, *Compliance Management*, 89 (Ch. 1, n. 26).

6. Tsay, "Designing an Internal Control," 54.

7. Ben-Chorin et al., "Auditing and Monitoring Activities," 71.

8. Ibid.

9. Tsay, "Designing an Internal Control," 54.

10. Silverman, *Compliance Management*, 264.

11. Tsay, "Designing an Internal Control," 54.

12. USSC, *Federal Sentencing Guidelines*, §8B2.1, Comm. 6 (Ch. 1, n. 24).

13. Peterson, "SEC Compliance Best Practices," 9 (Ch. 7, n. 22).

14. USSC, *Federal Sentencing Guidelines*, §8B2.1, Comm. 2(C)(iii).

Chapter Eleven: International Compliance

1. Lyn Boxall, in conversation with author, April 30, 2014.

2. Peter J. Henning, "Be Careful What You Wish For: Thoughts on a Compliance Defense Under the Foreign Corrupt Practices Act," *Ohio St. L. J.* 73, no. 883 (2012): 884.

3. Henning, "Be Careful What You Wish For," 883–884.

4. Ibid., 883–885.

5. 15 U.S.C. §§ 78dd-2(g)(2)(A); 15 U.S.C. §§ 78ff(a).

6. *See* FCPA Blog, available at http://www.fcpablog.com/blog/2012/2/28/a-survey-of-fcpa-sentences.html.

7. Gideon Mark, "Private FCPA Enforcement," *American Bus. L. J.* 49 no. 419 (2012): 419.

8. Departmet of Justice Criminal Division and Securities and Exchange Commission Enforcement Division, "FCPA: A Resource Guide to the U.S. Foreign Corrupt Practices Act," 21, last modified Nov. 14, 2012, http://www.justice.gov/criminal/fraud/fcpa/guide.pdf.

9. Ibid., 3.

10. Securities Exchange Act of 1934, 15 U.S.C. §§ 78dd-1(a).

11. Ibid.

12. DOJ et al., "FCPA: A Resource Guide," 12.

13. Ibid.

14. See generally, *United States of America v. Jefferson*, 674 F. 3d 332 (4th Cir. 2012).

15. Ibid., 14.

16. DOJ et al., "FCPA: A Resource Guide," 14.

17. Securities Exchange Act of 1934, 15 U.S.C. §§ 78dd-1(f)(1)(A).

18. Securities Exchange Act of 1934, 15 U.S.C. §§ 78dd-1(f)(1)(A)-(B).

19. *United States v. Esquenazi*, D.C. Docket No. 1:09-cr-21010-JEM-1 (App. Ct. 2014).

20. DOJ et al., "FCPA: A Resource Guide," 20.

21. *United States v. Esquenazi*, D.C. Docket No. 1:09-cr-21010-JEM-1 (App. Ct. 2014); see also *United States v. Carson*, No. 09-cr-00077-JVS (C.D. Cal. Feb. 16, 2012, Dkt. Entry No. 549, for similar factors.

22. DOJ et al., "FCPA: A Resource Guide," 21.

23. Ibid., 23.

24. Ibid., 23.

25. Ibid., 25.

26. Boxall, discussion.

27. This is a risk especially in countries where corruption is embedded into the government and into society.

28. APEC Anti-Corruption Code of Conduct for Business, 2007, available at http://www.apec.org/Groups/SOM-Steering-Committee-on-Economic-and-Technical-Cooperation/Task-Groups/~/media/Files/Groups/ACT/07_act_codebrochure.ashx.

29. DOJ et al., "FCPA: A Resource Guide," 27. (For more on the distinction between extortion and economic coercion, see *United States v. Kozeny*, available at http://www.justice.gov/criminal/fraud/fcpa/cases/kozenyv/10–13–08bourke-deny -motion.pdf).

30. Boxall, discussion.

31. Ibid.

32. Ibid.

33. Dave Senay, "Ethics as Culture," speech presented at St. Louis University, St. Louis, MO, April 23, 2014.

34. DOJ et al., "FCPA: A Resource Guide," 15.

35. Ibid., 15.

36. Ibid., 15.

37. Transparency International, Corruptions Perceptions Index 2013, available at http://www.transparency.org/cpi2013/results.

38. DOJ et al., "FCPA: A Resource Guide," 16.

39. Boxall, discussion.

40. DOJ et al., "FCPA: A Resource Guide," 11.

41. Ibid., 16.

42. Boxall, discussion.

43. DOJ et al., "FCPA: A Resource Guide," 19.

44. Foreign Corrupt Practices Act Review, Opinion Procedure Release: 10–02 (July 16, 2010).

45. Ibid., 39.

46. DOJ et al., "FCPA: A Resource Guide," 19.

47. A PwC Global Survey found that 90% reported the involvement of a third-party intermediary.

48. DOJ et al., "FCPA: A Resource Guide," 22.

49. Ibid., 60.

50. Ibid.

51. Ibid., 22–23.

52. Boxall, discussion.

53. DOJ et al., "FCPA: A Resource Guide," 60.

54. Ibid., 28.

55. Ibid., 28.

56. Ibid., 31.

57. Ibid.

58. Christopher M. Matthews, "Dun & Bradstreet Investigating FCPA Allegations," WSJ blogs, *Wall Street Journal,* March 19, 2012, http://blogs.wsj.com /corruption-currents/2012/03/19/dun-bradstreet-investigating-fcpa-allegations/.

59. DOJ et al., "FCPA: A Resource Guide," 30

60. Ibid., 39.

61. Ibid., 38.

62. Ibid., 39.

63. Ibid., 38.

64. Ibid., 40.

65. Export Administration Regulations, 15 C.F.R. § 730.3–730.4.

66. Bureau of Industry and Security, "Penalties," accessed June 26, 2014, https://www.bis.doc.gov/index.php/enforcement/oee/penalties.

67. Ibid., 15 C.F.R. § 734.3.

68. Ibid., 15 C.F.R. § 734.3 (Note that as used herein, "exports" is defined to include re-exports.)

69. Ibid., 15 C.F.R. § 734.3.

70. Ibid., Supp. No. 1 to EAR 734.

71. Ibid., 15 C.F.R. § 734.2.b.1.

72. Ibid.

73. Ibid., 15 C.F.R. § EAR 734.b.3.

74. Ibid., 15 C.F.R. § 734.2.b.4.

75. Ibid., 15 C.F.R. § 734.3.a.3.

76. Ibid., 15 C.F.R. § 730.7.

77. Ibid. (To view the full list, see https://www.bis.doc.gov/index.php /regulations/commerce-control-list-ccl.)

78. Ibid., 15 C.F.R. § 746.

79. Ibid., 15 C.F.R. § 744.8; 15 C.F.R. § 744.11; 15 C.F.R. § 744.12; 15 C.F.R. § 744.14; 15 C.F.R. § 744.15; 15 C.F.R. § 744.17.

80. The list is available at Supplement No. 4 to 15 CFR § 744.

81. Ibid., 15 C.F.R. § 736.2(b)(4); see generally 15 C.F.R. § 766.

82. Those subject to Denial Orders are listed on the BIS website at http://www .bis.doc.gov.

83. Ibid., 15 C.F.R. §744.2; 15 C.F.R. §744.3; 15 C.F.R. §744.4; 15 C.F.R. §744.5; 15 C.F.R. §744.7; 15 C.F.R. § 744.17; 15 C.F.R. §744.21.

84. Ibid. (This exception only applies to countries in Country Chart B at Supp. No. 1 to EAR 740. Country Chart B includes the vast majority of the world's countries.)

85. Ibid., 15 C.F.R. §740.3.

86. Ibid.

87. Ibid. (Identified by Country Chart B countries.)

88. Ibid., 15 C.F.R. §740.4.

89. Ibid. (This includes China, Russia, Mongolia, Vietnam, Iraq and others.)

90. Ibid., 15 C.F.R. §740.5.

91. Ibid. (Identified by Country Chart B countries.)

92. Ibid., 15 C.F.R. §740.6.

93. Ibid., see EAR 740 for the full list of exceptions to licensing requirements.

94. Compliance Guidelines: How to Develop an Effective Export Management and Compliance Program Manual, 11 (2011), http://www.bis.doc.gov/index.php /forms-documents/doc_view/7-compliance-guidelines.

95. EMCP 11.

96. Export Administration Regulations, Supp. No. 3 to 15 C.F.R. §732—BIS's "Know Your Customer" Guidance and Red Flags.

97. Ibid.

98. BIS, "Elements of an Effective Export Compliance Program," last modified Sept. 16, 2009, https://www.bis.doc.gov/index.php/enforcement/oac?id=289.

99. Export Administration Regulations, 15 C.F.R. §764.5(a).

100. Ibid., 15 C.F.R. §764.5(b)(4).

101. Ibid., 15 C.F.R. §764.5(c).

102. Ibid., 15 C.F.R. §762.2(a)(1–10).

103. Ibid., 15 C.F.R. §763.

104. BIS, "Elements."

105. For the full list of boycotting countries, see U.S. Government Printing Office, 78 FR 54370—List of Countries Requiring Cooperation with an International Boycott, http://www.gpo.gov/fdsys/granule/FR-2013–09–03/2013–21359 /content-detail.html.

106. BIS, "Elements."

107. Export Administration Regulations, 15 C.F.R. §760.1(e)(2).

108. Ibid., 15 C.F.R. §760.1(e).

109. Ibid., 15 C.F.R. §760.2(a)(1).

110. Ibid., 15 C.F.R. §760.2(a)(5).

111. Ibid., 15 C.F.R. §760.2.

112. Ibid., 15 C.F.R. § 760.2(xi).

113. Ibid., 15 C.F.R. §760.2(b)(1).

114. Ibid., 15 C.F.R. §760.2(b).

115. Ibid., 15 C.F.R. §760.2(b).

116. Ibid., 15 C.F.R. §760.2.

117. Ibid., 15 C.F.R. §760.2(c)(1).

118. Ibid., 15 C.F.R. §760.2(c).

119. Ibid., 15 C.F.R. §760.2(d)(1).

120. Ibid., 15 C.F.R. §760.2(d)(3).

121. Ibid., 15 C.F.R. § 760.2(d)(4).

122. Ibid., 15 C.F.R. §760.2(d).

123. Ibid., 15 C.F.R. §760.2(e)-(f).

124. Ibid., 15 C.F.R. §760.3(a)(2).

125. Ibid., see generally, 15 C.F.R. §760.3(a); 15 C.F.R. §760.3(b); 15 C.F.R. §760.3(c); 15 C.F.R. § 760.3(e); 15 C.F.R. § 760.3(f).

126. Ibid., 15 C.F.R. §760.3.

127. Ibid., 15 C.F.R. §760.3(a)(3) (citing to 15 C.F.R. §760.2(d)).

128. Ibid., 15 C.F.R. §760.3.

129. Ibid., 15 C.F.R. § 760.3(d)(1).

130. Ibid. This is a legally defined term at 15 C.F.R. §760.3(d)(8). Bona fide includes factors such as physical presence in the country, whether such residence is needed for legitimate business purposes, continuity of residency (though short-term residency is not an excluding factor by itself), intent to remain in the country, prior residence in the country, size and nature of presence in the country, whether the person is registered to do business or incorporated in the country, whether

the person has a valid work visa, and whether the person has a similar presence in both boycotting and nonboycotting foreign countries in connection with similar business activities.

131. Ibid., 15 C.F.R. §760.3(d)(4).

132. Ibid., 15 C.F.R. §760.3(d).

133. Ibid., 15 C.F.R. §760.3(d)(5).

134. Ibid., 15 C.F.R. §760.5(a).

135. Ibid., 15 C.F.R. §760.5(a)(4)(i).

136. Ibid., 15 C.F.R. §760.5(a)(4)(ii).

137. Mollie McGowan, "Between a Rock and a Hard Place: The Export of Technical Data Under the International Traffic in Arms Regulations," Geo. Wash. L. Rev. 76 no. 1327 (2008): 1327.

138. The United States Munitions List, 22 C.F.R. §120.3(a)

139. Military Export Controls, 22 C.F.R. §2278(b)(2).

140. Ibid., 22 C.F.R. §2278(c).

141. The United States Munitions List, 22 C.F.R. §120.17(a).

Chapter Twelve: Money Laundering

1. Federal Deposit Insurance Corporation (FDIC), "Bank Secrecy Act, Anti-Money Laundering, and Office of Foreign Assets Control," Section 8.1–39, accessed June 26, 2014, http://www.fdic.gov/regulations/safety/manual/section8–1.pdf.

2. New Zealand Ministry of Justice, "Money Laundering and Terrorism Financing," accessed June 26, 2014, http://www.justice.govt.nz/policy/criminal-justice/aml-cft/money-laundering-and-terrorism-financing.

3. United Nations Office on Drugs and Crime, "Money Laundering and Globalization" (2014), https://www.unodc.org/unodc/en/money-laundering/globalization.html.

4. International Money Laundering Information Network (IMOLIN), "Legislation/Regulations," accessed June 26, 2014, http://www.imolin.org/imolin/amlid/search.jspx?docType=document.

5. FDIC, "Bank Secrecy Act," 8.1–39.

6. Ibid.

7. Ibid.

8. Racketeering, 18 U.S.C. § 1956.

9. Racketeering, 18 U.S.C. § 1956(c)(7).

10. See *United States v. Floras*, 454 F. 3d 149, 155–156 (3d. Cir. 2006) (attorney convicted of willful blindness as to illegal source of client's money).

11. Records and Reports on Monetary Instruments Transactions, 31 U.S.C. § 5312(1).

12. Money and Finance: Treasury, 31 CFR § 103.121.

13. FDIC, "Bank Secrecy Act," 8.1–7.

14. Federal Financial Institutions Examination Counsel (FFIEC), "Bank Secrecy Act/Anti-Money Laundering Examination Manual," 55 (2010) available at https://www.ffiec.gov/bsa_aml_infobase/documents/BSA_AML_Man_2010.pdf.

15. Ibid., 57.

16. Ibid., 57.

17. Ibid., 64.

18. FDIC, "Bank Secrecy Act," 8.1–17.

19. FFIEC, "Bank Secrecy Act/Anti-Money Laundering Examination Manual," 24.

20. Ibid., 26.

21. Ibid., 26–27; see 2013 INCSR: Major Money Laundering Countries, last modified March 5, 2013, http://www.state.gov/j/inl/rls/nrcrpt/2013/vol2/204062.htm.

22. FFIEC, "Bank Secrecy Act/Anti-Money Laundering Examination Manual," 65.

23. Money and Finance: Treasury, 31 C.F.R § 103.181.

24. FDIC, "Bank Secrecy Act," 8.1–20.

25. Ibid., 8.1–45.

26. Ibid.

27. For the full list, see ibid., 8.1-4-45.

28. Ibid., 8.1–44.

29. FFIEC, "Bank Secrecy Act/Anti-Money Laundering Examination Manual," 69.

30. Ibid., 70.

31. Ibid., 71.

32. Ibid., 74.

33. Ibid.

34. FDIC, "Bank Secrecy Act," 8.1–46.

35. Ibid.

36. Money and Finance: Treasury, 31 C.F.R § 103.22.

37. Ibid., 8.1–1.

38. Ibid., 8.1–2.

39. Ibid.

40. Ibid.

41. Ibid.

42. Ibid., 8.1–31.

43. Ibid., 8.1–5–6.

44. Money and Finance: Treasury, 31 C.F.R §103.100.

45. FDIC, "Bank Secrecy Act," 8.15–13.

46. Ibid., 8.1–14.

47. Ibid., 8.1–15.

48. FFIEC, "Bank Secrecy Act/Anti-Money Laundering Examination Manual," 27.

49. FDIC, "Bank Secrecy Act," 8.1–32.

50. FFIEC, "Bank Secrecy Act/Anti-Money Laundering Examination Manual," 28–29.

51. FDIC, "Bank Secrecy Act," 8.1–33.

52. Ibid., 8.1–33.
53. Ibid., 8.1–34–35.

Chapter Thirteen: Health Care Concerns and Data Privacy

1. The FMLA also states that covered employers must also be engaged in "commerce," but the regulations go on to state that an employer with 50 or more employees is by definition engaged in commerce. See The Family and Medical Leave Act (FMLA), 29 C.F.R. §825.104(a).

2. Ibid., 29 C.F.R. §825.104(a).
3. Ibid., 29 C.F.R. §825.102.
4. Ibid.
5. Ibid.
6. Ibid., 29 C.F.R. §825.120(a).
7. Ibid., 29 C.F.R. §825.112.
8. Ibid., 29 C.F.R. §825.121.
9. Ibid.

10. Inpatient care means an overnight stay in a hospital or medical care facility, or any subsequent treatment in connection with such inpatient care. See ibid., 29 C.F.R. §825.114.

11. Continuing treatment includes: (1) a period of incapacity of more than three consecutive, full calendar days, and any subsequent treatment where that treatment occurs two or more times within 30 days of the first day of incapacity, or which results in continuing, supervised treatment; (2) any period of incapacity due to pregnancy or for prenatal care; (3) incapacity or treatment for incapacity due to a chronic serious health condition which requires treatment two or more times annually; (4) permanent or long-term conditions; (5) conditions requiring multiple treatments for surgery after an accident or other injury or a treatment that without the treatment would result in incapacity of more than three consecutive days. Incapacity, in turn, is defined to mean the inability to work or perform regular daily activities due to the serious health condition, treatment, or recovery. See ibid., 29 C.F.R. §825.113.

12. Ibid., 29 C.F.R. §825.114(d).
13. Ibid., 29 C.F.R. §825.122(d)(1).
14. Ibid., 29 C.F.R. §825.201.
15. For the full list, see ibid., 29 C.F.R. §825.126(b).
16. Ibid., 29 C.F.R. §825.127(c).
17. Ibid., 29 C.F.R. §825.202(a).
18. Ibid., 29 C.F.R. §825.205.
19. Ibid., 29 C.F.R. §825.202(a).
20. Ibid., 29 C.F.R. §825.202(b).
21. Ibid., 29 C.F.R. §825.202(c).
22. Ibid., 29 C.F.R. §825.204(a).
23. Ibid., 29 C.F.R. §825.204(c).

24. Ibid.
25. Ibid., 29 C.F.R. §825.204(e).
26. Ibid., 29 C.F.R. §825.204(b).
27. Ibid., 29 C.F.R. §825.207.
28. Ibid., 29 C.F.R. §825.214.
29. Ibid., 29 C.F.R. §825.214.
30. Ibid., 29 C.F.R. §825.216.
31. Ibid.
32. Ibid.
33. Ibid., 29 C.F.R. §825.218.
34. Ibid., 29 C.F.R. §825.209(a).
35. Ibid., 29 C.F.R. §825.210.
36. Ibid., 29 C.F.R. §825.209(a).
37. 770 F.Supp.2d 980 (2011).
38. FMLA, 29 C.F.R. §825.301(b).
39. Ibid., 29 C.F.R. §825.302(a).
40. Ibid., 29 C.F.R. §825.303.
41. Ibid., 29 C.F.R. §825.302(d) and 29 C.F.R. §825.303(c).
42. Ibid., 29 C.F.R. §825.304(a).
43. Ibid., 29 C.F.R. §825.312(a).
44. Ibid., 29 C.F.R. §825.123(b).
45. Ibid., 29 C.F.R. §825.305.
46. Ibid., 29 C.F.R. §825.312(c).
47. Ibid., 29 C.F.R. §825.300(b).
48. A health care clearinghouse receives information from a provider and transmits that information on the provider's behalf.
49. Health plans include self-funded employer plans, and medical, dental, and vision coverage, but do not include long-term and short-term disability policies or life insurance policies.
50. Though beyond the scope of this chapter, some readers may also recognize the affect of HITECH due to its emphasis on transferring PHI into electronic form.
51. HIPAA Administrative Simplification Regulations, 45 C.F.R. §160.103.
52. Ibid., 45 C.F.R. §164.502(a)(1).
53. Ibid., 45 C.F.R. §164.502(a)(1).
54. Ibid., 45 C.F.R. §164.502(a)(1).
55. Ibid., 45 C.F.R. §164.502(a)(1).
56. Ibid., 45 C.F.R. §164.508(c)(1)–(c)(2).
57. Ibid., 45 C.F.R. §164.508(b)(2).
58. Ibid., 45 C.F.R. §164.508(b)(5).
59. Ibid., 45 C.F.R. §164.508(c)(3).
60. Ibid., 45 C.F.R. §164.502(b)(6).
61. Ibid., 45 C.F.R. §164.520.
62. Ibid.
63. Ibid.

64. Ibid., 45 C.F.R. §164.524(b)(2).

65. Ibid., 45 C.F.R. §164.524(c)(2).

66. Ibid., 45 C.F.R. §164.502(c)(4).

67. Ibid., 45 C.F.R. §164.528(c); 45 C.F.R. §164.528(b).

68. Ibid., 45 C.F.R. §164.528(a)(1).

69. Ibid., 45 C.F.R. §164.528(b).

70. Ibid., 45 C.F.R. §164.306(a)(1–3).

71. Ibid., 45 C.F.R. §164.306(b)(2).

72. Ibid.

73. Available at: http://csrc.nist.gov/publications/nistpubs/800-66-Rev1/SP-800-66-Revision1.pdf.

74. Ibid., 45 C.F.R. §164.308(a)(1).

75. Ibid.

76. Ibid., 45 C.F.R. §164.308(a)(5).

77. Ibid.

78. Ibid., 45 C.F.R. §164.308(a)(6).

79. Ibid., 45 C.F.R. §164.308(a)(7).

80. Ibid., 45 C.F.R. §164.310(a)(2).

81. Ibid.

82. Ibid., 45 C.F.R. §164.312(c)(2).

83. Ibid., 45 C.F.R. §164.308(a)(5).

84. Ibid., 45 C.F.R. §164.402.

85. Ibid.

86. Ibid., 45 C.F.R. §164.404(a)–(b)(2).

87. Ibid., 45 C.F.R. §164.404(c).

88. Ibid.

89. Ibid., 45 C.F.R. §164.404(d)(1).

90. Ibid.

91. Ibid., 45 C.F.R. §164.406(a).

92. Ibid., 45 C.F.R. §164.408(b).

93. Ibid., 45 C.F.R. §164.408(c).

94. Ibid., 45 C.F.R. §164.414(b).

95. Ibid., 45 C.F.R. §164.404(b).

96. See generally ibid., 45 C.F.R. §164.408(a)–(e).

97. See generally ibid., 45 C.F.R. §164.404.

Chapter Fourteen: Fair Labor Standards Act

1. G. Calvasina, R. Calvasina, and E. Calvasina, "Complying with the Fair Labor Standards Act (FLSA): A Continuing Legal Challenge for Employers," *J. of Legal, Ethical, and Reg. Issues* 13, no. 41 (2010): 41.

2. Department of Labor, "Fair Labor Standards Act Advisor: Am I Covered by the FLSA?" accessed June 26, 2014, http://www.dol.gov/elaws/esa/flsa/scope/screen10.asp.

3. DOL, Wage and Hour Division (WHD), "Fact Sheet #14: Coverage Under the Fair Labor Standards Act (FLSA)," last modified July 2009, http://www.dol.gov/whd/regs/compliance/whdfs14.pdf.

4. DOL, WHD, "Fact Sheet #14."

5. Fair Labor Standards Act of 1938 (FLSA), 29 US.C. §206(a)(1)(c).

6. WHD, Minimum Wage Laws in the States—January 1, 2014: Texas, http://www.dol.gov/whd/minwage/america.htm#Texas.

7. FLSA, 29 US.C. §206(d)(1)(i–iv).

8. Ibid., 29 US.C. §206(d)(1)(i–iv).

9. Ibid., 29 US.C. §206(d)(1)(i–iv).

10. Ibid., 29 US.C. §203(l)(1–2).

11. FLSA, 29 C.F.R. §570.33(a–k).

12. Ibid., 29 C.F.R. §570.7(a).

13. FLSA, 29 US.C. §207(a)(1)

14. "2008 Statistics Fact Sheet," DOL, http://www.dol.gov/whd/statistics/2008FiscalYear.htm.

15. FLSA, 29 US.C. §207(e)

16. Calsavina et al., "Complying with the Fair Labor Standards Act," 45 (citing to Lisa Schreter, "Developing a Clock-Work State of Mind: Avoid Off-the-Clock Work Claims by Non-Exempt Employees," *SHRM Legal Report*, last modified Nov. 12, 2007.

17. FLSA, 29 C.F.R. §778.500(a).

18. Ibid., 29 C.F.R. §778.500(b).

19. Ibid., 29 C.F.R. §778.104.

20. Ibid., 29 C.F.R. §785.15.

21. Ibid., 29 C.F.R. §785.16.

22. Ibid., 29 C.F.R. §787.17.

23. The exception: as part of the Patient Protection and Affordable Care Act, employers now, under the FLSA, must provide nonexempt mothers with the time and space to express breast milk for one year after the birth of a child. See Jonathan A. Segel, "Give Me a Break," *HR Magazine* 58 no. 12 (Dec. 1, 2012).

24. Wage and Hour Division (WHD), "Minimum Paid Rest Period Requirements Under State Law for Adult Employees in Private Sector," January 1, 2014, http://www.dol.gov/whd/state/rest.htm.

25. FLSA, 29 C.F.R. §785.18.

26. Wage and Hour Division (WHD), "Minimum Length of Meal Period Required Under State Law for Adult Employees in Private Sector," January 1, 2014, http://www.dol.gov/whd/state/meal.htm.

27. Segel, "Give Me a Break."

28. Ibid.

29. Ibid.

30. Steve Bruce, "New Cottage Industry—Suits Over Small Wage and Hour Claims," HR.BLR.com, October 21, 2008, http://hr.blr.com/HR-news/Compensation/FLSA-Fair-Labor-Standards-Act/New-Cottage-Industry-Suits-over-Small-Wage-and-Hou#.

31. Segel, "Give Me a Break."

32. Calsavina et al., "Complying with the Fair Labor Standards Act," 48.

33. Ibid., 49.

34. FLSA, 29 US.C. §211(a).

35. See ibid., 29 C.F.R. 516.3.

36. Ibid., 29 C.F.R. §516.5–516.6.

37. FLSA, 29 US.C. §213(a)(1) and 29 US.C. §213(a)(17).

38. Or the equivalent of two full-time employees, such as four part-time employees. See ibid., 29 C.F.R. §541.104(a).

39. Ibid., 29 C.F.R. §541.100(a)(1–4).

40. Ibid., 29 C.F.R. §541.101.

41. Ibid., 29 C.F.R. §541.200.

42. Paul E. Prather and R. Alex Boals, "FLSA: It's Not Just an Administrative Issue—Misclassification Issues Under the Administrative Exemption," *HR Professionals Magazine*, accessed June 26, 2014, http://hrprofessionalsmagazine .com/flsa-its-not-just-an-administrative-issue-misclassification-issues-under-the -administrative-exemption/.

43. FLSA, 29 C.F.R. §541.202(b).

44. Ibid., 29 C.F.R. §541.203–204.

45. Ibid., 29 C.F.R. §541.300.

46. Ibid., 29 C.F.R. §541.301(d).

47. Ibid., 29 C.F.R. §541.304(a).

48. Ibid., 29 C.F.R. §541.302(c).

49. See FLSA, 29 U.S.C. §213—Exemptions (available at http://www.law .cornell.edu/uscode/text/29/213).

50. FLSA, 29 C.F.R. §541.500(c).

51. FLSA, 29 C.F.R. §541.500(a).

52. Ibid., 29 C.F.R. §541.502.

53. Ibid.

54. Prather et al., "FLSA: It's Not Just an Administrative Issue."

55. Ibid.

56. Diane Cadrain, "HR Magazine: Guard Against FLSA Claims," Society for Human Resource Management, last modified April 1, 2008, http://www.shrm .org/publications/hrmagazine/editorialcontent/pages/4compensation%20_%20 benefits%20agenda.aspx.

57. Prather et al., "FLSA: It's Not Just an Administrative Issue."

58. Calsavina et al., "Complying with the Fair Labor Standards Act," 49.

59. See Calsavina et al., "Complying with the Fair Labor Standards Act," 49. See also Lisa A. Schreter, "New Friends in the Lion's Den: Call the U.S. Labor Department Before It Calls You," *HR Magazine* 53 no. 12, last modified December 1, 2008, http://www.shrm.org/Publications/hrmagazine/EditorialContent /Pages/1208legal.aspx.

60. Because employees may be eligible for liquidated damages and other benefits arising from an assertion of purposeful misconduct, simply repaying back wages does not necessarily assure a future lawsuit will not be brought.

61. Cadrain, "HR Magazine: Guard Against FLSA Claims."

62. DOL, "Wage and Hour Division WHD: Fact Sheet #17G: Salary Basis Requirement and the Part 541 Exemptions Under the Fair Labor Standards Act (FLSA)," last modified July 2008, available at http://www.dol.gov/whd/overtime /fs17g_salary.htm.

63. Ibid.

64. Kirkpatrick and Lockhart Nicholson Graham, "Employment Law: Salary Deductions Under the FLSA: How Employers Can Stay Out of Trouble" (April 2006), http://www.klgates.com/files/publication/45df2781-cc77–4d5f-918a-436 b8f9bf306/presentation/publicationattachment/4aaeca49–3302–4a6e-a1f8–444a 8cb5acce/ela0406.pdf.

Chapter Fifteen: The Environmental Protection Act and Amnesty Provisions

1. John F. Steiner and George A. Steiner, *Business, Government and Society: A Managerial Perspective*, 13th ed. 447 (New York: McGraw-Hill Irwin, 2012).

2. Steiner et al., *Business, Government and Society*, 447.

3. Environmental Protection Agency, "NPDES Compliance Inspection Manual" (July 2004): 1–5, http://www.epa.gov/compliance/resources/publications /monitoring/cwa/inspections/npdesinspect/npdesinspect.pdf.

4. Environmental Protection Agency, "Understanding the Clean Air Act," last modified March 6, 2012, http://www.epa.gov/air/caa/peg/understand.html.

5. Steiner et al., *Business, Government and Society*, 447.

6. EPA, "Understanding the Clean Air Act."

7. Environmental Protection Act, "Permits and Enforcement," last modified March 6, 2012, http://www.epa.gov/airquality/peg_caa/permits.html.

8. See GPO, "Electronic Code of Federal Regulations, Title 40," http://www .ecfr.gov/cgi-bin/text-idx?SID=82f431dc8e79abd58bbd92ca6b21e726&node=40 :16.0.1.1.7&rgn=div5.

9. Steiner et al., *Business, Government and Society*, 450.

10. Ibid., 448.

11. Environmental Protection Agency, "Cleaning Up Commonly Found Air Pollutants," http://www.epa.gov/air/caa/peg/cleanup.html.

12. Steiner et al., *Business, Government and Society*, 448.

13. Ibid., 449.

14. Ibid.

15. Ibid.

16. Ibid.

17. Ibid., 450.

18. Ibid., 458.

19. Federal Water Pollution Control Act (CWA), 33 U.S.C. §304(a)(4) (2002).

20. Ibid., 33 U.S.C. §307(a)(1).

21. CWA, 40 C.F.R. §122.2.

22. EPA, "NPDES Compliance Inspection Manual," 1–1.

23. Ibid., 1–5.

24. Ibid., 3–5.

25. Ibid., 3–8.

26. Ibid., 3–1.

27. Ibid., 4–17.

28. Ibid.

29. Ibid., 4–20.

30. Ibid.

31. Steiner et al., *Business, Government and Society*, 459

32. GPO, "Environmental Protection Agency: Small Business Compliance Policy," Federal Register 65, no. 7 (April 11, 2000): 19634, http://origin.www.gpo.gov/fdsys/pkg/FR-2000–04–11/pdf/00–8955.pdf.

33. Ibid., 19632.

34. Ibid.

35. Ibid., 19630.

36. Environmental Protection Agency, "Incentives for Self-Policing: Discovery, Disclosure, Correction and Prevention of Violations, Environmental Protection Agency Final Statement Policy" (May 11, 2000): 14–15, http://www.epa.gov/compliance/resources/policies/incentives/auditing/finalpolstate.pdf.

37. Ibid., 15–16.

38. Penalties consist of a gravity-based component and an economic benefit component. The gravity component reflects the actual harm caused by the violation, while the economic benefit component seeks to recover on any economic advantage that went to the organization by virtue of its noncompliance. For example, if a business saved money by not having required machinery, then that is an economic benefit that the EPA may recover. The economic benefit component is rarely at issue, and therefore the fine-reduction program is extensive.

39. EPA, "Incentives for Self-Policing," 6.

40. Ibid., 10.

41. Ibid., 12.

42. Ibid., 17.

43. Ibid.

44. EPA, "NPDES Compliance Inspection Manual," 3–1.

45. Ibid., 4–18.

46. Ibid., 4–17.

47. EPA, "Incentives for Self-Policing," 19.

48. EPA, "Small Business Compliance Policy," 19630.

49. Ibid.

50. EPA, "Incentives for Self-Policing," 20.

51. Ibid., 21.

52. Ibid., 20

53. Ibid.

54. Ibid., 22.
55. Ibid., 23.
56. Ibid., 25.
57. Ibid.
58. Ibid.
59. EPA, "Small Business Compliance Policy," 19633.
60. Ibid., 19630.
61. EPA, "Incentives for Self-Policing," 25.
62. Ibid., 26.
63. Ibid., 27.
64. Ibid., 29.

Chapter Sixteen: Antitrust Compliance

1. See generally DOJ, "Price Fixing, Bid Rigging, and Market Allocation Schemes: What They Are and What to Look For," accessed June 26, 2014, http://www.justice.gov/atr/public/guidelines/211578.htm.

2. Keating, in e-mail to author, July 26, 2014.

3. Federal Trade Commission (FTC), "The Antitrust Laws," accessed June 26, 2014, http://www.ftc.gov/tips-advice/competition-guidance/guide-antitrust-laws/antitrust-laws.

4. Department of Justice, "Antitrust Enforcement and the Consumer," accessed June 26, 2014, http://www.justice.gov/atr/public/div_stats/antitrust-enfor-consumer.pdf (stating: "The Department has obtained price-fixing, bid-rigging or customer-allocation convictions in the soft drink, vitamins, trash hauling, road building and electrical contracting industries, among others, involving billions of dollars in commerce. And in recent years, grand juries throughout the country have investigated possible violations with respect to fax paper, display materials, explosives, plumbing supplies, doors, aluminum extrusions, carpet, bread, and many more products and services. The Department also investigates and prosecutes bid rigging in connection with government procurement.").

5. Keating, e-mail.

6. DOJ, "Price Fixing, Bid Rigging, and Market Allocation Schemes."

7. DOJ, "Antitrust Enforcement and the Consumer."

8. Ibid.

9. Ibid.

10. Department of Justice, "Corporate Leniency Policy" (August 10, 1993), http://www.justice.gov/atr/public/guidelines/0091.htm.

11. FTC, "The Antitrust Laws."

12. See generally Abbot B. Lipsky Jr., "Managing Antitrust Compliance Through the Continuing Surge in Global Enforcement," *Antitrust L.J.* 75 no. 965 (2008–2009).

13. DOJ, "Antitrust Enforcement and the Consumer."

14. FTC, "The Antitrust Laws."

15. Federal Trade Commission and Department of Justice, *Antitrust Guidelines for Collaborations Among Competitors*, 2000, available at http://www.ftc.gov/sites/default/files/documents/public_events/joint-venture-hearings-antitrust-guidelines-collaboration-among-competitors/ftcdojguidelines-2.pdf.

16. Ibid.

17. FTC, "The Antitrust Laws."

18. Keating, e-mail.

19. Ibid.

20. DOJ, "Antitrust Enforcement and the Consumer."

21. FTC, "The Antitrust Laws."

22. DOJ, "Price Fixing, Bid Rigging, and Market Allocation Schemes."

23. FTC, "The Antitrust Laws."

24. Ibid.

25. Ibid.

26. Ibid.

27. Keating, e-mail.

28. Ibid.

29. Ibid.

30. Keating, e-mail.

31. Ibid.

32. Ibid.

33. Ibid.

34. DOJ, "Antitrust Enforcement and the Consumer."

35. Ibid.

36. FTC, "The Antitrust Laws."

37. Ibid.

38. Ibid.

39. Ibid.

40. Federal Trade Commission Act Section 5: Unfair or Deceptive Acts or Practices, "Consumer Compliance Handbook," accessed December 11, 2014, http://www.federalreserve.gov/boarddocs/supmanual/cch/ftca.pdf.

41. Ibid.

42. FTC, "The Antitrust Laws."

43. Ibid.

44. Ibid.

45. Ibid.

46. Ibid.

47. Ibid.

48. For more about reporting thresholds and requirements, see FTC, "Premerger Introductory Guides," accessed June 26, 2014, http://www.ftc.gov/enforcement/premerger-notification-program/statute-rules-and-formal-interpretations/premerger.

49. FTC, "The Antitrust Laws."

50. *Motorola Mobility LLC v. AV Optronics Corp. et al.* Case Number 14-8003, U.S. Court of Appeals – 7th Circuit.

51. Keating, e-mail to author.

52. Rosa M. Abrantes-Metz, Luke M. Froeb, John F. Geweke, and Christopher T. Taylor, "A Variance Screen for Collusion," *Int'l J. of Industrial Org.* 24 (2006): 467–486.

53. Joe Murphy, "What Is an Antitrust Compliance Program?" accessed June 26, 2014, http://www.compliance-network.com/wp-content/uploads/2013/02/4th-edition-What-is-an-antitrust-compliance-program.pdf.

54. Rosa M. Abrantes-Metz, Patrick Bajara, and Joseph E. Murphy, "Antitrust Screening: Making Compliance Programs Robust" (July 26, 2010), http://ssrn.com/abstract=1648948.

55. See generally Lipsky Jr., "Managing Antitrust Compliance," 989 (arguing that global programs must reserve an influential role for local antitrust professionals).

56. Murphy, "What Is an Antitrust Compliance Program."

57. Abrantes-Metz et al., "Antitrust Screening: Making Compliance Programs Robust."

58. Murphy, "What Is an Antitrust Compliance Program."

59. Abrantes-Metz et al., "Antitrust Screening: Making Compliance Programs Robust."

60. Murphy, "What Is an Antitrust Compliance Program."

61. Abrantes-Metz et al., "A Variance Screen for Collusion."

62. Ibid.

63. Keith Read, "Looking Out for Number 1: Using Benford's Law in Compliance, Finance and Procurement," An LRN White Paper, accessed June 26, 2014.

64. Ibid.

65. Abrantes-Metz et al., "Antitrust Screening: Making Compliance Programs Robust" (stating that "studies have shown that the law applies to a surprisingly large number of data sets, including populations of cities, street addresses of the first 348 persons named in American Men of Science (1934), electricity usage, word frequency, the daily returns to the Dow Jones, and even the distribution of digits for the opening prices of 780 stocks on the Toronto Stock Exchange over a period of 300 days starting on June 30, 1998.").

66. Ibid.

67. DOJ, "Price Fixing, Bid Rigging, and Market Allocation Schemes."

68. Ibid.

69. Ibid.

70. Ibid.

Index

About the Authors

Nitish Singh (PhD/MBA/MA) is Associate Professor in Business at the Boeing Institute of International Business, St. Louis University. He developed and led one of the first university online certificate programs in ethics and compliance management. His compliance education efforts have helped executives from AT&T, Boeing, Dunkin Brands, Emirates National Oil, Johnson Controls, Monsanto, Northern Trust, Novartis, Suncor, and Verisign, among others. Dr. Singh is also the founder of the ethics and compliance consulting firm IntegTree LLC (www.integtree.com). He holds a PhD in business from St. Louis University and an MBA and MA from universities in India and the U.K. His educational efforts and programs have been supported by the U.S. Department of Education, Qatar Foundation, Adobe, AT&T, Nestlé Purina, and other organizations. He has published more than 50 academic papers and three books.

Thomas J. Bussen (JD/MBA/Certified in Ethics and Compliance) is a lawyer, consultant, and adjunct instructor at the Cook School of Business, Saint Louis University. His educational efforts have included teaching the Certificate in Ethics and Compliance Management, as well as a unique prison immersion MBA course on white-collar fraud. His corporate outreach includes helping companies develop their bribery and corruption compliance programs. He has written articles in the areas of ethics and compliance and is a regular contributor to the Corporate Ethics and Compliance Professor's blog. Finally, his social outreach efforts include serving as a business adviser in the Peace Corps, where he is enhancing his understanding of corruption and doing business in central Asia.